Robert Kipping

The Elements of Sailmaking for Historic Ships

Robert Kipping

The Elements of Sailmaking for Historic Ships

ISBN/EAN: 9783954273157
Erscheinungsjahr: 2013
Erscheinungsort: Bremen, Deutschland

www.maritimepress.de | office@maritimepress.de

Bei diesem Titel handelt es sich um den Nachdruck eines historischen, lange vergriffenen Buches. Da elektronische Druckvorlagen für diese Titel nicht existieren, musste auf alte Vorlagen zurückgegriffen werden. Hieraus zwangsläufig resultierende Qualitätsverluste bitten wir zu entschuldigen.

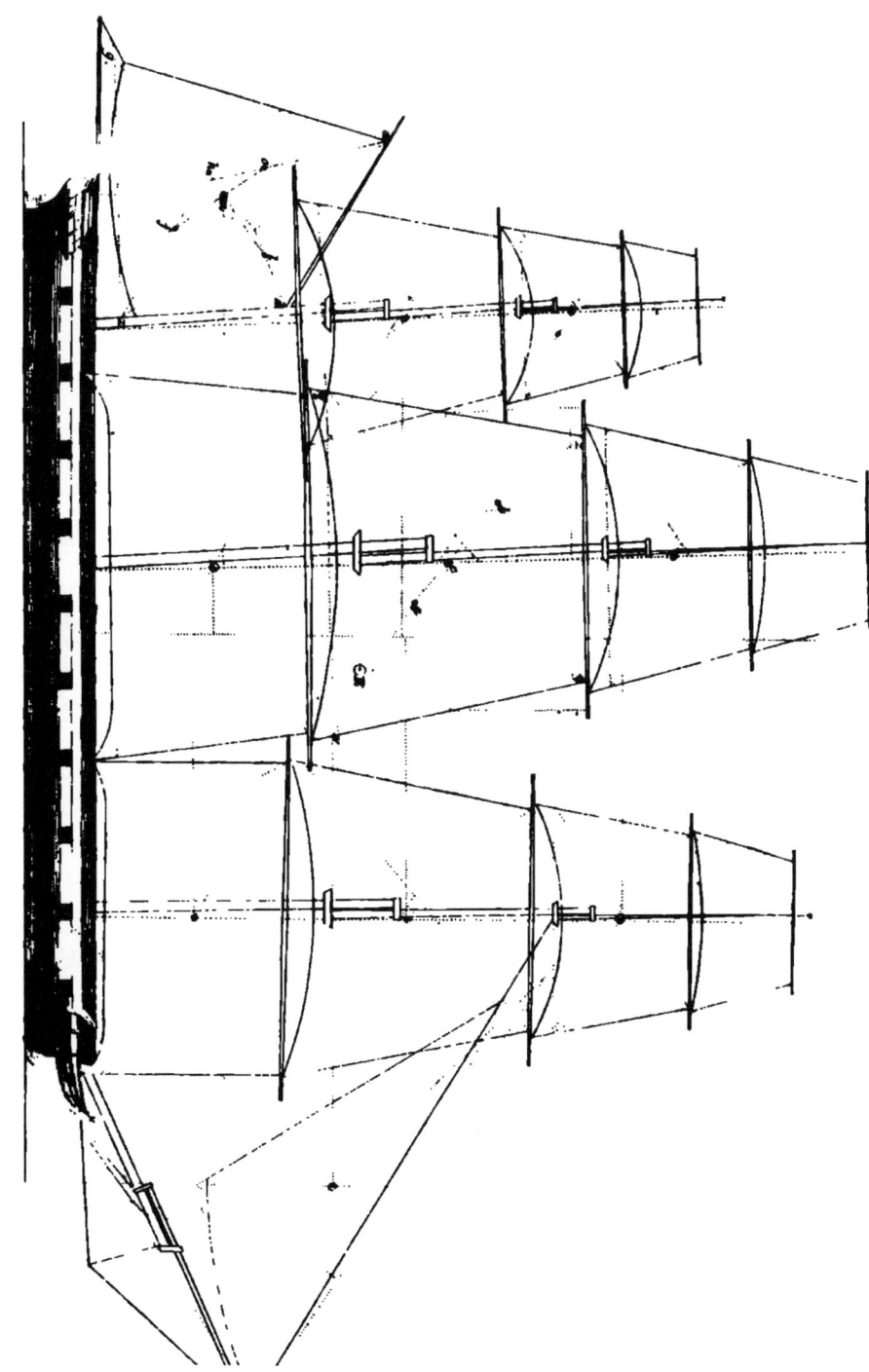

POSITIONS OF THE CENTRE OF GRAVITY, AND THE CENTRE OF EFFORT OF THE SAILS.

THE

ELEMENTS OF SAILMAKING,

BEING A

COMPLETE TREATISE ON CUTTING-OUT SAILS,

ACCORDING TO THE MOST APPROVED METHODS

THE MERCHANT SERVICE,

WITH DRAUGHTING, AND THE CENTRE OF EFFORT OF THE SAILS.

ILLUSTRATED BY ENGRAVINGS,

WITH FULL AND ACCURATE DIMENSIONS FOR JIBS, MAINSAILS, ETC., ETC.

BY ROBERT KIPPING,

(Sailmaker and Foreman to Messrs. THOMAS & WILLIAM SMITH, St. Peter's Dockyard,
Newcastle-upon-Tyne).

LONDON:

F. W. NORIE & WILSON, 157, LEADENHALL-STREET.

NEWCASTLE-UPON-TYNE: M. S. DODDS, QUAYSIDE.

NORTH SHIELDS: R. HARRISON.

ENTERED AT STATIONERS' HALL.

1847.

PREFACE.

THE writer of the ELEMENTS OF SAILMAKING, would merely observe, that as there was no existing work of the nature at all applicable to the present state of Sailmaking, nor was there ever any which contained the various calculations necessary for the scientific construction of sails, the opinion of many judicious friends coincided with his own, that such an obvious defect ought to be remedied; and as he has enjoyed very considerable experience during the last twelve years in the direction and cutting out of sails, he has been induced to write out the results of his experience and investigation, for publication, with strong hopes of success and approbation.

Sailmakers, in general, from the want of proper rules to calculate the dimensions for cutting out the sails, frequently find insurmountable difficulties, and, in consequence, are liable to many mistakes, and waste of canvass, which cannot be made without feelings of regret by those who have respect for their reputation. The great inconvenience arising from the want of these, was the cause of the author drawing up the following Rules for his own personal use; and having experienced the great advantage derived from them in fitting with sails the largest Indiamen afloat, built by and for Messrs. THOMAS & WILLIAM SMITH, the eminent Shipbuilders, and the great saving it has been to them, in preventing waste of canvass, he is induced, with the warm encouragement of them and Mr. ROBERT HANSELL, (with whom he served his Apprenticeship,) to submit his calculations to the Public, trusting they will be found useful. It is also the object of this work, to give a practical exposition in every department of, and every thing essential and expedient to, Sailmaking, with a view to the thorough SCIENTIFIC CONSTRUCTION,

and ultimately PERMANENT MAINTENANCE, strength, and stability of
the sails. It is also arranged with a view to afford some information to sailmakers who are in the habit of going foreign voyages, to
whom it is hoped that the book will be extremely useful.

Some portions of the work will be found to embrace rather difficult
formulæ, which, to the merely practical man, the Author is afraid
will be of no very great service; but he could not make easier for him
what required the aid of arithmetic and geometry. Those, however,
who have comparatively an elementary mathematical knowledge,
may not only understand the explanation of the manner of, and the
reasons for, performing the calculations, but also apply them to particular cases. In the mathematical investigations of the questions
involving the wind on the sails, a knowledge of the simple problems
which embrace the principles of the composition and resolution of
forces is necessary; and no person unacquainted with these principles can be said to be competent for the task.

Throughout the entire volume, every thing has been treated in a
consecutive manner, beginning with Section I., on the Description
and Use of Sails: then the Sections are divided into Chapters,
thus :—

Chapter I. On measuring Masts, Yards, &c., on Board.

Chapter II. On Finding the Number of Cloths, by new and very
simple Rules, with copious Examples illustrating their use.

Chapter III. On determining the Size of the Sail, from the
Dimensions as received from the Mastmaker, with the Form of the
Dimensions of a full-rigged Ship. The method by which the Sails
are determined, is so simple, that even a tyro may understand it; and
those fully conversant with fitting new ships will see immediately
how the results have been obtained.

Chapter IV. On Roaching the Sails, and the Mensuration of the
Gores. The observations and rules relative to roaching the sails
will be found very useful, as they are founded on long practice; and
the rules for calculating the gores are given in as simple a form as
they will admit. Appropriate examples are given under each head,
and the calculations are exhibited in a concise form, at the same
time that they are sufficiently obvious to any person who is acquainted with common arithmetic—which acquirement, together

with what may be considered an elementary knowledge of mathematics, will be essential in reading the whole of the Treatise.

Chapter V. Dimensions for Cutting the Sails. Finally, Part I. of the work concludes with Section Second, on Cutting out the Sails, with a valuable Table showing the Length of the Gores, corresponding to the Depth of the Selvage, and the Eating-in Seaming.

The greatest attention has been bestowed in preparing the several Plates for the Engraver, and in the revision of the proof-sheets of the press; and the Author confidently expects that no errors have been overlooked in either.

Diffident of venturing to publish the whole at once, as one who dares scarcely to anticipate what might be the extent of his success, he is induced to publish only in Parts, which shall be quickly brought forward; and he hopes that the continued portions of the work will be found to contain not only more principles, but also details of the practical execution of the different branches of Sail-making, together with voluminous tables of dimensions of sails for all classes of vessels, with Draughting, the Centre of Effort of the Sails, and all the technical minutiæ of the Art, explained in an alphabetical order.

St. Peter's Dockyard, Feb., 1847.

CONTENTS.

PART I.

SECTION FIRST.

THE DESCRIPTION AND USE OF SAILS.

ON MEASURING.

CHAPTER I.

CHAPTER II.

RULES FOR FINDING THE NUMBER OF CLOTHS, ETC.

CHAPTER V.

DIMENSIONS FOR CUTTING THE SAILS.

SECTION SECOND.

CHAPTER I.

ON CUTTING-OUT SAILS.

CHAPTER II.

OBSERVATIONS ON MATERIALS USED, ETC.

CHAPTER III.
PRACTICAL OPERATIONS IN SAILMAKING.

CHAPTER II.

ON DETERMINING THE SAILS, ETC., FOR A BRIG.

PART II.

SECTION FIRST.

ON DRAWING PLANS OF SAILS.

CHAPTER 1.

CHAPTER II.

ON THE CENTRE OF EFFORT.

ELEMENTS OF SAILMAKING.

PART I.

————————

SECTION FIRST.

ON DESCRIPTION AND USE OF SAILS.

ARTICLE 1. The first discoveries for impelling vessels by sails with the wind in different directions, were made, we can easily conceive, by those who would adopt the least complicated form—that of a single square sail erected on a single mast.* To the quadrangular we find added, at a very early period, the triangular sails. These have continued to constitute the forms of all sails up to the present time; and, according to the writers on the ancient navies, we find single sails of these forms were used, at very early periods, by the Egyptians, Carthaginians, and Greeks.†

2. The ancients, as they increased the size of their vessels, found it necessary to give them more than one sail. This we find was the case in the vessels which composed the fleets built by Ptolemy Philadelphus, (the second King of Egypt of that race,) and Hiero the Second, and also those which were sent against Syracuse, when besieged by the Romans under Marcellus, the Roman Consul, about 208 years B.C., for they had three and even four masts.

3. According to Hesychius, Isidorus, and Suidas, these masts were thus denominated: the mainmast, Acation; the mast placed at the

---

* Among the ancient Grecians, every ship had several masts. We are, nevertheless, informed by Aristotle, that at first there was only one mast, which, being fixed in the middle of the ship, the hole into which the foot of it was inserted they called μεσόδμη (mesodme); in Latin, *modius*; and in English, the step.

† Single sails were commonly called by the Greeks *Istia*, but sometimes *Fassones* or *Armenia*. The Carthaginians, on their *Exeres* and *Epteres*, appear to have formed a system of sails, supported by three masts. — *La Marine des Anciens Peuples*, Chap. I. and II., par M. Le Roy.

poop (which was second in size), Epidron ; that placed at the prow, Dolan ; and the fourth, which was made use of in some of the largest vessels, according to Sibius Italicus, Artimon ; a name still preserved by the French as their mizen.

4. The sail which was situated on the Acation was in the form of a triangle, with its vertex downwards, the upper part of which was placed horizontally ; above this sail, and fixed to the same yard, was the *sapparum*, a sail of similar form, with its vertex upwards. The sapparum, according to some authors, was only hoisted as a signal of victory ; but it appears to have been a sail too well disposed, and of too great an extent, not to have been used in navigating their vessels.

5. The sails affixed to the Dolan, Epidron, and Artimon, were likewise of a triangular form, but with their yards more or less elevated at the after-end, and their fore-ends brought to the deck, while they were slung or fixed to the masts near the middle. From these sails, it is most likely the lateen sails were derived, since they bear so near a resemblance, and especially as the Romans, in imitation of whom we use them, obtained all their maritime knowledge from the Carthaginians, Egyptians, and other ancient nations.

6. From the lateen sails were derived most of those of a triangular form ; for as vessels increased in size, and required a greater surface of canvas to impel them, it became necessary to give to the mast a greater support. With this increased support the lateen sails could not be so effectually used, which no doubt gave rise to the raking of the masts with Bermuda sails, to the various modifications which have taken place from time to time, and to the various methods which have been introduced of combining with them those of a quadrangular form ; whilst, by varying the number and disposition of those two kinds of sails, we are enabled to form numerous varieties, to be used according to the idea of the navigators, the services of the vessels, the places in which the vessels are employed, and the number of men that are to navigate them.

7. In every system, whatever may be the number or shape of the sails, they all contain either three or four sides—that is, are either triangular or quadrilateral. The former of these, or three-sided, are sometimes spread by a yard, as lateen sails, or by a stay, as staysails, or by a mast, as shoulder-of-mutton sails ; in all which cases the foremost leech or edge is attached to the yard, mast, or stay, throughout its whole length.

8. The latter, or those which are four-sided, are either extended by yards, as the principal sails of a ship, or by yards and booms, as the studding sails, drivers, ringtails, and all those sails which are set occasionally ; or by gaffs and booms, as the mainsails of sloops and brigantines.

9. The principal sails of a ship are—The courses, or lower sails ; the topsails, which are next in order above the courses ; and the topgallantsails, which are extended above the topsails.

10. The courses are—The mainsail and foresail, main-staysail, forestaysail, and mizen-staysail. The main-staysail is rarely used, except in small vessels.

11. In all quadrilateral sails, the upper edge is called the head ;

the sides, or skirts, are called the leeches; and the bottom, or lower edge, is termed the foot. If the head is parallel to the foot, the lower corners are denominated clues, and the upper corners earings.

12. In all triangular sails, and in those four-sided sails wherein the head is not parallel to the foot, the foremost corner at the foot is called the tack, and the after lower corner the clue. The foremost head is called the fore-leech, or luff, and the hindmost the after-leech.

13. The heads of most four-sided sails, and fore-leeches of lateen sails, are attached to their respective yards, or gaffs, by rope-yarns, called stoppers, or by a lacing; and the upper extremities are made fast by earings.

14. The staysails are extended upon stays between the masts, whereon they are drawn up or down; and their lower parts are stretched out by a tack and sheet.

15. The mainsail and foresail have a rope, and a large single block, or chain, made fast to each clue. The ropes or chains called tacks lead forward to the chess-trees and bumkins, and the block receives a thick rope from aft, which is termed the sheet.

16. The clues of the topsails are drawn out to the extremities of the sheave-holes, on the lower yards, by two chains called topsail-sheets; and the clues of the topgallant-sails are in like manner extended upon the topsail-yards, close home to the sheave-holes, by chains called topgallant sheets. The royals are set above the topgallant-sails, and skysails above the royals; and above them are sometimes sails called moonsails, and star-gazers; and the clues of the royal sails have sheets leading through sheaves, or holes, of the topgallant yard-arms.

17. Studdingsails are set beyond the leeches, or skirts, of the foresail, topsail, topgallant-sail, and royal, their upper and lower edges being extended by yards, and booms run out beyond the extremities of the yards for this purpose. These sails are, however, only used in favourable winds, and moderate weather.

18. All sails derive their names from the mast, yard, or stay upon which they are extended or attached. Thus the principal sail extended upon the mainmast is called the mainsail, or main-course; the next above, which stands upon the main-topmast, is termed the main-topsail; that which spreads across the main-topgallant-mast, is named the maintopgallant-sail; and the sails above it are called the main-royal and main-skysail. (Plate 2.)

19. In the same manner there are the foresail, or fore-course, foretopsail, fore-topgallant-sail, and fore-royal; the mizen, or driver, mizen-topsail, mizen-topgallant-sail, and mizen-royal. (Plates 3 and 4.) Thus, also, there are the fore-trysail, main-trysail, and mizen-trysail; or, as they are sometimes called, the fore-spencer, Duke of York, or main-spencer, and storm-mizen, or storm-driver, or spanker; the maintaysail, main-topmast-staysail, main-topgallant-staysail, and a middletaysail, which stands between the two last. All these staysails are between the main and fore masts.

20. The staysails are denominated from the stays; and there are the mizen-staysail, the mizen-topmast-staysail, the mizen-topgallant-staysail, and sometimes a mizen-royal-staysail, and main-spilling-staysail.

21. The sails between the foremast and the bowsprit are the fore-staysail, the fore-topmast-staysail, the jib, and the flying-jib, and even a middle-jib.

22. The studdingsails being extended upon the different yards of the mainmast and foremast, are also named according to their stations, as the lower-studdingsail, topmast-studdingsail, topgallant-studdingsail, and royal-studdingsail.

23. The ropes by which the lower yards of a ship are hoisted to their proper height on the masts, are called purchases. The sails are expanded by haliards, tacks, sheets, and bowlines, and are drawn up together, or trussed up, by buntlines, clue-garnets, leech-lines, reef-tackles, slab-lines, and spilling-lines. The studdingsails, and the jibs and staysails, are drawn down, so as to be taken in or reefed, by down-hauls; and the courses, topsails, and topgallant-sails hauled about the mast or the yards, so as to suit the various directions of the wind, by braces on the yards.

24. The *jib* is a sail of great command with any side wind, but espe-cially when the ship is close-hauled, or has the wind upon her beam; and its effect in casting the ship, or turning her head to leeward, is very powerful, and of great utility, particularly when the ship is working through a narrow channel.

25. The *flying-jib* is a sail much used in fine light winds, set upon a boom, and rigged out beyond the jib-boom; and sometimes an *inner-jib*, a similar sail, set between the fore-topmast-staysail and standing-jib, the tack of which is made fast near half-way down on the jib-boom.

26. The *after-sails*, which are those that belong to the mainmast and mizenmast, keep the ship to windward; on which account, ships sailing on a quarterly wind require a head-sail and an after-sail—one to coun-teract the other.

27. When a ship sails with a side wind, the clues of the fore and main courses are fastened by a tack and sheet, the tack being to wind-ward and the sheet to leeward. The tack is, however, only disused with a stern wind, whereas the sail is never spread without the assist-ance of one or both of the sheets.

28. It is under the topsails that many important evolutions are made, especially in time of emergency; and they are justly accounted the principal sails in a ship.

ON MEASURING.

CHAPTER I.

ON MEASURING MASTS, YARDS, BOOMS, &c., ON
BOARD.

29. The width of all sails are governed by the length of the yard, gaff, boom, and stay: the depth by the height of the mast. The total

extent of either is always taken, and the allowances for the sails stretching are left to the judgment of the sailmaker.

TOPSAILS.

Heads.—The topsail-yards are measured from cleat to cleat on the yard-arms

Feet.—The fore, main, and cross-jackyards are measured from pin to pin of the sheave-holes.

Hoists.—The topmasts are measured from the hounds down to the heel, and small vessels from the pin-holes down to the heel.

TOPGALLANT-SAILS.

Heads.—The topgallant-yards are measured from cleat to cleat on the yard-arms.

Feet.—The topsail-yards are measured from pin to pin of the sheaves.

Hoists.—The topgallant-masts are measured from the hounds down to the heel.

ROYALS.

Heads.—The royal-yards are measured from cleat to cleat on the yard-arms.

Feet.—The topgallant-yards are measured from pin to pin of the sheaves.

Hoists.—The royal-masts are measured from the hounds down to the heel.

COURSES :—*Fore-Course.*

Head.—The foreyard is measured from cleat to cleat on the yard-arms.

Depth.—The height of the centre of the yard from the deck, and the cat-head above the deck ; or, if the yard were sharply braced forward, measure the distance between the place of the earing and the bumkin-end.

BOOM-FORESAIL.

Head.—Measure the length of the foreyard between cleat and cleat.

Foot.—Measure the length of the boom between the two holes.

Depth.—The height of the centre of the yard from the mainstay.

Main-Course.

Head.—The mainyard is measured from cleat to cleat on the yard-arm.

Depth.—The height of the centre of the yard from the deck ; or, if the yard were sharply braced forward, the distance from the place of the earing to the chess-tree.

MAIN-STAYSAIL.

Stay.—The length of the mainstay between the mouse and the fore-mast.

Depth.—Measure from the place of the peek plumb down, so that the foot will clear the boat.

TRYSAIL.

Head.—Measure from the inside of the jaws of the gaff to the hounds.

Foot.—Measure the length of the boom from the afterside of the mast, or from the jaws to the sheave-hole at the end.

Fore-leech.—Measure from the under part of the hounds to the boom, or from the under part of the gaff, hoisted to its proper height, to the boom.

Cross-gore.—The diagonal length is taken from the throat, or height of gaff on the mast, to the place of the clue. This is done to get the proper foot-gore, and, if thought necessary, to make a draft.*

FORE-TRYSAIL.

Head.—Measure the length of the gaff.

Foot.—Measure from the mainstay, where it crosses the foremast, to the forepart of the gangway.

Mast.—The height of the gaff stands above the mainstay.

GAFF-TOPSAIL.

Mast.—Measure from the sheave-hole of the topmast, or the place the throat reaches, down to the gaff hoisted to its proper place.

Foot.—Measure the length of the gaff to the hounds.

Cross-gore.—Let the gaff be properly peeked, and measure the distance between the places of the throat and clue.

AWNINGS :—*Forecastle.*

Measure the *length* from the fore-end, or forestay, to the afterside of the foremast.

Breadths.—Measure the distances between the two cat-heads, middle-way, and fore-part of fore-rigging. The breadth of the fore-end is generally 3 feet.

Main-Deck Awning.

The *length* is taken from the afterside of foremast to afterside of mainmast.

The *breadths* are taken at the fore-part of fore-rigging and main-rigging.

Quarter-Deck Awning.

The *length* is taken from the afterside of the mainmast to the foreside of the mizenmast.

The *breadths* are at the fore-part of main-rigging and mizen-rigging.

Poop, or After-Awning.

The *length* is from the foreside of the mizenmast to the rake of the stern over the taffrail.

The *breadths* are at the fore-part of mizen-rigging and at the taffrail.

Curtains to Awnings.

Their depth is taken from the sides of the awning to the gunwale, supposing the awning to be in its place.

* The calculation from this measurement is shown in another part of this work.

CHAPTER II.

RULES FOR FINDING THE NUMBER OF CLOTHS, AFTER DETERMINING THE SIZE OF THE SAIL, FROM THE DIMENSIONS OF THE MASTS, YARDS, &c.

30. Sails have a double flat seam, and the breadths vary according to the size of the sail. The breadth of the seams of courses, topsails, and other sails in the merchant service, are as follows, viz., courses and topsails, for 500 tons and upwards, one inch and a half; and for 400 tons ships and under, one inch and a quarter at head and foot; all other square sails, one inch at head and foot. The tablings, too, vary proportionably to the size of the sail:—courses from 4 to 6 inches, topsails 3 to 5 inches, and topgallant-sails 3 inches, on the leeches.

RULES.

I. Heads of topsails and courses : $\frac{6}{11}$ of the width gives the number of cloths.

EXAMPLES.

1. Given the length on the head 40ft. 2in., to find the quantity of cloths?

	FT.	IN.
Here - -	40	2
Multiply by		6
Divide by -	11)241	0

22 cloths nearly.

2. Given the width of the head of a topsail, 21 feet: required the cloths?

	FT.
Here - -	21
Multiply by -	6
Divide by	11)126

$11\frac{5}{11}$ or $11\frac{1}{2}$ cloths.

₀ When there is a remainder, it must be multiplied by 2, and will give the number of inches of a cloth. Hence, it will be observed, that the above rule is quite general, answering for small as well as large ships' courses, topsails, and small topgallant-sails.

II. Heads of topgallant-sails : $\frac{6}{11}$ of the width gives the number of cloths.

EXAMPLES.

1. Given the length on the head, 23 feet, to find the number of cloths?

		FT.
(By Rule I.)	Here - -	23
	Multiply by -	6
	Divide by	11)138

$12\frac{6}{11}$ or $12\frac{1}{2}$ cloths.

2. Given the length on the head, 40ft. 4in.: requ red the number of cloths?

		FT.	IN.
(By Rule II.)	Here - -	40	4
	Multiply by -		8
	Divide by	15)322	8(21½ cloths.

```
15)322 8(21½ cloths.
   30
   ——
   22
   15
   ——
    7
   12
   ——
15)92(6in.   6 + 6 = 12in. or ½ cloth.
   90
   ——
   2 × 3 = 6in.
```

₊ When there is a remainder, it must be multiplied by 8, and it will give the inches of a cloth.

III. For the foot of topsails and topgallant-sails : $\frac{7}{13}$ of the length of the foot on a square gives the number of cloths.

EXAMPLES.

1. Given the length of the foot of a topsail, 39 feet, to find the spread of cloths?

	FT.
Here - -	39
Multiply by	7
Divide by	13)273(21 cloths.

```
13)273(21 cloths.
   26
   ——
   13
   13
   ——
```

2. Given the foot on a square of a topgallant-sail, 26 feet, to find the number of cloths the foot spreads?

	FT.
Here - -	26
Multiply by	7
Divide by	13)182(14 cloths.

```
13)182(14 cloths.
   13
   ——
   52
   52
   ——
```

IV. For the foot of topsails and topgallant-sails having cringles in lieu of turned clues, ⅘ of the length of the foot gives the requisite number of cloths. **EXAMPLES.**

1. Given the length of the foot of a topsail, 36 feet : to find how many cloths are required ?

	FT.
Here - -	36
Multiply by -	4
Divide by	7)144
	20 cloths.

2. Given the length of the foot of a topgallant-sail, 49 feet : how many cloths are required ?

	FT.
Here - -	49
Multiply by	4
Divide by	7)196
	28 cloths.

⁕ When there is not much slack to be marled in, ⅓ of a cloth less in the foot. It may, however, be observed, that it is a good plan to hold slack canvas in between the buntline holes, as it eases the canvas greatly from the tops and cross-trees, where the sail is generally much chafed when it is tight across.

THE RULES FOR FINDING THE CLOTHS OF FORE AND AFT SAILS.

31. The breadths of the seams being made broader on the head and foot, or foot only, are to be as follows, viz., trysails, mizens, and drivers, two inches and a half at the head, and three inches on the foot, except where the gores are stronger towards the mast, and the seams are one quarter to one half-inch broader ; the seams of *jibs* are three inches at the foot, increased towards the clue : but the seams ought to be creased, according to the roach with which the sail is cut, and thus eat up the irregular gores, and form a regular curve on the foot. The seams being made broader on the head and foot than the remaining part of the seam, forms what is called the belly part of the sail, restrained by the slack after-leech, which will be noticed afterwards.

I. For the foot of trysails and mizens, 2⅘ of the length of the foot gives the number of cloths.

EXAMPLES.

1. Given the length of the foot of a trysail, 29 feet : to find the number of cloths?

	FT.
Here - -	29
Multiply by	24
	116
	58
Divide by	43)696(16 cloths.
	43
	266
	258

C

2. Given the length of the foot of a mizen, 44 feet : to find the number of cloths ?

```
                                       FT.
            Here  -   -   -            44
            Multiply by  -             24
                                      ────
                                       176
                                       88
                                      ────
            Divide by  -     43)1056(24½ cloths.
                                   86
                                  ────
                                   196
                                   172
                                  ────
                                   24
```

II. For the heads of mizens, ⅕ of the length of the head, will give the number of cloths.

EXAMPLES.

1. Given the head of a mizen, 22 feet 6 inches : to find the number of cloths ?

```
                                    FT.  IN.
            Here   -   -            22   6
            Multiply by              5
                                   ─────────
            Divide by  -     9)112   6
                             ─────────
                              12½ cloths.
```

2. Given the head of a driver, 33 feet : to find the number of cloths ?

```
                                    FT.
            Here   -   -            33
            Multiply by             5
                                   ────
            Divide by      9)165
                           ────
                            18⅓ cloths nearly.
```

III. For the foot of a jib, 19/36 of the length of the foot, will give the number of cloths.

EXAMPLES.

1. Given the length of the foot of a jib 26 feet 6 inches, to find the number of cloths ?

```
                                    FT.  IN.
            Here  -   -   -         26   6
            Multiply by  -              19
                                   ─────────
                                    243   6
                                    26
                                   ────
            Divide by       36)503(14 cloths.
                              36
                             ────
                              143
                              144
```

2. Given the length of the foot of a jib, 32 feet : to find the number of cloths ?

	FT.
Here - -	32
Multiply by	19
	288
	32
Divide by	36)608(17 cloths nearly.
	36
	248
	252

ON FINDING THE NUMBER OF CLOTHS IN THE CLOSE REEF, AND THE QUANTITY OF HOLLOW IN THE TWO LEECHES OF A TOPSAIL.

32. Given the number of cloths in the head and foot and the length of the reef, to find the hollow in the two leeches.

EXAMPLE.

Given the head 15 cloths, foot 24 cloths, and the length of the low reef at 1 foot above half way of the leech, 32 feet ?

	FT.		
Here - -	Reef 32	Head 15 cloths.	
Multiply by	6	Foot 24 ditto.	
	—		
	11)192	½)39 sum.	
	—.		
	17¼ cloths.	19½ mean cloths.	
		17¾	
		Diff. 2 cloths.	

Hence, the hollow on each leech will be one cloth, or 2 feet.

** The method of fixing the length on the head of the topsail, or the distance of the head of the sail from the cleats on the topsail-yard, will cause the hollow given to the leeches of the topsails always to be more or less, according as the lengths of the lower yards exceed the lengths of the topsail-yards, which, in some cases, may give a very considerable hollow, as in the example shown above. The hollow given to the leeches of topsails appears to have originated in the topsail-yard-arms not being sufficiently long without the sail to take the lowest reef; but if the length of the arms beyond the head of the sail had been increased to lessen the hollow, or to have made the leeches straight, as those of other sails, the topsails would not only have stood better, but have had a better appearance, without occasioning any practical disadvantage, besides that of the increased weight of the additional length of the yard-arm.

CHAPTER III.

ON DETERMINING THE SIZE OF THE SAIL FROM THE
DIMENSIONS AS RECEIVED FROM THE MASTMAKER.

33. Having in the preceding chapter given Rules and Examples on the finding of the number of cloths after having determined the size of the sails from the measurement of the yards, &c., on board, we shall now proceed to determine the size of the sail, from the extreme dimensions of the masts, yards, &c., as received from the mast-maker, and apply these rules in finding the number of cloths.

FORM OF THE DIMENSIONS OF A FULL-RIGGED SHIP.

DIMENSIONS OF MASTS, YARDS, ETC.							
MASTS.	Extreme Length.	Headed Length.	YARDS.	Extreme Length.	Yard-arms.	Pin of sheave hole within the hounds.
	Ft. In.	Ft. In.		Ft. In	Ft. In.	Inches
Main Mast	82 10	13 4	Main Yard........	73 6	4 3	10
Topmast	49 6	7 9	Topsail-yard	57 10	4 9	8
Topgallant-mast ..	26 0		Topgallant-yard	41 7	2 8	6
Royalmast	18 0		Royal-yard	29 6	1 9	
Fore Mast	77 6	13 0	Fore Yard........	65 8	4 0	10
Topmast	45 6	7 3	Topsail-yard	52 6	4 6	8
Topgallant-mast ..	24 0		Topgallant-yard	37 8	2 5	6
Royalmast	16 6		Royal-yard	26 0	1 9	
Mizen Mast	60 0	9 9	Cross-jack-yard ..	58 8	6 6	8
Topmast	37 6	5 10	Mizen Topsail-yard	4) 9	3 3	6
Topgallant-mast ..	19 10		Topgallant-yard	29 8	1 11	5
Royalmast	13 0		Royal-yard	21 0	1 8	
Housing of mainmast..	21 6.		Bowsprit	50 0	End.	
Foremast	27 0		Jib-boom	45 0	2 0	
Mizenmast	14 6		Flying jib-boom ..	49 0		
Outrigger.			Gaff............	41 4½	6 4½	

The mainmast steps into a chock upon the top of the keelson, which is 1 feet 6 inches thick, and a mortoise 8¼ inches, for the tenon at the heel of the mast. Foremast the same way. The mizenmast steps on the hold beam, and the tenon is 4 inches.

34. From the foregoing (Chapter I.) we have simply to determine the rounded lengths of the masts and yards, and allow for the sail stretching; or fix the places for the head of the courses, topsails, &c., within the cleats on the yard-arms, and the clues to the sheave holes on the yards. We shall now exhibit the process.

COURSES.
RULE.

1. The depth of the *leech* is found by adding the length of the mast-head, the slings* below the bottom of trestle-trees, the housing of the

* The distance the cat-harpin legs, or place of the centre of the yard, is below the top of cheeks, and is generally about ⅓ the hounded length of the topmast.

mast, and the chess-tree above the deck, the sum of which, subtracted from the extreme length of the mast, and 20 inches or 2 feet from the remainder, for the *length of the leech.*

2. The *head.* Subtract the two yard-arms from the whole length of the main-yard, gives the hounded length, and 3 *feet* or 18 inches within each of the cleats on the yard-arms, for the *length on the head.* Thus:

MAIN COURSE.

	FT.	IN.	FT.	IN.			FT.	IN.
Mainmast	82	10	- 13	4	head.	Mainyard - -	73	6
"			5	2	sling.	" two arms	8	6
"			20	8	housing.			
"			2	0	chess-tree.	" hounded	65	0
						" within clts.	3	0
	41	2						
						Head	62	0
	41	8					6	
Stretching	1	8				Divide by 11)372	0	
Leech -	40	0						
						33 $\frac{2}{11}$ or 34 cloths		

	FT.	IN.		IN.
Housing	21	6	- - 18	chock.
			sub. 8	tenon.
	10			
Housing of mast 20	8			

Foot, 38 cloths.

FORE-COURSE.

	FT.	IN.	FT.	IN.			FT.	IN.
Foremast	77	6	13	0	head.	Foreyard - -	65	8
"			5	0	sling.	" two arms -	8	0
"			27	0	housing.			
	45	0				" hounded -	57	8
						" within the		
Leech	32	6				clts. the		
						earings	3	0
							54	8
							6	
						Divide by 11)328	0	

TOPSAILS.
29 $\frac{7}{11}$ or 30 cloths
RULE.

1. The *hoist.* The hounded length of the topmast, or mast-head, deducted from the extreme length of the topmast.

2. *Head.* Subtract the two yard-arms from the whole length of the yard, gives the hounded length, and 3 *feet* for the earings within the cleats on the yard-arms is the *length of the head.*

3. *Close-reef.* Subtract 4 feet from the whole length of the topsail-yard.

4. *Foot.* Subtract the two yard-arms from the length of the lower-yard, and the distance of the two pins of the sheave-holes is within the hounds, gives the *foot on a square.* Thus—

MAIN-TOPSAIL.

	FT.	IN.
Main-topmast - -	49	6
"　　head -	7	9
hounded -	41	9 hoist.

	FT.	IN.
Main-yard hounded - - - -	65	0
"　distance of the two pins within the hounds -	1	8
pin and pin	63	4 foot.
	4	

Divide by 7)253　4

　　36 cloths in the foot.

	FT.	IN.
Main-topsail-yard - -	57	10
"　　two arms -	9	6
	48	4
within the cleats the earings	3	0
Head	45	4
	6	

Divide by 11)272　0

24.⁴⁄ cloths.

Low-reef at half-way of the leech　- 54 feet.

FT.	
Here - Reef 54	Head 24 cloths.
Multiply by 6	Foot 36 ditto.
Divide by 11)324	(Art. 32)　½)60 sum.
	30 cloths the mean.
29½ cloths.	Reef 29½ ditto.

Diff.　½ cloth = 12in.
Hollow on each leech = 6in.

FORE-TOPSAIL.

	FT.	IN.
Fore-topmast - -	45	6
" head -	7	3
hounded	38	3 hoist.

	FT.	IN.
Fore-yard hounded - - - -	57	8
" distance of the two pins within the hounds -	1	8
" pin and pin	56	0 foot.
	4	
Divide by 7)224	0	

32 cloths in the foot.

	FT.	IN.
Fore-topsail-yard - - - -	52	6
" two arms -	9	0
" hounded - - - • • •	43	6
" within the cleats the earings -	3	0
Head	40	6
	6	
Divide by 11)243	0	

22 cloths.

Low-reef at half-way of the leech   -   48ft. 6in.

	FT.	IN.
Here - Reef	48	6
Multiply by	6	
Divide by 11)291	0	
	26¼ cloths.	

Head 22 cloths.
Foot 32 ditto.
½)54 sum.
27 cloths the mean.
Reef 26¼

Diff.   ¼ cloth = 12in.
Hollow on each leech = 6in.

MIZEN-TOPSAIL.

		FT.	IN.
Mizen-topmast	-	37	6
" head		5	10
" hounded		31	8 hoist.

		FT.	IN.
Cross-jack-yard	- - -	58	8
" two arms		13	0
" hounded	- - - -	45	8
" distance of the two pins within the hounds	-	1	4
pin and pin		44	4 foot.
			4
Divide by 7)177			4

25 cloths in the foot.

		FT.	IN.
Mizen-topsail-yard	- - - -	40	9
" two arms	-	6	6
" hounded	- - - - -	34	3
" within cleats the earings		3	0
Head		31	3
			6
Divide by 11)187			6

17 cloths.

Low-reef at 18 inches above half-way of leech - - 37ft. 6in.

	FT.	IN.
Here - Reef	37	6
Multiply by		6
Divide by 11)225		0
20½ cloths.		

Head 17 cloths.
Foot 25 ditto.

½)42 sum.

21 cloths the mean.

Reef 20½ cloths.

Diff. ½ cloth = 12in.
Hollow on each leech = 6in.

TOPGALLANT-SAILS.

RULE.

1. The *hoist*. The hounded length of the topgallant-mast, with one foot added.

2. The *head*. Subtract the two yard-arms from the whole length of the yard, gives the hounded length, and 18 inches for the earings to come within the cleats on the yard-arms, for the *length on the head*.

3. *Foot*. Subtract the two yard-arms from the length of the topsail-yard, and the distance of the two pins of the sheave-holes within the hounds gives the length of the foot for sheeting home. Thus—

MAIN-TOPGALLANT-SAIL.

	FT.	IN.	
Main-topgallant-mast - -	26		feet.
Add	1		
	27		hoist.
Main-topsail-yard, hounded - - -	48	4	
" distance of the two pins within the hounds -	1	4	
pin and pin	47	0	foot.
	4		
Divide by 7)188	0		
	26		cloths in the foot.
Main-topgallant-yard - -	41	7	
" two arms	5	4	
hounded - - - -	36	3	
within cleats the earings -	1	6	
Head	34	9	
	8		
Divide by 15)278	0		(18½ cloths.
15			
128			
120			
$\frac{8}{15}$ or ½ cloth.			

D

FORE-TOPGALLANT-SAIL.

Fore-topgallant-mast -   - - 24 feet.
                                        Add   1
                                              ———
                                              25 hoist.

	FT.	IN.
Fore-topsail-yard, hounded - - -	43	6
" distance of the two pins		
within the hounds -	1	4
" pin and pin	42	2	foot.
		4

Divide by 7)168 8
                ———
              24 cloths in the foot.

	FT.	IN.
Fore-topgallant-yard - -	37	8
" two arms	4	10
	32	10
hounded - - -		
earings within the		
cleats - - -	1	6
Head	31	4
		8

Divide by 15)250   8(16½ cloths.
            15
           ———
            100
             90
           ———
             10
             12
           ———
      15)128(8in., or ½ cloth nearly.
         120
         ———

MIZEN-TOPGALLANT-SAIL.

	FT.	IN.
Mizen-topgallant-mast - -	19	10
Add	1	0
	20	10 hoist.

	FT.	IN.
Mizen-topsail-yard, hounded - - -	34	3
" distance of the two pins within the hounds -	1	0
pin and pin	33	3 foot.
		4
Divide by 7)133		0
	19 cloths in the foot.	

	FT.	IN.
Mizen-topgallant-yard -	29	8
" two arms -	3	10
hounded - - - - - -	25	10
within the cleats the earings	1	6
Head	24	4
		6
Divide by 11)146		0
	13¼ cloths.	

ROYALS.

RULE.

1. The *hoist*. The hounded length of the royal-mast.

2. The *head*. Subtract the two yard-arms from the whole length of the yard, gives the hounded length, and 1 foot for the earings to come within the cleats on the yard-arms, which gives the *length on the head*.

3. The *foot*. Subtract the two yard-arms from the length of the top-gallant-yard, and the hounded length gives the *length of the foot* sheeted home.

MAIN-ROYAL.

Main-royal-mast - - - 18 feet the hoist.

FT. IN.

Main-topgallant-yard, hounded -　36　3
"　distance of the two pins within the hounds - - -　1　0

pin and pin -　35　3 foot.
7

Divide by 13)246　9(19 cloths in the foot.
13

116
117

FT. IN.

Main-royal-yard　-　29　6
"　two arms　3　6

hounded - - - - -　26　0
earings to come within the cleats - - - - - -　1　0

Head　25　0
8

Divide by 15)200　0(13⅓ cloths.
15

50
45

$\frac{5}{15} = \frac{1}{3}$.

FORE-ROYAL.

Fore-royal-mast   -   16ft. 6in. the hoist.

	FT.	IN.
Fore-topgallant-yard, hounded - -	32	10
" distance of the two pins within the hounds -	1	0

pin and pin   31 10 foot.
7

Divide by 13)222 10(17 cloths in the foot.
13

92
91
—
1

	FT.	IN.
Fore-royal-yard - - -	26	0
" two arms	3	6
hounded - - - - -	22	6
earings to come within the cleats - - - - -	1	0
Head	21	6
		8

Divide by 15)172 0(11¾ cloths.
15

22
15
—

$\frac{7}{15}$ or ¾ cloths nearly.

Mizen-royal-mast   - - -   13 feet the hoist.

	FT.	IN.
Mizen-topgallant-yard, hounded -	25	10
" distance of the two pins		
within the hounds -	0	10
pin and pin	25	0 foot.
	7	

Divide by 13)175(13½ cloths in the foot.
13

45
39

$\frac{6}{13}$ or ½ cloth.

	FT.	IN.
Mizen-royal-yard - -	21	0
" two arms	2	6
hounded - - - - - -	18	6
earings to come within the		
cleats - - - - - -	1	0
Head	17	6
	8	

Divide by 15)140   0(9⅓ cloths.
135

$\frac{5}{15} = \frac{1}{3}$ cloth.

DRIVER.

RULE.

1. To determine the *height* of the nook of the sail, or gaff, on the mast. Add the length of the mast-head, the sling of the cross-jack yard, and the housing of the mizen-mast, and subtract the sum from the whole length of the mizen-mast, the remainder gives the height of the cross-jack-yard, on a level with the cat-harpin legs, when the gaff is worked on a trysail-mast; but when worked on the standing mast, it can seldom be got so high.

2. The *luff* or *depth* of the mast. The distance from the nook to 1 foot 4 inches, or to 1 foot 9 inches, above the boom, which the height of the saddle will determine, which is about 5 feet 6 inches above the deck in flush-deck vessels, and in poop-deck ships as low as the boom can be conveniently worked over the poop or barricading.

3. To determine the *length on the head.* Subtracting the outer end (for

displaying signals) from the length of the gaff, gives the hounded length or place of the cleat, and 1¼ inch in every 3 feet is allowed for the head of the sail stretching, which is about 1 foot 8 inches in small vessels, and 2 feet in larger, what the head comes within the cleat or hound.

4. The *length of the foot* is short of the length of the boom 3¼ inches in every 3 feet, for the foot of the sail stretching.

5. For the *proportion* of the *after-leech* to the *luff*, which determines the *peak*, one and three-fifths the luff. Thus—

	FT.	IN.	FT.	IN.	
Mizen-mast	60	0	9	9	head.
"			3	0	sling.
"			14	5	housing.
	27	2			
			32	10	height of cross-jack-yard from the poop-deck.
			6	0	height of tack from the deck.
Depth of mast	26	10			

	FT.	IN.
Gaff - -	41	4½
" end -	6	4½
" hounded - - - - - - -	35	0
" earing to come within the hound	2	0
Head	33	0
		5

Divide by 9)165

18⅓ cloths.

Distance of outrigger-end to the mast, 49 feet, and $\frac{49}{3}$ = 16 yards, which, multiplied by 3¼ inches = 5 feet, the foot is to be short of the boom ; or, the length of foot of sail is 44 feet. $\frac{44 \times 24}{43}$ = 24½ cloths in the foot. (See p. 12.)

Leech = 27 + $\frac{27 \times 3}{5}$ = 43 feet.

STANDING JIB.

RULE.

The *foot* to be one cloth less than five-sixths of the length of the jib-boom.

The *depth of the leech* :—as many yards in length, within one, as there are cloths in the foot.

The *luff* or *stay* :—about one-fourth more than the length of the leech.*

The *foot* is obtained thus—Jib-boom, 45 feet, and $\frac{45 \times 5}{6} = 37$ feet, equal to 20 cloths; leech, $19\frac{3}{4}$ yards, cut; and stay, 25 yards.

STAYSAILS.

FORE-TOPMAST STAYSAIL.

RULE.—The *length of the leech* :—the hounded length of the fore-topmast. The *foot* :—the same number of cloths as the leech in yards. Thus—fore-topmast, hounded, 38 feet 3 inches; or leech, 13 yards, cut; foot, 13 cloths.

FORE-STAYSAIL.

RULE.—The *foot* of this sail to have two cloths more than half the number of cloths in the head of the fore-course, cut straight. The *depth of the leech* :—the same as the fore-course.

MAIN-STAYSAIL.

RULE.—The *foot* to be five-eighths the number of cloths in the head of the main-course, and to be cut straight. The *depth of the leech* :— the same as the main-course.

MIZEN-STAYSAIL.

RULE.—The *foot* to be equal to one-half the number of cloths in the head of the main-course. The *depth of the leech* to be seven-eighths of the depth of the main-course. The *mast* to be two-thirds the depth of the leech, having two mast-gores.

STUDDINGSAILS.

LOWER-STUDDINGSAIL.

RULE.—The *number of cloths* to be two-thirds of the quantity of cloths in the head of the foresail, with two cloths more in large ships. The *depth of the leech* :—the same as the fore-course.

MAIN-TOPMAST AND TOPGALLANT STUDDINGSAILS.

RULE.—The *maintop and topgallant studdingsails* are one-half the respective cloths in the head of fore-topsail and topgallant-sails. Four cloths are gored on the outer-leech of the topmast-studdingsails, and three cloths of the topgallant-studdingsails.

FORE-TOPMAST AND TOPGALLANT STUDDINGSAILS.

RULE.—One *cloth* less than the maintop and topgallant studdingsails. The *depth of the inner leeches* :—9 inches longer than the leeches of the respective topsails and topgallant-sails.

* The complaint of jibs, which do not stand well, is very often from the clue being too low ; and when the jib-sheet is carried too far aft, the sail is always drumming with a slack leech. (See Art. 43.)

CHAPTER IV.

ON ROACHING THE SAILS, AND THE MENSURATION
OF THE GORES.

35. What is here meant by *roaching*, is the arc of a circle passing through the middle at the foot and clues of the sails, as topsails, top-gallant-sails, &c., for clearing the several stays which reach between the masts and bowsprit, and standing above the yards.

36. The height of the lower part of the topsails, topgallant-sails, &c., at the middle, is governed by the height of the stays standing above the yards, on which they are extended.

37. The height of the lower part of the courses at the middle, in small vessels, is governed by the height of the boats, for the main, and by the mainstay, when it is carried to the stem, for the fore; and, in large ships, the foot of the courses stands about 6 inches above the bulwarks or hammock-rails. The roach, however, of the foot of the courses is *not* circular: ¼ of its breadth at the middle is made parallel to the head, from which place the clues are carried down to give the roach. The reason why there are so many square cloths in the centre of the course, is to prevent leeward pressure, thereby equalizing the pressure of the wind on the surface of the sail—the same means clearing the height of the boats, and not throwing the foot so high up into the wind.

38. That the courses may stand well, it requires an equal strain to be brought on the foot and leech ropes; for if the sail is acted on too much up and down, the foot will become slack, or, if too much in a fore-and-aft direction, the leeches will become slack; consequently, too much care cannot be taken in fixing these blocks for the tacks and sheets, or, if the blocks are fixed, in cutting the sail to them.

39. The foot of the foresail is sometimes narrowed, for bringing the tack to the boomkin:—formerly, 3 feet 9 inches on each leech, and, in some ships, about 2 feet, or two cloths in the foot less than the head. This quantity, however, may not be invariable; for when the boomkin can be carried sufficiently forward to bring the tack properly down, it will be better to lessen the narrowing, not only on account of gaining sail, and for appearance, but the sail will, in general, stand better with parallel leeches.

40. The roach of the mainsail, in 1,500 tons ships, is 3 feet 9 inches, and in smaller ships, 3 feet; and the roach of the foresail, 3 feet, and in small vessels, 2 feet 6 inches. The roach of the mainsail and foresail should, however, be such, that when the depth at the middle is fixed, as well as the tack and sheet blocks, the foot and leech ropes shall be properly acted on.

41. The roach commonly given to topsails is about 1 foot 9 inches for main and fore topsails, and 3 feet for mizen-topsails. The topsails of brigs are usually roached about 2 feet 6 inches to 3 feet.

42. The quantity of roach given to topgallant-sails, for large ships,

E

is 4 feet, and for small ships, about 3 feet. The roach here given is for clearing the topmast stays, when the topsails are reefed. To lessen the roach in the topgallant-sails would be somewhat advantageous with whole topsails; but when the topsails are reefed, the topgallant-sails must be kept higher, and not sheeted home. The mizen-topgallant-sail is commonly roached as much as 5 feet 6 inches, on account of the standing part of the main-topgallant braces leading to the mizen-topmast stay, and, particularly so, to allow the sheets to come home over the single-reefed mizen-topsail.

43. The royals are also roached as much as 1 foot 6 inches the main and fore, and 2 feet the mizen, in large ships; but brigs are commonly roached only 6 inches.

44. The remaining sails, by which the gore on the foot gives the position of the clues, are the jib and driver. The position of the clue of the jib will be according to the steave of the bowsprit, and the angle formed by the jib-stay and the fore-topmast. The flatter the jib-stay, or the greater angle the jib-stay makes with the fore-topmast, the greater foot gore is required, and shorter leech; and, also, the less the steave of the bowsprit, the shorter the length of the leech, and more foot gore will the jib require. The height of the clue, however, should be such as to prevent the foot-rope being slack, or the sail drumming with a slack leech.

45. The common size given to the jib at the foot is $\frac{1}{6}$ the length of the jib-boom, and one cloth less for small ships; for the leech, as many yards in length within one as there are cloths in the foot; and for the luff or stay, every cloth is roached 3 inches, or the fore-edge of each cloth is carried down 3 inches, on an average, without a perpendicular from its edge, and the most round on the stay is nearly one-third up from the tack, to a line stretched from the tack to the peak; but, if we desire the element to which its dimensions bear the best relation, and take ·27, the length of the water-line, for the foot of the jib, ·8, or nearly the length of the topmast-stay, for the luff, and ·8 of the luff for the leech, we shall have a well-proportioned jib, which will stand well, provided the proper round in the luff and foot be given. The leech, however, may be somewhat longer, (when the bowsprit steaves a great deal,) to avoid carrying the jib-sheet too far aft, and to prevent the leech-rope from being slack. The longer the leech and foot of the sail are, the less foot-gore is required; and the foot, to form the proper round, must be made to cut the stay from 6 to 9 inches above the jib-boom; or the foot of the jib should be like a driver foot.

46. The amount of the foot-gores in the driver, which determines the position of its clue, can only be governed by the number of cloths in the mast-leech or luff, and the rake of the mast. The foot-gore must vary inversely as to the rake of the mast. The greater the rake, the less the foot-gore; but the boom, which rises with the sheer of the deck, will also diminish the foot-gore. Hence, care must be taken in giving the proper foot-gore to suit the rake which the mast has, and the number of cloths in the mast-leech. Again, when the mast cloths are several, and the mast has little rake, the gore of the foot can be made

less, by dividing the cloths between the mast-leech and after-leech:—say, if there were 9 cloths difference between the foot and head, let 3 goring-cloths be brought on the after-leech (see Plate 6), and that will diminish the foot-gore considerably; also, the fewer the mast cloths, the greater is the head-gore, and the less the foot gore, for giving the sail peak.

47. The proportion of the leech to the luff or mast-leech, which determines the peak, varies according to fancy. When with a narrow head, the sail has a handsome appearance, having a deal of peak; but a wide head and little peak is better adapted for quick sailing. In the merchant service, the proportion of the length of the after-leech in large ships' drivers, is one and three-fifths the luff; and in brigs, about one-half longer than the depth of the fore-leech. The head is within the cleats, in large ships, 2 feet, and in all smaller vessels about 1 foot 8 inches, for stretching. The head, foot, mast-leech, and after-leech are roached (see Plate 6). The latter of these is by means of gathering slack canvas in the seaming-up of the after-leech, or *puckering* the seams, in a gradual manner. The slack, however, should be held on all above the reefs; that is, 1 inch in every 3 feet down from the head to the upper reef in the leech seam, and 1 inch less in the next seam, and so on, one inch less in every seam from the leech; but when the sail has a narrow head, and a long leech, the slack is more quickly diminished. The seams thus sewed, and the slack allowed in the cutting out, form the curve on the leech, which, rightly managed, will be an extremely near approximation to a circular arc. The same means give the utmost freedom to the after-leech, thereby taking out the belly which was made by the broad seams, and bringing it back, as near as possible, to a perfect plane; besides, the straining of the leech into a hollow is completely avoided—at least, so far as it is practicable. (See Art. 31.)

48. In determining the gores for sails, no general rule appears to be known among sailmakers, and only such figures are used by them which their own experience has discovered, without attempting at figures founded on mathematical principles. It is here intended to show, that all the gores can be calculated for every sail, the sizes of which have already been determined, according to the preceding rules. Previous, however, to these being worked out, it will be necessary to give a few preliminary examples.

ON FINDING THE DEPTH OF THE GORES, FOR CUTTING THE HOLLOW ON THE LEECHES OF A TOPSAIL.

49. Given the depth of the leech, the number of cloths, and the hollow on the leech, to find the depth of each gore.

EXAMPLE.

Given the depth of the leech, 32 feet, the number of goring cloths, four and a half, equal to 9 feet wide, and the hollow at half-way down on the leech, 2 feet?

(Plate 1.) Let the right angled triangle ABC, Fig. 1, represent the leech, when straight. Upon AC, as a chord with the height or given hollow, describe the arc ANC, of which O is the centre, and ON the radius. Draw OE, AF, and OF parallel to BC and AB respectively. Divide the base BC, which is equal to the width of the cloths, into as many equal parts as there are cloths in the leech, which, in the present example, are four and a half, being designed for a small topsail with a deal of hollow. (See Art. 32.) Through the points of division draw lines perpendicular to BC, to meet on OE, then will the differences of the perpendiculars within ANCB be the gored cloths, and the depth of each is easily found by the following.

CALCULATION OF THE DEPTH OF THE GORES.

Here $AC = \sqrt{(AB^2 + BC^2)} = 33\cdot24$, the length of the chord of the arc ANC. From the chord of the arc equal $33\cdot24$ feet, and the height or hollow 2 feet, will be found the radius of the sweep $ON = \frac{1}{2}$ $(IN + \frac{AI^2}{IN}) = \frac{1}{2} (2 + \frac{16\cdot62^2}{2}) = 70\cdot056$. And, by similar triangles ABC, AIG, and OGF, we have $BC : AB :: AI : IG$ and $AC : BC ::$ $OG : OF$; or, $IG = \frac{32 \times 16\cdot62}{9} = 59\cdot09$, $OG = 70\cdot056 - (59\cdot09 + 2)$ $= 8\cdot966$, and $OF = \frac{9 \times 8\cdot966}{33\cdot24} = 2\cdot42$, the distance from the centre to the half chord AF, and $AF = \sqrt{(70\cdot05^2 - 2\cdot42^2)} = 70\cdot01$. Hence, the length of the perpendiculars within ANCD are as follow :—

$$\sqrt{(70\cdot056^2 - 68\cdot01^2)} - 2\cdot42 = 14\cdot38$$
$$\sqrt{(70\cdot056^2 - 66\cdot01^2)} - 2\cdot42 = 21\cdot05$$
$$\sqrt{(70\cdot056^2 - 64\cdot01^2)} - 2\cdot42 = 26\cdot05$$
$$\sqrt{(70\cdot056^2 - 62\cdot01^2)} - 2\cdot42 = 30\cdot17$$
$$\sqrt{(70\cdot056^2 - 61\ 01^2)} - 2\cdot42 = 32\cdot$$

And the depth of the gores are thus found, as the

		FT. DEC.		FT.	IN.
1st gore -	- - - - - -	14·38	=	14	4
2d ditto -	21·05—14·38 =	6·67	=	6	8
3d ditto -	26·05—21·05 =	5·	=	5	0
4th ditto	30·17—26·05 =	4·12	=	4	0
½ ditto -	32· —30·17 =	1·83	=	2	0
	Leech			32	0

ON FINDING THE DEPTH OF THE GORES, FOR CUTTING THE ROACH OF THE FORE-LEECH OF A DRIVER.

50. Given the length on the mast, the number of mast cloths, and the round or height of the roach, to find the depth of each gore.

EXAMPLE.

Given the depth of the mast, 26 feet, the number of mast cloths, five and a half, equal to 11 feet, and the roach 6 inches?

(Plate 1.) Here AC, Fig. 1, $= \sqrt{(CD^2 + AD^2)} = 28\cdot2$, the length of the chord of the arc ANC, $\therefore$ the radius $ON = \frac{1}{2}(\cdot5 + \frac{14^2}{\cdot5}) = 199\cdot34$. And by similar triangles ACD, AIG, and OGF, we have AD : CD :: AI : IG, and AC : AD :: OG : OF, or $IG = \frac{26 \times 14\cdot1}{11} = 33\cdot35$, OG $= 199\cdot34 - (33\,35 + \cdot5) = 165\cdot49$, and $OF = \frac{11 \times 165\cdot49}{28\cdot2} = 64\cdot55$, the distance from the centre to the half chord AF, and $AF = \sqrt{(199\cdot34^2 - 64\cdot55^2)} = 188\cdot6$. Hence, the lengths of the perpendiculars within ANCD are respectively—

$$\sqrt{(199.34^2 - 186\cdot6^2)} - 64\cdot55 = 5\cdot57$$
$$\sqrt{(199\cdot34^2 - 184\cdot6^2)} - 64\cdot55 = 10\cdot67$$
$$\sqrt{(199\cdot34^2 - 182\cdot6^2)} - 64\cdot55 = 15\cdot41$$
$$\sqrt{(199\cdot34^2 - 180\cdot6^2)} - 64\cdot55 = 19\cdot83$$
$$\sqrt{(199\cdot34^2 - 178\cdot6^2)} - 64\cdot55 = 23\cdot98$$
$$\sqrt{(199\cdot34^2 - 177\cdot6^2)} - 64\cdot55 = 26\cdot0$$

And the depth of the gores are thus found, as the

			FT. DEC.	FT.	IN.
1st mast gore	- - - - - -		5·57 =	5	6
2d ditto	- -	10·67— 5·57 =	5·10 =	5	0
3d ditto		15·41—10·67 =	4·74 =	4	9
4th ditto	-	19·83—15·41 =	4·42 =	4	6
5th ditto	-	23·98—19·83 =	4·15 =	4	2
½ ditto	-	26· —23·98 =	2·02 =	2	0
		Mast -		26	0

ON FINDING THE DEPTH OF THE LEECH GORES, WHEN THE LEECHES ARE CUT STRAIGHT.

51. Given the depth of the leech, and the number of cloths gored on the leech, to find the depth of each gore.

RULE.—Divide the depth of the leech by the number of cloths gored on the leech, and it will give the depth of each gore.

EXAMPLES.

1. Given the depth of the leech of a main-course, 40 feet, and having two goring cloths, that is, three-quarters of a cloth at the earing, and one-quarter of a cloth at the clue?

<pre>
Here   -   Divide by 2)40 feet.   And ¼)20 feet.
                     —   Subtract 5 "
                    20   —
       First, three-quarter cloth   15 gore.
       Second, a whole cloth   -   20   "
       Third, a quarter cloth -   5   "
                                           —
                           Leech   40 feet.
</pre>

2. Given the hoist of a topsail, 32 feet, and three and three-quarters cloths on each leech; that is, half of a cloth at each earing, and one quarter of a cloth at the clues?

<pre>
Here   -   Divide by 3¾)32 feet.
                    4   4
                   —   —
              15)128(8 feet 6 inches.
                 120
                 ——
                   8
                  12
                 ——
              15)96(6
                 90
                 ——
                  6
                 ——
</pre>

<pre>
                                           FT. IN.
And   Divide by ¼)8   6
                                     ——————
       First, half a cloth   -   4   3 gore.
       Second, a whole cloth -   8   6   "
       Third, ditto ditto   -   8   6   "
       Fourth, ditto ditto   -   8   6   "
       Fifth, a quarter cloth   2   0   "
                                      ——————
                   Leech   - 32   0
</pre>

3. Given the hoist of a topgallant-sail, 20 feet 6 inches, and two and five-eighths cloths on the leech ; that is, equal to 15 inches wide the cloth at the earing, and one quarter of a cloth at the clue ?

	IN.	
Thus	24	- equal to one cloth.

	IN.	
	12	equal to one-half of a cloth.
	3	equal to one-eighth of a cloth.

Sub.	15	equal to five-eighths of a cloth.
	9	equal to three-eighths of a cloth.

And 9 inches, or $\frac{3}{8}$ of a cloth, are cut off the full cloth at the earing, and brought on at the clue for the one quarter cloth.

Here - Divide by 2⅝)20 6
                      8   8

21)164 0(7 feet 9½ inches.
   147
   ——
    17
    12
   ——
21)204(9½
   189
   ——
    15
   ——

	FT.	IN.
Therefore - - - - -	7	9½ .
Multiply by		3
Divide by 8)23		4½

First, three-eighths of a cloth	2	11	gore.
Second, a whole cloth - - -	7	9½	"
Third, ditto ditto -	7	9½	"
Fourth, one quarter cloth -	2	0	"
Leech -	20	6	

ON FINDING THE NUMBER OF SQUARE CLOTHS TO PUT IN THE ROACH OF THE FOOT OF SAILS.

52. Given the number of cloths in the foot of a topsail, or any four-sided sail, and the height of the arc, or amount of the foot-gore, to find what number of square cloths there ought to be, so that the foot shall be nearly circular, and the first gore, from the sides of the squares, cut with 1 inch gore.

EXAMPLES.

1. Given the number of cloths in the foot of a topsail, 43, and foot-gore, 1 foot 9 inches; required the number of squares?

(Plate 1.) Let AB, Fig 2, represent the half of the foot, and BC the height of the arc, or total amount of the foot-gore. Draw the radius OE, and from E draw EI parallel to AC, and EI will be half of the squares, and IB $=$ 1 inch, the first gore.

Here, 43 cloths $=$ 86 feet, the half of which is 43 feet, the chord AC, and 1 foot 9 inches $=$ 1·75 $=$ BC, the height of the arc, and 1 inch $=$ ·08$\not{3}$. From the chord of the arc equal 43, and the height 1·75, the radius is thus found for the foot, viz., OE $= \frac{1}{2}$ (BC $+ \frac{AC^2}{BC}$).

Thus	43		And	529·16	radius.
	43		Sub.	·08$\not{3}$	BI

$$\text{Thus} \quad \begin{array}{r} 43 \\ 43 \\ \hline 129 \\ 172 \\ \hline \end{array}$$

$$\text{And} \quad 529\cdot16 \text{ radius.}$$
$$\text{Sub.} \quad \cdot08\not{3} \text{ BI}$$
$$529\cdot07\not{3} \text{ OI}$$

Therefore EI $= \sqrt{(OE^2 - OI^2)} = 9$ feet.

$$1\cdot75)1849(\quad \begin{array}{r} 1056\cdot57 \\ 1\cdot75 \end{array}$$

$$\begin{array}{r} 175 \\ \hline 990 \\ 875 \\ \hline 1150 \\ 1050 \\ \hline 1000 \\ 875 \\ \hline 1250 \\ 1225 \\ \hline 25 \end{array}$$

$$\tfrac{1}{2})1058\cdot32$$
$$529\cdot16 \text{ radius.}$$

Hence, the number of squares is nine cloths.

2. Given 28 cloths in the foot of a topgallant-sail, and gore of the foot, 4 feet; to find the requisite number of squares?

Here, OE $= \frac{1}{2}$ (4 $+ \frac{14^2}{4}$) $=$ 100, the radius, and 1 inch $=$ ·08$\not{3}$ feet, $\therefore$ 100$-$·08$\not{3} =$ 99·91$\not{3} =$ OI; therefore EI $= \sqrt{(100^2 - 99\cdot91\not{3}^2)}$ $=$ 4 feet.

Hence, the number of square cloths is *four*.

ON FINDING THE LENGTH OF THE ARC OR ROACH ON THE FOOT OF A TOPSAIL, TOPGALLANT-SAIL, &c.

53. Given the length of the foot, sheeted home, and height, or total amount of the foot-gore, to find the length on the roach or curve of the foot.

RULE.—From eight times the chord of half the arc, subtract the chord of the whole arc, and one-third of the remainder will be the length of the arc *nearly.*[*]

EXAMPLES.

1. Given the length of the foot of a topsail, 32 feet, and height of the foot-gore, 3 feet; what length ought the foot to measure, when marled or fixed in?

(Plate 1.)   Here $\frac{1}{2}$)32 the length of the foot.   AB (Fig. 2) =

— $\sqrt{(16^2 + 3^2)} = 16\ 2785.$

16 half the chord or AC.

Therefore   16·2785 chord of half arc.

Multiply by   8

130·2280

Subtract   32·0000 chord of whole arc.

Divide by 3)98·2280 diff.

32·7426 = 32 feet 9 inches.

Hence, the foot is 9 inches longer on the roach than it is upon a square, or distance the clues are on the yard.

2. Given the length of the foot of a mizen topgallant-sail, 32 feet, and height of the foot-gore, 5 feet 6 inches; to find the measure on the roach for fixing the foot?

Here $\frac{1}{2}$)32 and $\sqrt{(16^2 + 5\cdot5^2)} = 16\cdot9189$, chord of half arc.

—

16

Therefore   16·9189 chord of half arc.

·Multiply by   8

135·3512

Subtract   32·0000 chord of whole arc.

Divide by 3)103·3512 diff.

34·4504 = 34 feet 5 inches.

Hence, the roach is 2 feet 5 inches longer than the foot on a square.

[*] This rule was first given by Huygens, a Dutch mathematician.

ON FINDING THE FOOT-GORE, FROM THE MEASUREMENT OF THE CROSS-GORE OF A TRYSAIL. (See p. 8.)

54. Given the length on the head, foot, and mast leech, the number of mast cloths, and cross-gore, to find the foot-gore.

EXAMPLE.

Given the length on the mast-leech, 22 feet 6 inches; head, 20 feet; foot, 29 feet; cross-gore, 35 feet; and five mast cloths (per rules page 11); to find the foot-gore?

(Plate 1.)   As the three sides of the triangle CAB, Fig. 3, are given, we may find the angle ABC; and in the right-angled triangle APB, AB and BP are given, and, therefore, the angle ABP, and the difference of the angles ABC and ABP, will equal the angle CBE; so that we shall have in the right angled triangle BEC, the side BC, and the angles to find CE.   The computation will, therefore, be as follows:—

By a well-known rule in trigonometry—

$$\text{Cos. ABC} = \frac{AB^2 + BC^2 - AC^2}{2\, AB \cdot BC} = \text{cos. } 09367 = 84° \ 38'.$$

Again, by Rule 1, page 9, *five cloths* equals $\dfrac{5 \times 11}{6} = \dfrac{55}{6} = 9$ feet 2 inches equal BP, $\therefore$ angle ABP $= \dfrac{BP}{AB} = $ cos. $40740 = 65° \ 58'$, and angle CBE $= 84° \ 38' - 65° \ 58' = 18° \ 40'$, $\therefore$ CE $=$ BC sin. CBE $= 29 \times$ ·32006 $= 9·28$, or 9 feet 3 inches the *foot-gore.*

$$\text{PF} = \text{BP} \frac{\sin. \text{ B}}{\cos. \text{ B}} = \text{BP tan. CBE} = 3 \text{ feet 1 inch.}$$

Remark.—In this example the mast cloths equal the foot-gore; but, when the foot is longer, it increases the cross-gore, and also the foot-gore; consequently, the mast cloths alone are no rule for determining the foot gore.   For further remarks, see Art. 46.

ON FINDING THE FOOT-GORE, FROM THE RAKE OF THE MAST AND MAST CLOTHS. (See Art. 46.)

55. Given the length of the mast-leech, foot, the rake of the mast to the foot, and the number of mast cloths, to find the foot-gore.

EXAMPLE.

The rake of the mast, in the above example, is $1\frac{1}{8}$ inch to the foot. Then the mast-leech, 22·5 feet, $\times$ $1\frac{1}{8}$ inch $= 2·11$ feet, $\therefore$ angle included between the perpendicular and mast is equal to tan. $\dfrac{2·11}{22·5} = 5° \ 22'$, which subtracted from 90° gives 84° 38', ABP (above example) $= 65° \ 58'$, and CBE $= 18° \ 40'$, $\therefore$ CE $= 9$ feet 3 inches the foot-gore.

ON FINDING THE FOOT-GORE, WHEN THE MAST STANDS UPRIGHT.

56. Given the length of the mast-leech, foot, and the number of mast cloths, to find the foot-gore.

RULE.—The length of the foot multiplied by the width of the mast cloths (by a thread of the weft), and divided by the length of the mast-leech, gives the *foot-gore*, supposing the boom on a level with the water; but if the boom has an elevation aft, which it commonly has, and varying from about 1 foot in 12 to 1 foot in 10 above the level of the water, this quantity must be deducted.

EXAMPLE.

Given same as in the first example,

	FT.	IN.	
Then - - -	9	2 = 5 mast cloths.	
Multiply by - -	29 = length of foot.		

FT. IN.
Divide by 22 6)265 10
2 2

FT. IN.
45 0)531 8(11 9⅞ foot gore·
45

81
45

36
12

440(9
405

$\frac{35}{45} = \frac{7}{9}$

ON FINDING THE HEAD-GORE.

57. RULE.—Multiply the sum and difference of the cross-gore and head, and divide the product by the length of the leech: the quotient halved and subtracted from the half length of the leech, gives the head-gore.

EXAMPLE.

The dimensions the same as the preceding. Leech, 33 feet 9 inches, (Art. 47). Here $(35 + 20) (35—20) = 825$, and $\frac{825}{33\cdot75} = 24\cdot4$, $\therefore$
$\frac{1}{2}(33\cdot75—24\cdot4) = 4\cdot6$, or 4 feet 7 inches the *head-gore.*

ON FINDING THE GORES FOR CUTTING A CIRCULAR FOOT TRYSAIL, JIB, &c.

58. Given the total amount of the foot gores, the number of cloths in the foot, and the round up at the clue, to find what distance the *square* cloth ought to be from the leech, and the gore on each cloth, so that the foot shall be *circular*.

EXAMPLE.

Given the foot-gore of a trysail, 9 feet; the number of cloths, 16; and cut up at the clue, 6 inches?

(Plate 1.) Let the arc of the circle BIC represent the foot of the trysail ABCD, BE = 16 cloths across, or 32 feet, IL = 9 feet the height of the arc, or total amount of foot-gore. From C draw CK parallel to BE, and IK = 6 inches, and CK will be the distance of the square cloth. The distance of the square cloth is found thus—viz.,

$CK = \frac{BE}{CE}(\sqrt{IL \cdot IK} - IK)^* = 6$ feet, or 3 cloths; that is, the fourth cloth from the leech must be cut a square. Hence, BL = 12 cloths, or 24 feet, and the radius of the foot is, $OI = \frac{1}{2}(9 + \frac{24^2}{9}) = 36 \cdot 5$; and, similarly to Art. 50, we find the foot-gores.

	FT. DEC.	IN.
1st gore (next the tack)	1·6 =	19
2d ditto - - - -	1·432 =	17
3d ditto	1·222 =	15
4th ditto	1·052 =	13
5th ditto	·902 =	11
6th ditto	·762 =	9
7th ditto	·633 =	8
8th ditto	·507 =	6
9th ditto	·390 =	4
10th ditto	·280 =	3
11th ditto	·165 =	2
12th ditto	·055 =	1
13th ditto - - -	·000 =	0
14th ditto (reversed)	=	1
15th ditto - - -	=	2
16th ditto -	=	3

9 feet.

Similarly, the foot-gores of a jib may be calculated, and likewise the gores on the stay, with sufficient data. It is the curvilinear branch of this art in sailmaking which particularly calls for arithmetical and geometrical knowledge; for, without their aid, sailmakers must frequently feel their deficiency, when curved edges mingle with straight-sided sails.

* *Demonstration.*—Let $a-x =$ half chord of the arc, $b =$ its height, $c =$ the difference between the height and the ordinate at the distance of x from the middle of the chord, and D the diameter. Then will $(D-b)b = (a-x)^2$ and $(D-c)c = x^2$, or $Db = a^2 - 2ax + x^2 + b^2$, and $Dc = x^2 + c^2$, from which we get $\dfrac{a^2 - 2ax + x^2 + b^2}{b}$

CHAPTER V.

DIMENSIONS FOR CUTTING THE SAILS.

59. The two preceding chapters are the basis on which to complete our other dimensions for cutting the sails, and roaching, according to the size of the ship (Art. 37 to 46). The gores are calculated in a similar manner as in the last chapter, and the dimensions for cutting may be put like the following :—

MAIN-COURSE.

	FT.	IN.	
Head	62	0	equal to 34 cloths.
Foot	70	6	equal to 38 cloths.
Leech	41	0	cut, and 40 feet tabled.
Gore	3	0	
Middle - - - - -	38	0	cut.

For the number of squares   -   38 cloths.

(Art. 37.)

Divide by 5)114 over 3

23 squares, and gores 1, 2, 3, 4, 5-7, 9, 5 inches.

Leech gores   10, 20, and 10 = 40 feet.

FORE-COURSE.

	FT.	IN.	
Head	54	8	equal to 30 cloths.
Leech	32	6	tabled to the cringle holes.
Gore	3	0	
Middle - - - - -	30	6	cut.

For the number of squares   30 cloths.

(Art. 37.)

Divide by 5)90 over 3

18 squares, and gores 2, 3, 5, 7, 9, 11 inches.

MAIN-TOPSAIL.

Foot-gores.

	FT.	IN.		IN.
Head	45	6	equal to 24 cloths.	1
Reef	54	0		1
Foot -	63	4	equal to 36 cloths.	1
Hoist -	41	9		1
Gore -	1	9		1
Middle	40	0	cut—8 squares.	1
				2
				2

Leech-gores.

—	FT. DEC.		FT.	IN.
2—	8·11	=	8	1
2—	7·52	=	7	6
2—	7·07	=	7	1
2—	6·67	=	6	8
3—	6·35	=	6	4
3—	6·04	=	6	1
—	—		—	—
24	41·76	=	41	9

FORE-TOPSAIL.

Foot-gores.

	FT.	IN.		IN.
Head	40	6	equal to 22 cloths.	1
Reef	48	6		1
Foot	56	0	equal to 32 cloths.	1
Hoist	38	3		1
Gore -	1	9		2
Middle	36	6	out—8 squares.	2
				2

Leech-gores.

—	FT. DEC.		FT.	IN.
2—	9·07	=	9	1
2—	8·19	=	8	2
2—	7·5	=	7	6
3—	6·97	=	7	0
3—	6·52	=	6	6
—	—		—	—
22	38·25	=	38	3

MIZEN-TOPSAIL.

Foot-gores.

	FT.	IN.		IN.
Head	31	3	equal to 17 cloths.	1
Reef -	37	6		2
Foot -	44	4	equal to 25 cloths.	2
Hoist - -	31	8		3
Gore - -	3	0		3
Middle	28	8	out—5 squares.	4 Leech-gores.

	FT. DEC.		FT.	IN.
4—	9·6	=	9	7
5—	8·17	=	8	2
5—	7·22	=	7	3
6—	6·52	=	6	6
36	31·51		31	6

MAIN-TOPGALLANTSAIL.

Foot-gores.

	FT.	IN.		IN.
Head -	34	9	equal to 18½ cloths.	1
Foot -	47	0	equal to 26 cloths.	2
Hoist -	27	0		2
Gore -	4	0		3
Middle	23	0	cut—4 squares.	3
				4
				5 Leech-gores.

		FT.	IN.
6 —		5	6
7 —		7	2
7 —		7	2
8 —		7	2
48		27	0

FORE-TOPGALLANTSAIL.

Foot-gores.

	FT.	IN.		IN.
Head	31	4	equal to 16½ cloths.	1
Foot	42	2	equal to 24 cloths.	2
Hoist	25	0		3
Gore	4	0		4
Middle	21	0	cut—4 squares.	5
				5 Leech-gores.

		FT.	IN.
6 —		5	0
7 —		6	8
7 —		6	8
8 —		6	8
48		25	0

MIZEN-TOPGALLANTSAIL.

	FT.	IN.		Foot-gores. IN.
Head	24	4	equal to 13¼ cloths.	2
Foot	33	3	equal to 19 cloths.	3
Hoist	20	10		5
Gore	5	6		7
Middle	15	4	cut—1 square.	7
				9 Leech-gores.

		FT.	IN.
11	—	6	4
13	—	7	3
15	—	7	3
72		20	10

MAIN-ROYAL.

	FT.	IN.		Foot-gores. IN.
Head	25	0	equal to 13⅜ cloths.	1
Foot	35	3	equal to 19 cloths.	1
Hoist	18	0		2
Gore -	1	6		2
Middle	16	6	cut—3 squares.	3 Leech-gores.

		FT.	IN.
3	—	5	4
4	—	6	4
4	—	6	4
20		18	0

FORE-ROYAL.

	FT.	IN.		Foot-gores. IN.
Head	21	6	equal to 11¾ cloths.	1
Foot	31	10	equal to 17 cloths.	2
Hoist -	16	6		2 Leech-gores.
Gore -	1	6		
Middle	15	0	cut—4 squares.	

		FT.	IN.
3	—	0	10
4	—	6	3
5	—	6	3
3	—	3	2
20		16	6

MIZEN-ROYAL.

	FT.	IN.		Foot-gores.
				IN.
Head -	17	6	equal to 9½ cloths.	2
Foot -	25	0	equal to 13½ cloths.	3
Hoist -	13	0		5 Leech-gores.
Gore -	2	0		FT. IN.
Middle	11	0	cut—3 squares.	7 — 5 3
				7 — 6 3
				8 — 1 6
				27 13 0

DRIVER.

	FT.		Cloths.	Foot-gores. IN.	Mast-gores. FT. IN.
Head -	33	equal to 18½ cloths.	½	12 —	2 9
Foot -	44	equal to 24¼ cloths.	1	23 —	5 0
Leech -	45 6	cut—44ft. 3in. tabled.	2	21 —	4 9
Mast -	26 10	tabled.	3	19 —	4 6
			4	16 —	4 2
			5	14 —	3 6
			6	12 —	1 2
				Mast	25 10

Foot-gores. IN.	Head-gores. IN.		Cloths.
	4		- ½
10	- - 10		7
10	- 8		8
9	- 8		9
9	- 6		10
8	- 6		11
8	- - 4	-	12
7	- 3	- - - -	13
7	- 2	Slack seams.	14
5	1	IN.	15
4	0	1	16
3	0	2	17
2	1	3	18
1	2	4	19
0	2	5	20
1	3	6	21
2	3	7	22
3	4	8	23
4	4	- 10	24

STANDING-JIB.

Leech	19¾ yards cut : 56 feet tabled.
Stay	26⅛ yards tabled.
Foot	- 12⅝ yards, equal to 20 cloths.

Cloths.	Stay-gores. FT.	IN.	Foot-gores. IN.
1	11	0	3
2	6	4	2
3	4	9	0
4	4	9	1
5	4	0	2
6	4	0	3
7	3	6	4
8	3	6	5
9	3	2	6
10	3	2	7
11	3	0	8
12	3	0	9
13	2	10	10
14	2	10	11
15	2	8	13
16	2	8	15
17	2	6	17
18	2	6	19
19	2	6	21
20	2	6	24

FLYING-JIB.

Leech	17¾ yards cut.
Stay	22⅛ yards tabled.
Foot	- 9 yards, equal to 14 cloths.

Cloths.	Stay-gores. FT.	IN.	Foot-gores. IN.
1	9	0	0
2	7	0	1
3	6	0	2
4	5	0	3
5	4	8	4
6	4	8	5
7	4	6	7
8	4	6	9
9	4	0	11
10	4	0	13
11	3	6	15
12	3	0	18
13	2	6	21
14	2	6	24

FORETOPMAST-STAYSAIL.

		Stay-gores.		
Leech	39 feet cut : 37 feet 6 inches tabled.			
Stay	47 feet tabled.	Cloths.	FT.	IN.
Foot -	24 feet, equal to 13 cloths.	1st -	6	6
Foot-gores -	2 inches per cloth.	2nd -	5	0
		3rd	4	0
		4th	3	6
		5th	3	3
		6th -	3	3
		7th -	3	0
		8th	3	0
		9th	2	9
		10th	2	9
		11th	2	6
		12th	2	6
		13th	2	6

LOWER-STUDDINGSAIL.

Head, 45 feet 6 inches, equal to 24 cloths : cut, 33 feet.

MAIN-TOPMAST-STUDDINGSAIL.

Head, 11 cloths ; foot, 15 cloths ; and cut, 42 feet 6 inches *inner* leech.

Head-gore, 4 inches per cloth, decreasing to the outer earing.

Foot-gore, 5 inches per cloth, increasing the depth of the inner leech.

FORE-TOPMAST-STUDDINGSAIL.

Head, 10 cloths ; foot, 14 cloths ; and cut, 39 feet the *inner* leech.

Head-gore, 4 inches, and foot-gore, 5 inches per cloth, respectively.

MAIN-TOPGALLANT-STUDDINGSAIL.

Head, 8 cloths ; foot, 11 cloths ; and cut, 27 feet 9 inches the *inner* leech.

Head and *foot gores*, 6 inches per cloth.

FORE-TOPGALLANT-STUDDINGSAIL.

Head, 7 cloths ; foot, 10 cloths ; and cut, 25 feet 9 inches the *inner* leech.

Head and *foot gores*, 6 inches per cloth.

AWNINGS.

The canvas is cut in lengths, agreeably to the breadths measured (see page 8), and 3 feet taken off the length and breadths for stretching. Let the dimensions for the awnings be the following, viz. :—

Main-Deck Awning.

		FT.	IN.		FT.	IN.
Fore-rigging to fore-rigging	- -	30	6	cut	27	6
Main-rigging to main-rigging	-	27	6	- cut	24	6
Length (see page 8) measured	-	62	0	- cut	59	0

Then, per Rule I., page 9, $59 \times \frac{6}{11} = 32$ cloths.

	FT.	IN.	
Fore-end	27	6	14 squares, cut 27ft. 6in.
After-end -	24	6	After-end 18 gores, 1 inch each.

$\frac{1}{2}$)3   0   32 cloths.

1   6 or 18 inches gore each side.

Quarter-Deck Awning.

		FT.	IN.		FT.	IN.
Breadth at fore-end	- - - -			cut	24	6
Mizen-rigging to mizen-rigging	-	27	0	- cut	24	0
Length (see page 8) measured	-	43	6	- cut	40	6

Then, per Rule I., page 9, 40 feet 6 inches $\times \frac{6}{11} = 22$ cloths.

	FT.	IN.	
Fore-end -	24	6	19 squares, cut 24ft. 6in.
After-end -	24	0	After-end 3 gores, 1 inch per cloth.

$\frac{1}{4}$)6   22 cloths.

3 inches gore on each side.

Poop or After-Awning.

Breadth at fore-end		- - -	cut 24 feet.
Breadth at the taffrail	- - -	17 feet.	cut 15 feet.
Length (see page 8) measured	34 feet.	-	cut 31 feet.

Then, per Rule I., page 9, $31 \times \frac{6}{11} = 17$ cloths.

Fore-end - 24 feet.   1 square, cut 24 feet.
After-end - 15 feet.

Decreasing to after-end.
  { 1 gore, 1 inch per cloth.
  3 gores, 2 inches ditto.
  5 gores, 3 ditto ditto.
  4 gores, 4 ditto ditto.
  3 gores, 5 ditto ditto.

$\frac{1}{2}$)9

4ft. 6in. gore

17 cloths.

Forecastle Awning.

		FT. IN.		FT. IN.
Fore-end - - - - - -			cut	3 0
Cathead to cathead - - - -		23 0	cut	20 0
Fore rigging to fore-rigging - -		30 6	cut	27 6
Length (see page 8) - - - - - -		41 0	cut	38 0

Then, per Rule I., page 9, $38 \times \frac{6}{11} = 21$ cloths.

		FT. IN.
And - 20 feet.		27 6
Subtract 3 feet.		20 0

$\frac{1}{2})17$ $\frac{1}{2})7\ 6$

              3 9

8 feet 6 inches.

2 squares, cut 27ft. 6in.

{ 3 gores, 2, 4, 6 inches.
4 gores, 8in. per cloth.
12 gores, 8½in. ditto.

21 cloths.

CONCENTRATED JIB (SEE PLATE 5),

EQUAL TO 11 CLOTHS JIB.

		Stay-gores.		Cloths.
		FT. IN.		
Leech	36 feet cut.			
Stay -	49 feet tabled.	3	4 peak.	1
Foot	22 feet, equal to 11 cloths.	2	10 -	2
Square	17 feet opposite to the clue.	2	4 -	3

DIRECTIONS.

In cutting from the square cloth, cut each cloth longer, to allow for *eating-up* in seaming. Cut from the square or 13th cloth both ways.

The round of the foot is formed by the selvage of the cloth, that is, by cutting a hollow off the canvass to join the next cloth. This tightens the foot, and prevents its shaking.

There is no waste attending cutting a sail on this plan.

Stay-gores.		Cloths.
FT. IN.		
2	0 -	4
2	0 -	5
1	4 -	6
1	4 -	7
1	0 -	8
1	0	9
0	6	10
0	6	11
0	2	12
0	0	13
0	2	14
0	2	15
0	6 -	16
0	6 -	17
0	10 -	18
0	10 -	19
1	0	20
1	0	21
1	0	22

SECTION SECOND.

CHAPTER I.

ON CUTTING-OUT SAILS.

60. Sails are cut out, cloth by cloth, to the respective number of cloths in the head, foot, and stay: the depth, to the height of the mast, or leech. Sails called

SQUARE-HEADED SAILS,

as topsails, topgallant-sails, and other four-sided sails. The cloths in the centre are cut square to the depth. The first square cloth cut, is the guide or regulator to cut all the other squares by; and, to prevent any mistake, *a mark may be put on it.* From each side of the square cloths cut, the gores are cut to give the roach.

61. Every cloth gored should be marked from the squares—the first gore (1), and the succeeding cloths cut by it (2), (3), (4), &c.—to avoid confusion and mistake.

62. The gores on the leeches, or appendages, when straight, are found by dividing the depth of the sail by the number of cloths gored in the leech, which gives the length of each gore. (See Art. 51.)

63. In cutting the leeches, the foot gore is cut first on the canvass, and the length of the longest selvage of the head earing cloth serves to measure the shortest selvage on the canvass; and the first leech-gore is set down from a thread of the *weft* with the opposite selvage. The canvass being cut diagonally, the one gore cuts the gore for the other leech, the longest selvage serving to measure its length, having the same gore cut on the foot. The gore left on the canvass is altered (if necessary) to meet the increased gore; and the length of the shortest selvage of the first leech-gore serves to measure the shortest selvage on the canvass, and the gore set down as before, from the thread of the weft with the opposite selvage. The gore cut through, the two long gores, or points, are put together, and measured both of the same length, and having the same foot-gore cut. Consequently, one gore cuts the other, for both sides of the sail, without waste.

64. In leeches of topsails cut with a hollow or circular, the upper gores are always longer than the lower ones, which are easily calculated, as is shown in an example. (See Art. 49.)

65. Sails gored with a sweep on the head and foot, or foot only, have received the name of

FORE-AND-AFT SAILS,

as mainsails, misens, drivers, jibs, gaff topsails, &c. The first cloth next the mast-leech is cut first. Thus, the foot-gore is cut upon the end of the canvass, and the length of the tack-gore is measured up the short side on the selvage, and carried across by a thread of the weft to the opposite selvage, and cut diagonally; then the longest gored side of the first cloth measures the length of the shortest side of the next. The canvass is again taken across by a thread, and the length of the second foot-gore is measured down on the opposite selvage, and cut diagonally; consequently, the first gored cloth being cut, the longest selvage of it serves to measure the shortest selvage of the next, and so on, until the whole of the cloths in the mast-leech are cut to the given number, and its length, when care must be taken that the whole of the gores do not exceed the depth of the luff; and it is better to measure them over, to see whether they will make out the length, before proceeding with cutting the head cloths, even if the gores should all be rightly calculated.

66. In cutting all fore-and-aft sails, a long gore and a short gore are always brought together, and the breadth of the seams of the sail allowed for eating-in seaming.

67. The additional parts of sails, made to fasten with latchings to the foot of the sails, and which are exactly similar to the foot of the sails they are intended for, constitute

SAILS THAT HAVE BONNETS,

as jibs, drivers, &c., in lieu of having one or two reefs in the sail. The bonnets are cut out the whole depth of the sail, allowing enough for the tablings on the foot of the sail, and head and foot of the bonnet; then, after the sail is sewed together, the bonnet is cut off the depth required, generally 9 feet. Bonnets have a head tabling, $2\frac{1}{4}$ inches broad, on which a line of 12-thread, named *keel-line*, for forming the latchings, is sewed in bights. These latches are six inches asunder, and six inches long, except the two middle ones, which are eighteen inches long, to fasten off with. In fastening it, the loops are alternately reeved through holes in the foot of the sail, and through each other, and fastened by the two long loops in the middle with two half-hitches, by the loosening of which they unreeve themselves. The tabling on the foot of the jib, when the bonnet is cut off, is six inches wide. The holes are wrought up from the edge close to the tabling stitches, the same distances as are the length of the latchings. Also, the leech, foot, and stay are tabled, roped, &c., similar to the jib the bonnet is intended for. A strengthening band extends from the clue over two cloths less than half the number of cloths in the foot. Earings are made on the head of the bonnet, six inches short of the top part, for the seizing of it to the clue and tack cringles of the sail.

68. For the length of gores corresponding to the depth on the selvage of canvass, 24 inches wide, observe the table on the following page, which will be found useful in finding the length on the stay of a jib, or the length of the mast-leech of a fore-and-aft mainsail; and, when the gores are cut longer, for the eating-up in seaming.

TABLE—Showing the length of any gore by its depth, from 1 inch to 12 feet, advancing by 1 inch in depth on the selvage of the canvass 24 inches wide; and also showing the length on the selvage of the eating of any gore from the creasing of the seams, in widths from 1 inch to 4 inches wide the seams, advancing by ¼-inch;

Depth down the Selvage.	Length of the Gore.	Length of the Eating-in Seaming on the Selvage of the Width of the Seams.												
		In. 1	Ins. 1¼	Ins. 1½	Ins. 1¾	Ins. 2	Ins. 2¼	Ins. 2½	Ins. 2¾	Ins. 3	Ins. 3¼	Ins. 3½	Ins. 3¾	Ins. 4
Ft In.	Ft. In.	Ins.	Ins	Ins	Ins.	Ins.	Ins.	Ins.	Ins.	Ins.	Ins.	Ins.	Ins.	Ins.
0 1	2 0	0	0	0	0	0	0	0	0	0	0	0	0	⅛
0 2	2 0	0	0	⅛	⅛	⅛	⅛	⅛	⅛	¼	¼	¼	¼	¼
0 3	2 0⅛	⅛	⅛	⅛	⅛	¼	¼	¼	¼	⅜	⅜	⅜	½	½
0 4	2 0¼	⅛	⅛	¼	¼	¼	⅜	⅜	⅜	½	½	½	⅝	⅝
0 5	2 0⅜	⅛	¼	¼	⅜	⅜	⅜	½	½	⅝	⅝	⅝	¾	¾
0 6	2 0½	¼	¼	⅜	⅜	½	½	⅝	⅝	¾	¾	⅞	⅞	1
0 7	2 0¾	¼	¼	⅜	½	½	⅝	⅝	¾	⅞	⅞	1	1	1⅛
0 8	2 1⅛	¼	⅜	½	½	⅝	¾	¾	⅞	1	1	1⅛	1¼	1¼
0 9	2 1½	⅜	⅜	½	⅝	¾	¾	⅞	1	1⅛	1⅛	1¼	1⅜	1½
0 10	2 1⅞	⅜	½	⅝	⅝	¾	⅞	1	1⅛	1¼	1¼	1⅜	1½	1⅝
0 11	2 2¼	⅜	½	⅝	¾	⅞	1	1⅛	1¼	1⅜	1½	1½	1⅝	1¾
1 0	2 2¾	½	⅝	¾	⅞	1	1⅛	1¼	1⅜	1½	1⅝	1¾	1⅞	2
1 1	2 3¼	½	⅝	¾	⅞	1	1⅛	1¼	1⅜	1⅝	1¾	1⅞	2	2⅛
1 2	2 3¾	½	⅝	⅞	1	1⅛	1¼	1⅜	1½	1¾	1⅞	2	2⅛	2¼
1 3	2 4¼	⅝	¾	⅞	1	1¼	1⅜	1½	1⅝	1⅞	2	2⅛	2¼	2½
1 4	2 4¾	⅝	¾	1	1⅛	1¼	1½	1⅝	1¾	2	2⅛	2¼	2½	2⅝
1 5	2 5¼	⅝	⅞	1	1⅛	1⅜	1½	1¾	1⅞	2⅛	2¼	2⅜	2⅝	2¾
1 6	2 5¾	¾	⅞	1⅛	1¼	1½	1⅝	1⅞	2	2¼	2½	2⅝	2¾	3
1 7	2 6¼	¾	1	1⅛	1⅜	1½	1¾	2	2⅛	2⅜	2½	2¾	3	3⅛
1 8	2 7	¾	1	1¼	1⅜	1⅝	1⅞	2	2¼	2½	2⅝	3	3⅛	3¼
1 9	2 7¾	⅞	1	1¼	1½	1¾	2	2⅛	2⅜	2⅝	2¾	3	3¼	3½
1 10	2 8½	⅞	1⅛	1⅜	1⅝	1¾	2	2¼	2½	2¾	3	3⅛	3⅜	3⅝
1 11	2 9¼	⅞	1⅛	1⅜	1⅝	2	2⅛	2⅜	2⅝	2⅞	3	3⅜	3½	3¾
2 0	2 10	1	1¼	1½	1¾	2	2¼	2½	2¾	3	3¼	3½	3¾	4
2 1	2 10¾	1	1¼	1½	1¾	2	2⅜	2½	2⅞	3⅛	3⅜	3⅝	4	4⅛
2 2	2 11½	1	1¼	1⅝	1⅞	2⅛	2⅜	2⅝	2⅞	3¼	3½	3¾	4	4¼
2 3	3 0¼	1⅛	1⅜	1⅝	1⅞	2¼	2½	2¾	3	3⅜	3⅝	4	4⅛	4½
2 4	3 1	1⅛	1⅜	1¾	2	2¼	2⅝	2⅞	3⅛	3½	3⅝	4	4⅜	4⅝
2 5	3 1¾	1⅛	1½	1¾	2⅛	2⅜	2⅝	3	3¼	3⅝	3⅞	4⅛	4½	4¾
2 6	3 2½	1¼	1½	1⅞	2⅛	2½	2¾	3⅛	3½	3¾	4	4⅜	4¾	5
2 7	3 3¼	1¼	1⅝	1⅞	2¼	2½	2⅞	3⅛	3½	3⅞	4⅛	4½	4¾	5⅛
2 8	3 4⅛	1¼	1⅝	2	2¼	2⅝	3	3¼	3⅝	4	4¼	4⅝	5	5¼
2 9	3 5	1⅜	1⅝	2	2⅜	2¾	3	3½	3¾	4⅛	4⅜	4¾	5⅛	5½
2 10	3 5⅞	1⅜	1¾	2⅛	2½	2¾	3⅛	3½	3⅞	4¼	4½	4⅞	5¼	5⅝
2 11	3 6¾	1⅜	1¾	2⅛	2½	2⅞	3¼	3⅝	4	4⅜	4¾	5⅛	5⅜	5¾
3 0	3 7⅝	1½	1⅞	2¼	2⅝	3	3⅜	3¾	4⅛	4½	4⅞	5¼	5⅝	6

nd in depths of gores from 1 inch to 3 feet; and from 1 inch to 1½ inches wide the seam dvancing by ¼-inch; and in depths of gores from 3 feet 1 inch to 12 feet. The depths o he gores are arranged in the first column, and the length of the gores alongside of it; th ength of the eatings are under the widths of the seams, and in a line with the gores.

Depth down the Selvage.	Length of the Gore.	Length of Eating &c. In. 1	Length of Eating &c. Ins 1¼	Depth down the Selvage.	Length of the Gore.	Length of the Eating, &c. In. 1	Length of the Eating, &c. Ins. 1¼	Length of the Eating, &c. Ins. 1½	Depth down the Selvage.	Length of the Gore.	Length of the Eating Width of Seam. In. 1	Length of the Eating Width of Seam. Ins. 1¼	Length of the Eating Width of Seam. Ins 1½
Ft. In.	Ft. In.	Ins.	Ins.	Ft. In.	Ft. In.	Ins.	Ins.	Ins.	Ft. In.	Ft. In.	Ins.	Ins.	Ins.
3 1	3 8⅛	1½	1⅞	6 1	6 4¾	3	3¾	4½	9 1	9 3½	4½	5⅝	6¾
3 2	3 9¼	1½	2	6 2	6 5⅝	3	3¾	4⅝	9 2	9 4½	4½	5⅝	6⅞
3 3	3 10¼	1⅝	2	6 3	6 6⅝	3	3⅞	4⅝	9 3	9 5½	4⅝	5¾	6⅞
3 4	3 11⅛	1⅝	2	6 4	6 7⅝	3⅛	3⅞	4¾	9 4	9 6½	4⅝	5¾	7
3 5	4 0	1⅝	2⅛	6 5	6 8⅝	3⅛	4	4¾	9 5	9 7½	4⅝	5⅞	7
3 6	4 0⅞	1¾	2⅛	6 6	6 9½	3⅛	4	4⅞	9 6	9 8½	4¾	5⅞	7⅛
3 7	4 1¾	1¾	2¼	6 7	6 10⅛	3¼	4	4⅞	9 7	9 9⅜	4¾	6	7⅛
3 8	4 2⅝	1¾	2¼	6 8	6 11½	3¼	4⅛	5	9 8	9 10⅜	4¾	6	7¼
3 9	4 3½	1⅞	2⅜	6 9	7 0⅜	3⅜	4⅛	5	9 9	9 11⅜	4⅞	6	7¼
3 10	4 4⅜	1⅞	2⅜	6 10	7 1⅜	3⅜	4¼	5⅛	9 10	10 0⅜	4⅞	6⅛	7⅜
3 11	4 5¼	1⅞	2⅜	6 11	7 2⅜	3⅜	4¼	5⅛	9 11	10 1⅜	4⅞	6⅛	7⅜
4 0	4 6⅛	2	2½	7 0	7 3¼	3½	4⅜	5¼	10 0	10 2⅜	5	6¼	7½
4 1	4 7	2	2½	7 1	7 4¼	3½	4⅜	5¼	10 1	10 3¼	5	6¼	7½
4 2	4 7⅞	2	2½	7 2	7 5¼	3½	4⅜	5⅜	10 2	10 4¼	5	6¼	7⅝
4 3	4 8¾	2⅛	2⅝	7 3	7 6¼	3⅝	4½	5⅜	10 3	10 5¼	5⅛	6⅜	7⅝
4 4	4 9⅝	2⅛	2⅝	7 4	7 7⅛	3⅝	4½	5½	10 4	10 6¼	5⅛	6⅜	7¾
4 5	4 10½	2⅛	2¾	7 5	7 8⅛	3⅝	4⅝	5½	10 5	10 7¼	5⅛	6½	7¾
4 6	4 11⅜	2¼	2¾	7 6	7 9⅛	3¾	4⅝	5⅝	10 6	10 8¼	5¼	6½	7⅞
4 7	5 0¼	2¼	2⅞	7 7	7 10	3¾	4¾	5⅝	10 7	10 9¼	5¼	6⅝	7⅞
4 8	5 1⅛	2¼	2⅞	7 8	7 11	3¾	4¾	5¾	10 8	10 10⅛	5¼	6⅝	8
4 9	5 2	2⅜	3	7 9	8 0	3⅞	4¾	5¾	10 9	10 11⅛	5⅜	6⅝	8
4 10	5 2⅞	2⅜	3	7 10	8 1	3⅞	4⅞	5⅞	10 10	11 0⅛	5⅜	6¾	8⅛
4 11	5 3¾	2⅜	3	7 11	8 2	3⅞	5	5⅞	10 11	11 1⅛	5⅜	6⅞	8⅛
5 0	5 4⅝	2½	3⅛	8 0	8 2⅞	4	5	6	11 0	11 2⅛	5½	6⅞	8¼
5 1	5 5½	2½	3⅛	8 1	8 3⅞	4	5	6	11 1	11 3	5½	6⅞	8¼
5 2	5 6⅜	2½	3¼	8 2	8 4¾	.4	5	6⅛	11 2	11 4	5½	7	8⅜
5 3	5 7¼	2⅝	3¼	8 3	8 5¾	4⅛	5⅛	6⅛	11 3	11 5	5⅝	7	8⅜
5 4	5 8⅛	2⅝	3¼	8 4	8 6¾	4⅛	5⅛	6¼	11 4	11 6	5⅝	7	8½
5 5	5 9	2⅝	3⅜	8 5	8 7¾	4⅛	5⅛	6¼	11 5	11 7	5⅝	7⅛	8½
5 6	5 10	2¾	3⅜	8 6	8 8¾	4¼	5¼	6⅜	11 6	11 8	5¾	7⅛	8⅝
5 7	5 11	2¾	3½	8 7	8 9¾	4¼	5⅜	6⅜	11 7	11 9	5¾	7⅛	8⅝
5 8	6 0	2¾	3⅝	8 8	8 10⅝	4¼	5⅜	6½	11 8	11 10	5¾	7¼	8¾
5 9	6 1	2⅞	3⅝	8 9	8 11⅝	4⅜	5⅜	6½	11 9	11 11	5⅞	7¼	8¾
5 10	6 2	2⅞	3⅝	8 10	9 0½	4⅜	5½	6⅝	11 10	12 0	5⅞	7⅜	8⅞
5 11	6 3	2⅞	3⅝	8 11	9 1	4⅜	5½	6⅝	11 11	12 1	5⅞	7⅜	8⅞
6 0	6 4	3	3¾	9 0	9 2½	4½	5⅝	6¾	12 0	12 2	6	7½	9

USE OF THE FOREGOING TABLE.

69. In the first column, find the depth given, and the second column will show the corresponding length; and, immediately under the width of the seam, and in a line with the gore, is the length of the eating-in seaming, or what the gore flies beyond the creasing of the seam. Suppose the depth to be 6 feet 4 inches, and the width of the seam 1¼ inches, opposite to it and under the width of the seam will be found 6 feet 7⅝ inches and 4¾ inches respectively.

70. This table will be found of great use when cutting out a jib, beginning at the tack. The breath of the seam on the foot requires to be allowed before the gore is cut, and the quantity of inches corresponding to the gore is found under the width of the seam in the table. Thus:—Suppose the foot-gore 1 foot 10 inches, and the seam 3¼ inches broad, then, under 3¼ inches is found 3 inches, to be measured on the canvass before the gore is set up on the opposite selvage.

71. It is also well adapted for ascertaining the exact length on the stay and leech of a jib, the mast of a driver, and luff of a gaff-topsail. Rules:—1. Place in parallel columns the depths of the gores on the stay and foot, and, opposite to them, the lengths of the gores and eating-in of the seaming, found in the table in different columns parallel to the former.—2. Add up the several columns, subtract the sum of the foot-gores from the sum of the depth of the stay-gores, and 18 inches for tabling gives the *length of the leech*.—3. For the length on the stay, subtracting the sum of the eating-in of the seaming on the stay, from the sum of the lengths of the stay-gores, and 18 inches for tabling from the remainder, gives the *length on the stay*.—4. For the mast of a driver, subtract the sum of the eating-in of the seaming from the sum of the lengths of the mast gores, and 8 inches for tabling gives the *length on the mast*.

EXAMPLES.

Jib, 15 cloths.
Leech, 47 feet 6 inches tabled.
Stay, 64 feet tabled.

GORES.

Number of Cloths.	Depth of Stay Gores. Ft.	In.	Depth of Foot Gores. In.	Length of Stay Gores. Ft.	In.	Length of Eating-in of Seaming. 1 inch Seam on the Stay. In.	Length of Eating-in of Seaming. 3 inches Seam on the Foot. In.
1	10	0	2	10	2⅜	5	¼
2	6	0	0	6	4	3	0
3	5	0	2	5	4⅜	2½	¼
4	4	9	3	5	2	2⅜	⅜
5	4	0	4	4	6⅛	2	½
6	4	0	5	4	6⅛	2	⅝
7	3	6	6	4	0⅞	1¾	¾
8	3	6	8	4	0⅞	1¾	1
9	3	0	10	3	7⅝	1⅝	1¼
10	3	0	13	3	7⅝	1½	1⅜
11	2	9	15	3	5	1⅜	1⅞
12	2	9	17	3	5	1⅜	2⅛
13	2	6	20	3	2½	1¼	2½
14	2	6	22	3	2½	1¼	2⅝
15	2	6	24	3	2½	1¼	3
Total..	59	9	147	67	11⅝	12)29⅞	18⅜
			18⅜	2	5⅞	2 5⅞	
	10	8⅜	=128⅜	65	6		
				1	6 tablings.		
	49	0⅜					
	1	6 tablings		64	0 tabled—stay.		
Leech	47	6 tabled.					

Gaff-topsail, 12 cloths.
Leech .... 35 feet tabled.
Mast .... 46 ditto ditto.

GORES.

Number of Cloths.	Depth of Mast Gores. Ft.	In.	Depth of Foot Gores. In.	Length of Mast Gores. Ft.	In.	Length of Eating-in of Seaming. 1 inch Seam on the Mast. In.	Length of Eating-in of Seaming. 3 inches Seam on the Foot. In.
1	7	0	2	7	3¼	3½	¼
2	6	0	0	6	4	3	0
3	5	0	1	5	4⅝	2½	0
4	4	0	2	4	6⅛	2	¼
5	3	6	3	4	0⅞	1¾	⅜
6	3	0	4	3	7⅝	1½	½
7	2	6	5	3	2⅛	1¼	⅝
8	2	6	7	3	2½	1¼	⅞
9	2	0	9	2	10	1	1⅛
10	2	0	12	2	10	1	1⅜
11	2	0	15	2	10	1	1⅞
12	2	0	18	2	10	1	2¼
Total	41	6	74	48	11⅝	12)20¼	9⅜
			9¼	1	8¾	1 8¼	
	5	4⅜	=64⅜	47			
				1	3 tablings.		
	36	1⅞					
	1	0 tablings		46	0 tabled—stay.		
Leech	35	1⅜ tabled.					

GORES.

Number of Cloths.	Depth of Mast Gores. Ft. In.		Length of Mast Gores. Ft. In.		Length of Eating-in of Seaming. 1½ inch Seam on the Mast. In.
1	5	6	5	10	3½
2	5	0	5	4½	3½
3	5	0	5	4½	3¼
4	4	6	4	11½	2¾
5	4	0	4	6½	2½
½	2	0	2	3	
Total ..	26	0	28	3½	14⅞
			1	2¾	
			27	1	
				8	tablings.
			26	5	
				4	head gore.
Mast ..			26	9	tabled.

node is very ingenious, embrac
o prevent leeward pressure, th
he vessel—the same means inc
ails."

There is, however, an object
lrawing must be made of every
aining the gores ; and, therefo
lepend entirely upon the accur
s, as yet, an advocate for the
ierein described.

CHAPTER II.

GENERAL OBSERVATIONS ON THE MATERIALS USED,
AND INSTRUCTIONS FOR MAKING SAILS.

THE MATERIALS—CANVASS, &c.

72. *Canvass.*—To obtain the best canvass for the making of sails is of the first importance to the owner, not only on account of its great expense, but because the safety of a ship, in tempestuous weather, frequently depends on its quality; and, besides, the cost for making is not more for a good article than it is for a very bad one. Hence, the best canvass is by far the cheapest in the end. The canvass which is generally used in the merchant service, is *twenty-four* inches wide, and it is certainly the strongest for all purposes. Sometimes, however, jibs and drivers are made of *eighteen* inches wide canvass, to ensure greater strength and a better appearance.

73. There are six to eight (and some lighter) sorts of canvass, viz.:— Nos. 1, 2, 3, 4, 5, 6, 7, and 8, weighing respectively (or ought to do) 46℔, 41℔, 38℔, 35℔, 32℔, &c., per bolt of 40 yards each. The warp or chain of every piece or bolt of the first three numbers should be wholly wrought, and made of double yarn, and contain in every piece or bolt, of 24 inches wide, at least 560 double threads of yarn; and both the warp, and shoot or weft yarn, ought to be made of long flax, without any mixture of tow, and this of strong staple, fresh, sound, and good in its kind. It should also be well dressed, properly cleansed, even spun, and well twisted; and all the weft yarn should be fully as strong as the warp yarn, and close struck.

74. In selecting canvass for making up into sails, considerable practice and close observation are required, as well as a general acquaintance with the manufacture of canvass. The experienced sailmaker forms his opinion of the quality and strength of canvass, not only from its being even spun and well struck together, but he takes two persons' canvass, of the same No., and makes a slit in each, and knots them together: he then hangs weights to the loose parts, and finds which bears the most. Another trial is by boring a *fid* through the canvass, when the threads of bad canvass are easily broken; and the workman can tell the difference in this way, when working holes in a sail. A testing machine is also an excellent plan. Again, for knowing the quality, draw a few threads, and examine whether they are composed of long flax, without mixture of tow, and try if it be of strong staple, fresh, sound, and well cleansed.

75. It is of importance for canvass to have a good and even selvage, and free from tightness, because of the seaming, which it is awkward to have slack in seams unnecessarily. It may, however, be observed, that there is a deal of difference in canvass for stretching. Generally, canvass badly struck together stretches most.

76. *Twine.*—The edges of the cloths or pieces of which a sail is composed, are sewed together with a double seam, and should be sewed

with the best twine (made of flax), of three folds, spun from 360 fathoms to 430 fathoms to the pound; and one pound of twine will sew four bolts of canvass, or 160 yards in lengths. In the merchant service, the twine is dipped in tar, softened with a proper proportion of oil.

77. *Bolt rope.*—Bolt-rope should be well made of fine yarn, spun from the best Riga rhine hemp, well topped, and tarred in the best Stockholm tar. It is the erroneous practice of some ropemakers, in the closing of the strands, to have too much tension on the strands, which causes the rope to be hard to sew on. There is no necessity for this; only he ought to put plenty of foreturn, and use as little power as possible in keeping the strands tight, so as to close the rope soft. The hard-stranded and flexible rope will last longer than the hard-closed rope, which will generally break before it bends, and wears badly. Bolt-ropes formerly were stoved in a stove, by the heat of a flue, and tarred afterwards. Mr. Daniel Burn, of London, was famed for stoved ropes on his sails; and it is the opinion of many that white rope, tarred, answers best for hot climates.

MAKING OF SAILS:—SEAMS.

78. The *seams* of sails are sewed twice from the foot to the head[*]— that is, the edges of the cloths are creased to the required breadths (see Art. 30 and 31), and, when finished, are well rubbed down with a rubber, and turned over to sew the second side, and again rubbed down. There ought to be from one hundred and twenty-four to one hundred and forty-four stitches in every yard in length.

79. The *creasing of seams* is a very important thing in fore and aft sails, and requires good judgment. The *breadth* of the seams on the foot of a jib or driver ought to be made according to the roach with which the sail is cut, and thus eat up the irregular gores, so as to form a regular curve on the foot. The *length* run up from the foot should be for a jib at the clue thus—$3\frac{1}{2}$ inches broad by 3 feet up, next $4\frac{1}{2}$ feet, 5 feet, and 6 feet the rest: the remaining breadths at the foot 3 inches. Driver seams are thus, viz.—$3\frac{1}{2}$ inches broad and run up, 2 feet, 3 feet, $4\frac{1}{2}$ feet, $5\frac{1}{2}$ feet, and 6 feet the mast part; and 3 inches broad by 2 feet, 4 feet, $5\frac{1}{2}$ feet, and 6 feet from the foot and the leech, and continued 3 inches broad and 6 feet up between the leech and mast; also, at the head $2\frac{3}{4}$ inches broad, decreasing to the peak to $2\frac{1}{4}$ inches, and creased down 4 feet: the remaining part of the seam $1\frac{1}{4}$ inches broad.

TABLINGS.

80. The *widths* of the tablings of all sails are according to the size of the sail, and stuck or stitched down on the edge or on the top (long-work), with 72 to 110 stitches in a yard. (For widths, see Art. 30.)

81. The *breadths* of the tablings of fore and aft sails, as jibs and drivers, are thus:—*Jib*, a 3 inches tabling on the *leech* and the stay; $2\frac{1}{4}$ inches, doubled into the rope or bite of the canvass, the *foot*. The leech tabling is sometimes banded or doubled again. *Driver.*—The

---

[*] The Scotch fashion is to sew down from the head.

leech tabling is made broader at the clue and peak, to make the leech round and keep the corners in proper form: the remaining part of the leech tabling about 3¼ inches wide. The *head* and *mast tablings* are from 4 to 5 inches wide; and the *foot* 2¼ inches—like the jib, or rather narrower.

LININGS.

82. In order to strengthen and preserve them from chafing, sails have *linings* in various parts: such as the reef-bands, middle-bands, reef-tackle pieces, leech-linings, bunt-line cloths, foot-bands, corner-pieces, &c.; all of which are particularly noticed in their respective places, as well as is shown on the finished plans. The shaded parts on the plates exhibit the linings.

83. These linings are all seamed on the sails, except the reef-bands, which are tabled on the fore-side of the sail. Top-linings, mast-cloths, and corner-pieces are put on the aft-side of the sail; and, when there is not a middle-band on the topsail, the reef-tackle pieces are seamed on the aft-side, and reach the top of the top-lining. (See Plate 4, mizen-topsail.)

84. It may be necessary to observe, that linings ought not to be put on too taut, or flat; they require to be put on *easy*, as they are generally of lighter canvass than the sail, and not capable of bearing the same strain as the sail; besides, they run up a great deal by wet.

HOLES AND GROMMETS.

85. *Holes* are cut by a knife, and stretched or rounded up by a fid or a marline spike, and are fenced round by stitching the edge of the hole to a *grommet*, made like a ring of three strands, with rope-yarns; when finished, they should be well stretched.

86. The holes in sails have received particular names; as, head, reef, cringle, bowline, clue-cringle, clue-garnet, bunt-line, spilling, bunt-jigger holes, &c., all of which are hereinafter mentioned.

87. Sails have the holes in the heads and reefs of topsails, courses, &c., placed thus:—One hole is made near the seam on each side of the middle cloth, or two holes in the cloth and one in the next, on both sides; and so on, one and two holes, from the middle; and in the centre of the head is stuck a small cringle, for making the middle fast, as also useful for a guide in bending the sail square to the yard. Holes in the stays of jibs, staysails, &c., are one yard apart, excepting at the peak, when the hole is about 2 feet distant.

88. *Reef* and *head-holes* of large sails, have grommets of bolt-rope yarns, made thick in the rim, and worked round with 18 to 21 stitches. Small sails have grommets of small bolt-rope yarns, worked with 16 to 18 stitches, or as many as shall cover the grommet. Holes ought not to be larger than what is necessary for the points getting through. Clue and buntline holes are the largest in the sail for admitting the rope or cringles passing through them.

POINTS.

89. White-line, from 5 to 8 thread-hook, is what is generally used

for *points*. The lengths are about twice the circumference of the yards ; each reef the points are 6 inches shorter, and the aft-legs are 1 foot longer, excepting the close reef points are halved and put through every grommet, and securely sewed to it on the aft-side of the sail, by opening the strands a little, by a pricker, so as to sew the point to the grommet.

BOLT ROPE :—SEWING IT ON.

90. The flexibility of *bolt-rope* should be always considered in taking in the slack, which must rest on the judgment of the sailmaker, and it should be neatly sewed on through every cuntline of the rope ; and to avoid getting a turn, the rope must be kept tightly twisted while sewing on ; but to rope, without a turn in it, can only be acquired by practice. In roping, care must be taken that neither too much nor too little slack is taken in, but a regular slack held on all the way on the leeches of square-sails. The leeches of fore and aft sails ought to be straight-roped, without any slack, with a shallow stitch and a stout thread. All jibs should be roped straight round the sail ; the foot-rope the slackest, when the foot is cut with a curve. In the foot of trysails, it is the erroneous practice of some sailmakers to curl the rope in sewing it on : all foot-ropes on drivers, trysails, &c., should be sewed on very round, with a slight hold of the canvass, and for the canvass just to carry the strain. Mast-ropes ought to be nearly straight roped on, and the headlines one inch in every yard slack canvass. Many a well-cut sail is spoiled by the roping.

CLUES.

81. In the merchant service, the rope is carried round the sail without forming the *clue* with a seizing, but cringles are stuck through holes, with a thimble, for the sheet, in the same manner as the reef-cringles ; the sheet, by this mode, having a fairer strain than by any seized clue.

92. In the *clues* of *main-courses*, the clue-cringles are the same size as the rope which goes round the sail for 500 tons and upwards ; and for 400 tons ships and under, the thickness is one inch larger than the bolt-rope. The whole length of the foot-rope, from clue to clue, and from 2 to 3 feet up each leech from the clue, is parcelled over with worn canvass, well tarred—and served over that with spunyarn ; it is then marled on the sail with marline or houseline, as far as it is served.

93. The *cringles* for the tack and sheet-blocks of fore-courses, the rope the same size as the rope which goes round the main-course. It is prepared, and the cringles stuck in other respects like the clues of main-courses. The serving on the leeches of small-courses is only 18 inches from the clue.

94. The *hole* for the clue-garnet of the courses is made close down to the cringle holes, the block-strop is placed through the hole and clue thimble, and the block seized in the strop on the aft-side with several turns of spunyarn, and strained tight with three or more cross-turns.

95. The *clues* of *main* and *fore topsails* :—The cringles are the same size as the rope which goes round the sail. They are tight stuck through two holes, and well stretched ; then parcelled and served with spun-

yarn, and a thimble knocked in. The whole length of the foot-rope, and from 18 inches to 3 feet up the leech from the clues, is parcelled over with worn canvass, well tarred, and served over that with three or four yarns spun yarn. It is then marled on to the sail with strong marline or houseline, as far as it is served ; and the hole for the clue garnet is prepared for the strop in the same way as those of main and fore courses.

96. The *clue* cringles of *mizen-topsails* are similar to those of main and fore topsails, except at the clues: 18 inches to two feet up the leech from each of them is parcelled and served, as the foot: a hole for fixing the clue-garnet close to the cringle is made.

97. The *clues* of *topgallant-sails* and *royals* are similar to those of topsails. The cringles are one inch larger than the rope which goes round the sail. The whole length of the foot-rope, from clue to clue, and 18 inches up the leech from each of them, is served. A hole for the clue-garnet is prepared, in every respect the same as the topsails. The clues only are parcelled with worn canvass. Sometimes the whole length of the foot-rope of the royals, from clue to clue, and one foot up each leech, is served with small spun yarn, and marled on to the sail ; but, generally, the clues of small royals are formed of the bolt-rope, sewed home to the clues. The clues only are served with spun yarn, and seized with houseline or marline.

98. The *clues* of *main, fore,* and *mizen staysails,* and *main* and *fore-topmast staysails.*—The cringles are half an inch larger than the clue-rope. The clue-rope splices into the foot and after-leech rope, and the cringle is stuck through holes made in the corner of the clue. The ends of the cringle are passed through the bolt-rope three times each way, and the tacks have cringles stuck in the same manner as the clues, and earings at the peak, with iron thimbles in each of the corners.

99. The *clues* of all *studdingsails* have cringles stuck through holes, and the ends passed into the bolt-rope. The tacks only of topmast-studdingsails, topgallant-studdingsails, &c., are made of the bolt-rope, parcelled, and served with spun yarn. The canvass is marled on to the rope about 18 inches, equally distant from the clue, or the extent of it served.

100. The *clues* of *ships' drivers* and *trysails, barques' mizens* and *trysails, brigs' mainsails,* &c.—These are made with cringles, about half an inch larger than the clue rope. The mast-rope on the driver of large ships should be taken round the tack and neck ; also, the peak rope round the corner, and spliced in the head-rope ; and cringles stuck in all the corners, with the ends passed into the bolt-rope. The tack of the driver should be strong, as it is frequently hauled to the weather-mizen rigging. The tacks of large jibs should have a rope spliced into the foot and stay-rope, as large as the clue-rope, with a cringle : the clues to be fixed about two feet equally distant from the clue, and the cringle half an inch less than the clue-rope, stuck twice through the holes, and the ends passed into the cringle, or into the bolt-rope.

101. The *clues of sloops' topsails,* and *topsails* and *other sails* of *colliers,* are mostly formed by the rope going round the sail, which is left

sufficiently long to form the clues. The advantage of cringles in lieu of turned clues, is, that they are more readily replaced when the clues break; besides, more sail is gained in not having those long clues. The more compact clues can be made, the stronger they will be, with the clues coming nearer in the sheave-holes in the yards, and to avoid the complaint made of " the clues always breaking."

102. *Cringles* should be made of the strands of new bolt-rope, half an inch smaller than the bolt-rope on the sail in which they are stuck, excepting the clue-cringles, which cannot be too strong.

103. The *earing-cringles* are made of an additional length of 15 to 18 inches of the leech-rope left at the head of the sails, which, being turned back to the size of eight twists or turns, forms the cringle by splicing its ends into the leech rope, and cross-stitching the whole of the splice. The first stitch at the head is double, and all the cross-stitches hove tight. The ends of the head-line are spliced into the earings, and one strand is turned back and spliced in the head-rope, for preventing the head-line drawing out of the earings. All earings are served over with spun yarn, when finished.

104. *Reef* and *reef-tackle cringles* are stuck through holes made in the tablings, and the lower ends are put through the bolt-rope once more than the upper ends, being more liable to be drawn out. Sometimes the cringles are stuck twice through the holes, and the ends worked up into the cringle. Eyelet-holes, thus worked in the sail for cringles to be formed through, are an excellent plan, as the cringle is then made round the entire rope, and not between the strands, which must give the leech ropes better lead, and less injury to the rope.

105. The *bowline-cringles* of courses and topsails are stuck the same way as the reef-cringles; and topgallant-sails and royals are stuck in the bolt-rope on the sail, at the distance of four turns or one strand clear in the bolt-rope asunder. The ends are first stuck in an opening made with a fid, under two strands of the bolt-rope. The two ends are then passed over each other, one of them being the longest. The long end is thrust through two strands, and worked back into a three-stranded rope. The ends are then stuck under two strands, and again passing over one strand, they are finally stuck under two : all bowline-cringles are served as those of earings.

SPLICES.

106. *Splices* are made by opening the ends of two ropes, and placing the strands between each other, openings being made in the untwisted part of the rope, near the thickest end, with a fid. The strands are thrust through them; and the large ends are regularly tapered from the thick rope, by cutting away some of the yarns every time they are thrust through. The small strands, as those of the foot or leech rope, are stuck twice through the openings made in the large rope; and the large strands are tapered on to the small rope for about 15 to 18 inches. The left-handed splices are the best for roping straight, and look much better, being passed too and keeping the form of the strands, and scarcely showing that there is a splice. All splices are cross-stitched as far as they run, and some only at the ends.

CHAPTER III.

PRACTICAL OPERATIONS ON EVERY SAIL, IN PUTTING TOGETHER, LINING, AND FINISHING THEM.

MAIN-COURSE (PLATE 2).

107. This sail is quadrilateral, square on the head, (some cut it down at the earings,) and is made of No. 1 or 2 canvass. It bends at the head to the jackstay on the mainyard, which hangs to the mast at right angles, and parallel to the deck. The earings come 18 inches within each of the cleats on the yard-arms, and drop to clear the height of the boat. (See Art. 37.)

Gores.—One to two cloths are gored on each *leech;* and the gore on the *foot* is such, that when the depth at the middle is fixed, as well as the tack and sheet blocks, the clues are carried down to give the roach, at the rate of so many inches per cloth. (See Art. 59.)

For seams, tablings, reef and head holes, &c., see the general instructions at pages 56, 57, &c.

This sail has, in very large ships, two *reef-bands,* of one-third the breadth of a cloth. The upper reef is 6 feet 6 inches, and the lower reef-band is 7 feet distance from the upper one. The ends go under the leech-linings to the rope, which are tabled twice down. Ships of 900 tons and under have only one reef-band, about 6 feet down from the head. The *reef-tackle cringle* is 3 feet below the reef. The sail has also a *middle-band,* of one breadth of cloth, half-way between the lower reef-band and the foot. It is first folded and creased down at one-third of the breadth, then tabled small (long) work on the top of the selvage; and it is then turned down, and seamed both the selvage and double part, leaving open in the way of the tops of the buntline cloths, to be stitched down twice underneath. A half of a breadth middle-band is put on small courses, half-way between the reef-band and the foot.

Linings are of one breadth of cloth, from the clue to the earing on the leeches. The foot is lined from clue to clue with half of a breadth of canvass.

Four *buntline cloths* are placed at equal distances between the clues, extending from the foot to underneath the lower side of the middle-band, which is tabled down upon the ends of the buntline-cloths; and the feet of the buntline-cloths are tabled down over the foot-band. The outer buntline-cloths are put on two cloths of the sail, goring inwards; and the middle two are straight up and down.* (See Plate 2.) When

---

* Rule for finding the gore at the *top* of *buntline-cloths* inclined inwards:—Divide the number of cloths the buntline-cloth is gored inwards, by 1⅓ times the depth in yards, and the quotient will give the gore at the head in terms of a cloth. Thus— Suppose the buntline-cloth is gored one cloth and a half in the middle of the sail, and the perpendicular depth of it is 3 yards 1 foot, then $3\frac{1}{3}$ yards $\times 1\frac{1}{3} = \frac{10}{3} \times \frac{4}{3} = \frac{40}{9}$, and 1½ cloth $= 3$ feet $= 36$ inches. Therefore 5)36

7 inches gore for the head of the buntline-cloths.

there are four buntline-cloths in the sail, divide the foot into five equal parts ; for two bunts, divide the foot into three parts. In small courses there are only two buntline-cloths, run up about one yard and a half.

Reef-cringles are made on each leech, one at each reef-band ; *reef-tackle cringles* at 3 feet below ; and three *bowline-cringles*, the upper at 3 feet above half-way of the leech, and the other two equally divided between it and the clue.

Holes are made on the foot, one at the middle of each buntline-cloth.

The *clues* have a *casing* of the same canvass as the lining on the sail, extending 18 inches each way from the clue over the spun yarn. The *clue-cringles* are described at page 58.

In sewing on the bolt-rope, three inches of *slack cloth* are taken up in every yard in the leeches, and one inch in every cloth marled in the foot.

. The foot-rope ought to be well stretched before it is marled.

FORE-COURSE (PLATE 3).

108. This sail is made of canvass No. 1 or 2. It is bent, at the head, to the jack-stay on the foreyard, which hangs at right angles to the mast, and parallel to the deck. It hauls out at the earings within 18 inches of the hounds on the yard arms, and drops to clear the mainstay, when carried to the stem.

Gores.—(See Article 39.)—A gore is made on the *foot*, to drop the clue, usually 2 feet 6 inches to 3 feet, beginning at the three fifths of the foot. Instructions for seams, tablings, holes, &c., are given in the last chapter. Two *reef bands*, of one-third the breadth of a cloth, are put on large ships' courses, at the distance of 6 feet and 6 feet 6 inches asunder, the upper one being 6 feet from the head ; the ends go to the rope under the leech linings, which are tabled twice over them. Ships of small tonnage have only one reef-band, 5 feet or 5 feet 6 inches below the head.

A *middle-band*, of one breadth of canvass, is put on half way between the reef-band and the foot, of No. 5 canvass. It is put on in the same way as that of the main-course. In smaller vessels half of a breadth of canvass extending from leech to leech under the linings :—often none at all.

Linings on the leeches are of one breadth of cloth, extend from the clue to the earing ; and on the *foot* half of a breadth from clue to clue. In coasters, foot bands are seldom used ; and, when any, it is one-third of a cloth.

Four *buntline-cloths*, at equal distances ; or, the foot divided into five parts, are carried up to the lower side of the middle band; the outer ones are put on one and half cloth goring inwards, and the middle two straight up and down (see Plate 3); the middle band is tabled upon the ends of the buntline-cloths, and the buntline-cloths are tabled over the foot-band. *Two* buntline-cloths only are put on small courses, run about 1 yard or 1¼ yards up from the foot.

Reef cringles are made on the leeches, one at the end of each reef-band, stuck through holes close to the rope or room to take half of a stitch : *reef-tackle cringle* 3 feet below the reef ; as also are two *bowline-cringles*, the upper bowline-cringle being made in the middle of the leech, and the lower one equally distant from the upper one and the clue : a *hole* is also made at the end of each buntline-cloth on the foot, in the middle.

Cringles are also made in lieu of turned clues (see page 58), and a large *hole* worked in close down to the cringle, for the clue-garnet block strop. The *clues* are *cased* with canvass half of a yard each way over the spunyarn.

In sewing on the bolt-rope, three or four inches of *slack-cloth* should be taken up in every yard in the leeches, and one inch up in every cloth in marling the foot. The foot-rope ought to be well stretched before it is marled.

SHIP'S CROSS JACKSAIL.

109. This sail is made of canvass No. 3. The head is bent to the jack-stay on the cross jack-yard, and it drops at right angles with the ship's mizenmast, and parallel to the deck, extending within 12 inches of the hounds on the yard-arms. The depth of this sail at the middle is made to clear 6 or 7 feet of the deck, so that it is cut with a deal of roach on the foot.

Gores.—Two *goring cloths* are on each *leech ;* and the gore on the *foot* is 6 feet, beginning at the buntline-cloth, and increasing to give the drop at the clues. The gores are found in a similar way to those of the main-course.

For *seams, tablings,* &c., consult the last chapter.

This sail has one *reef-band,* of one-third the breadth of a cloth, at 5 feet 6 inches down from the head. The ends go four inches under the leech-linings, which are tabled twice over them. A reef in this sail is not of any use : it is merely for the sake of uniformity with the other courses that it is put on. Like a small main-course, it has no *middle-band.*

Linings are of one breadth of cloth from the clue to the earing on the *leeches,* and half of a breadth of cloth from clue to clue on the *foot.*

Two buntline-cloths are placed at equal distances between the leeches, or the foot is divided into three parts, extending from the foot to one-fourth up the sail.

A *reef-cringle* is made on each leech, one at each end of the reef-band, stuck through holes made in the tablings ; two *bowline-cringles,* the upper one made in the middle of the leech, and the lower one equally distant from the upper one and the clue : a *buntline-hole* is also made at the end of each buntline-cloth on the foot, in the middle.

Cringles are also made in preference to turned clues ; the clues are *cased* with canvass, as those of the main and fore courses, over the spunyarn ; and a *hole* for the clue-garnet, which should be close to the cringle-holes.

In sewing on the *bolt-rope,* a regular slack is taken up in the leeches and head, and one inch in every cloth in marling the foot throughout.

MAIN-TOPSAIL (PLATE 2).

110. This sail is made of No. 2 or 3, and lined with No. 5 or 6 can-

vass. It has three or four *reef-bands*, put on at 18 inches above, or at half-way the *close-reef*, when there are four reefs in the sail; and the upper-reef is 4 feet distance from the head: the others are divided equally between it and the lower-reef, and they extend from leech to leech underneath the linings. They are each half of a breadth of canvass, put on double: the first side is stuck twice long-work, and the last turned over and tabled close-work, which gives strength to the eyelet-holes for the reef-points.

A *middle-band* is put on half-way between the lower reef-band and the foot, and is made and put on in the same way as that of the main-course.

Linings.—The *leeches* are lined from clue to earing with one breadth of cloth, and the *foot* is lined from the clue under the leech lining to the buntline-hole with half a breadth. Two *buntline-cloths* are put on the fore-side of the sail, at one-third the foot: their ends go over the foot-band-end, and are carried up under the middle-band, which is tabled twice on them.

The *reef-tackle cringle* is 3 feet below the lower-reef. The *reef-tackle pieces* are put on the fore-side of the sail, and are so cut and sewed as, when put on, to be two-thirds broad at the leeches, and one-third at the end which reaches to the top of the buntline cloth, and tabled twice, under the middle-band.

Also, a *top-lining* on the aft-side, which covers one-third of the cloths in the foot, and is carried up so as to sew the top-edge to the centre of the middle-band, and *two cloths* run up to the head, covering the centre cloths of the sail.

Three *bowline-cringles*,* the upper one being 2½ feet below the reef-tackle, and the other two equally distant from each other between the upper one and the clue. One *buntline-hole* is made in the middle of each buntline-cloth; and, also, a hole in the middle of the foot, for the spilling-line.

The *bolt-rope* along the foot, and for 3 feet up each leech, is parcelled and served; and before it is marled to the sail, the foot-rope should be well stretched, and the length of the foot of the sail set off.

Cringles are made on the leeches at the end of each reef-band, and in lieu of turned clues, which are described in the foregoing chapter.

Beckets for *bunt-jigger.*—Work *two holes* on each side of the centre seam, in the first and second reefs; the first for furling with one reef, and the second with two.

FORE-TOPSAIL (PLATE 3).

111. This sail is made of No. 2 or 3, and lined with No. 5 or 6 canvass. It has the same number of *reefs* in it as those of the main-topsail; and the *linings*, &c., are exactly similar to those of the main-topsail.

MIZEN-TOPSAIL (PLATE 4).

112. This sail is made of canvass No. 3, and lined with No. 5. It has

* Two are much better with using the reef-tackle cringle for the upper bowline.

*three reef-bands,** put on as those of the main-topsail. A *middle-band* is only put on sometimes, and likewise *buntline-pieces.*

The *reef-tackle cringle* is 3 feet below the close-reef, and *two bow-lines,†* the upper one 3 feet below the reef-tackle. The *reef-tackle pieces* are put on the aft-side of the sail, extending from the leech to the top-lining.

The *top-lining* is put on the aft-side, and covers one-third tho foot, and is carried up half-way between the lower-reef and foot. Two *mast-cloths* are put on in the middle of the sail, on the aft-side, between the foot and head.

Linings on the *leeches* and *foot*, the same as the main-topsail.

Cringles are made on the leeches, stuck through holes worked at the end of each reef-band, reef-tackle piece, and bowlines; *cringles*, also, are in lieu of turned clues. One *buntline hole* is made at the top lining on each side, to take the end of the foot-band.

The *bolt-rope* along the foot, and for 18 inches to 2 feet up each leech, is parcelled and served, and is marled to the sail, as for the main-topsail.

MAIN-TOPGALLANT-SAIL (PLATE 2).

113. This sail is made of No. 4 or 5 canvass, and lined with No. 6 canvass.

Three bowline cringles are made on each leech, the upper one in the middle, and the others equally divided between that and the clue.

Linings on the *leeches* are of half a breadth, extend from the clue to the earing; and the *foot-band* of the same breadth extends from the clue (underneath the leech lining), to one-third the foot along. Also, a *top-lining* on the aft-side of the sail, which covers one-third of the cloths in the foot, and runs up one third the depth of the middle. One *buntline-hole* is made at the one-third of the foot, on each side of the top-lining, and to take the foot-band end.

One *mast cloth* is put on the middle of the sail, on the aft-side between the top-lining and head.

Cringles are made in lieu of turned clues, and a *hole* for the clue-garnet.

The whole length of the foot-rope, from clue to clue, and 18 inches up each leech, is served and marled to the sail; the clues only are parcelled before they are served.

FORE-TOPGALLANT-SAIL (PLATE 3).

114. This sail is made of No. 4 or 5, and lined with No. 6 canvass: it has the same number of bowlines in it as those of the main-topgallant-sail.

The *linings*, &c., are exactly similar to those of the main-topgallant-sail. It may, however, be observed, that it is *best* to make the sail with an odd number of squares, so that the *mast-cloth*, on the aft side, shall cover the centre-cloth in the sail, which answers better for wear.

* They may be fitted with *four*, which, except for the sake of uniformity, is not of much use.
† Sometimes *three.*

MIZEN-TOPGALLANT-SAIL (PLATE 4)

115. This sail is made of No. 5, and lined with No. 6 canvass.

Two *bowline cringles* are made on each leech, the upper one in the middle, the other half way between it and the clue.

The *linings* are the same as for the main-topgallant-sail. Also, a *top lining* on the aft-side of the sail, which covers one-third the cloths in the foot, and run up one yard the short-cloths and centre cloth rom the foot to the head.

The *foot rope* is marled to the sail, as the main-topgallant-sails. *Cringles* are stuck for the sheets, and a *hole* for the clue-garnet.

MAIN-ROYAL (PLATE 2).

116. This sail is made of No. 6 canvass. Two *bowline cringles* are stuck in the leech-ropes, the upper one in the middle, and the other half way between it and the clue.

Linings.—The *foot* is lined with one-third of a breadth of cloth from clue to clue: pieces are put on at the *earings*. Cringles are stuck for the sheets. There are not any buntline holes made in the foot; and the foot is fixed as that of the mizen topgallant-sail. (See Art. 97)

FORE-ROYAL (PLATE 3).

117. This sail is made of No. 6 canvass: it is precisely the same way finished as the main-royal.

MIZEN-ROYAL (PLATE 4).

118. This sail is made of No. 6 canvass. *Pieces* are put on at all the corners, and the clues only are served and marled in, having *cringles* stuck for the sheets.

FORE-TOPMAST-STAYSAIL (PLATE 5).

119. This sail is made of No. 1 or 2 canvass. The *clue-piece* is from two to three yards long, and the *peak* and *tack-pieces* are one yard; and in general, the tack-piece is so cut as to form the piece for that at the peak. *Holes* on the stay are one yard apart: two *holes* are worked at the clue and tack for cringles with thimbles.

The thickness of the *clue-rope* is one inch larger than the rope which is put on the leech, and is described in the last chapter.

STANDING-JIB (PLATE 5).

120. This sail is made of No. 4 or 5 canvass. Its proportions are given at page 28, art. 45.

Gores.—The stay and foot are cut with a roach for making it set. (See dimensions for cutting one, page 44.)

For *seams* and *tablings* consult the last chapter.

The *clue-piece* is five yards, and the peak and tack-pieces are one yard, cut diagonally. For small jibs, the *clue-piece* is two yards. A *strengthening band* is carried over one-half the cloths in the foot, so cut and sewed, as when put on, to be two-thirds of a cloth broad at the clue, and one-third of a cloth broad at the end : the selvage on the canvass is kept next to the foot, and sewed nearly by a thread of the weft from the clue. (See the shaded part on the drawing.)

Two holes are made at the *clue* and *tack*, for the cringles, and one hole is made in every yard up the *stay*.

The *clue-rope*, which is spliced into the leech and foot-ropes, is one inch thicker than the leech rope : the *tack rope* should be as stout as the clues. In sewing on the bolt-rope, not any slack cloth should be taken up, but just what the stitch (sinking in the cuntlines) gathers, which easily stretches out again. A jib will never stand tightly roped.

Iron thimbles are put in the cringles at the clue and tack, and the earing at the peak.

FLYING JIB.

121. This sail is made of No. 5 or 6 canvass, and is better than two-thirds of the size of the standing-jib. It is the foremost sail, and hoists on the flying-jib-stay, which is attached to the fore topgallant-mast-head. The leech has two or three yards more allowed for than the foot has cloths.

Gores.—(See dimensions for cutting, at page 44.)

The *clue-piece* is from two to three yards in length, and the peak and tack-pieces cut out each other, three-quarters of a yard.

A *strengthening-band* at the clue, 18 inches broad and 6 inches the end, extending one-half across the foot, the selvage gored one inch per cloth to the foot : it is precisely finished as for the jib preceding.

DRIVER (PLATE 4).

122. This sail is made of No. 3, and lined with No. 5 canvass : the essential particulars are given at pages 28 and 29—Articles 46 and 47.

The *gores* for cutting-out one are on page 43.

For *seams*, *tablings*, &c., consult the last chapter.

It has *two reefs*, 6 feet 6 inches, and 6 feet parallel to the foot, which have one hole made in every seam of the sail.

Linings.—The after-leech is *lined* with one breadth of cloth, from the clue to one yard above the upper-reef ; six inches off the lining is cut down at the top (the long gore on the leech) ; the *peak-piece* is one and a half-yard in length, and gored up as the clue-piece : and the fore-leech is lined with a whole, and sometimes a half, breadth of cloth, from the tack to the nock.

Two holes are made in the leech, for the brails—one a foot shorter down the leech than the length of the head, and the other hole half-way between it and the peak. Also, a small hole, or a cringle stuck through one hole in the middle of the foot, for the tricing line, which is for hauling the foot of the sail up, clear of the man's head at the helm, in calms. *Holes* are made for the reefs, clue, and tack-cringles.

Bolt-ropes.—The *clue-rope* is one inch thicker than the leech and mast-ropes ; the *peak* and *tack* half an inch less than the clue-rope ; *head-line* half an inch less than the leech-rope ; and *foot-line* half an inch less than the head-line. For sewing on the rope, see last chapter, (Art. 90).

Iron thimbles are generally put in the cringles stuck at the tack, nock, clue, and reefs: the peak-earing-cringle is served.

Cringles for the lacing are made above the upper-reef on the mast-leech, 30 inches asunder: the one next the nock ought not to be less than a yard from the nock. These cringles are stuck two high in the strands.

LOWER-STUDDINGSAIL (PLATE 7).

123. This sail is made of No. 4 or 5 canvass, and spreads beyond the leeches of the fore-course. The half of the head is bent to the studdingsail-yard, and the foot extended on the boom, and sometimes further extended by jack-yards. The Rule for determining the size of it is given on page 26.

Pieces, three-quarters of a yard in length, are put on the corners, and a *piece,* half a yard long, on the middle of the head.

Holes are made on half of the head, and two in each clue, and two in the centre of the head, for the cringles.

In sewing on the bolt-rope, a regular *slack* should be taken up round the sail. Sometimes the middle cloths in the foot (one quarter), are served and marled on the sail, to protect the bolt rope from being chafed in the way of the guy for steadying the boom.

Cringles with iron thimbles are stuck in the clues, the earings being served, as well as the cringle, in the centre of the head.

MAIN-TOPMAST-STUDDINGSAIL (PLATE 7).

124. This sail is made of No. 4 or 5 canvass, and spreads beyond the leeches of the main-topsail, the head being bent to its yard. The inner-earing covers two cloths of the topsail, and the foot, extended on the boom, covers one cloth of the topsail-clue. To find the size, refer to Rule on page 26, and gores at page 45.

A *reef-band,* 6 inches broad, is put on at 5 feet down from the head: *pieces* on the four corners. Two holes are made at the clue, for the cringle; and two holes for the downhauls on the outer leech, at one-third the depth of the leech from the head of the upper one, and the other half-way between it and the tack.

The *head-holes* are cut one and two in each cloth respectively.

In sewing on the bolt-rope, a regular *slack* should be taken up in the foot and goring-leech, and none in the square-leech. The *tack* is served and marled for 18 inches each way.

One *reef-cringle* is made on the leeches at each end of the reef-band, and one at the clue. The earings are served, and the cringles have iron thimbles knocked in.

FORE-TOPMAST-STUDDINGSAIL (PLATE 7).

125. This sail is made of No. 4 or 5 canvass, and spreads beyond the leeches of the fore-topsail, the head being bent to its yard. The inner-earing covers two cloths of the topsail, and the foot is extended on the boom to cover one cloth of the topsail-clue. To find the size, refer to Rule at page 26, and gores at page 45. It is finished precisely in the same way as the preceding.

Some ships have *mizen-topmast-studdingsails*, but they are rarely used.

MAIN-TOPGALLANT-STUDDINGSAIL (PLATE 7).

126. This sail is made of No. 6 canvass, and spreads beyond the leeches of the main-topgallantsail, the head being bent to its yard. The inner-earing covers one and a half cloths of the head of the topgallantsail, and the foot is extended on the boom to cover three-quarters of a cloth of the clue of the topgallantsail. To find the size, refer to Rule at page 26, and gores at page 45.

Pieces on the four corners of the sail. Two holes are made in the clue for a cringle, and holes in the head, cut one and two in each cloth respectively.

In sewing on the bolt-rope, a regular *slack* should be taken up in the foot and gored-leech, but none in the square-leech. The tack is served and marled on the sail for 12 inches each way.

Iron thimbles are put in the cringle at the clue and tack, the earings being served.

FORE-TOPGALLANT-STUDDINGSAIL (PLATE 7).

127. This sail is made of No. 6 canvass, and spreads beyond the leeches of the fore topgallantsail, the head being bent to its yard. The inner earing covers one and a half cloths of the head of the topgallantsail, and the foot is extended on the boom to cover three quarters of a cloth of the topgallantsail-clue. To find the size, refer to Rule at page 26, and gores at page 45. It is precisely the same way finished as the main.

ROYAL-STUDDINGSAILS (PLATE 7).

128. These sails are made of No. 7 canvass, and spread beyond the leeches of the royals. They are finished in the same way as the preceding. To obtain the size, refer to Rule at page 26, which is applicable to all studdingsails.

AWNINGS.

129. (See pages 46–7.) These are made of canvass No. 3 or 4. They spread flat over the ship above the deck, for protection from the rays of the sun in hot climates, and are sewed together athwartship with an inch *seam*, and *tabled* at the ends with a three-inch tabling; then *lined* with half of a breadth of canvass A whole breadth is sewed along the *ridge* of each awning. Valances are attached to the side, of one-third of a breadth of canvass, which are sometimes scalloped, and bound with baize of some fancy colour. The diameter of the masts is cut out in the middle at each end, and lacing holes are made across the ends, one foot distant, to connect one awning with the other.

On the upper part, along the middle of the ridge-lining, two small holes are made in every seam, about one inch apart, and two at each end, to which the ridge-rope is seized on, in lieu of being roped on. Round the margins of each awning and mast-holes is sewed one-and-a-half or two-inch rope. *Cringles* are stuck at the end of each seam, and small earings with iron thimbles in the four corners. Sometimes *holes* are worked in lieu of small cringles, and the valances are attached within the holes.

WINDSAIL.

130. The windsail, or ventilator, is made of canvass No. 5. It is employed to convey a stream of fresh air downwards into the lower apartments of a ship, being let down through the hatches, and is in the form of a wide tube or funnel. It is kept distended by *circular hoops*, made of ash, and sewed to the inside—one at the top, and one at every six feet distance. The upper part or top is covered with a circular piece of canvass, and below the top is an open on one side, to which *wings* are sewed, of two breadths of canvass each, tapering to a point, which are braced to the wind so as to receive the full current of air, which fills the tube, and rushes downwards into the lower regions of the ship. Large merchantmen have generally, in hot climates, three or four of these windsails, for the preservation of the health of the crew.

These windsails are about 8 yards in length; and four breadths are sewed together with a half-inch seam. In joining them, one cloth is left, or cut four feet short at the top. A three-inch tabling goes round the top and bottom; and, at every six feet distance, a six-inch band is tabled for the hoops, which are sewed to the inside. The *wings* are cut thus :—One breadth of cloth, 4 feet 6 inches long, has a gore of 16 inches cut off at each end, then laced together, and sewed to it, thus making two breadths tapered to a point. A small rope is sewed all round the edge of the wings and opening of the tube, and an eye or clue formed at the points of the wings. At the top a diamond piece is stitched on, for working in a grommet for a becket, which is spliced with a stopper-knot, for the windsail to hang by. Two or three holes are worked in the edge of the tabling, at the bottom, to keep it steady.

STAYSAILS :—MAIN-STAYSAIL.

131. This sail is made of canvass No. 1 or 2, and is in the form of a right-angled triangle. It is extended upon a springing-stay, alongside of the main standing-stay, between the main and fore masts, so that the foot will clear the boat; and the sheet is hauled aft to the gangway. This sail is seldom used now, as ships generally carry a fore-trysail in lieu.

Referring to Rule at page 26 :—Let there be in the head of the main-course 32 cloths. Then $32 \times \frac{5}{8} = \frac{160}{8} = 20$ cloths; and the depth of the middle of the main-course 33 feet 8 inches = the leech of the main-staysail cut.

Stay-gores.—Divide the depth of the leech by the number of cloths.

FT. IN.

Thus 20)33   8(1 foot.
      20

      13
      12

     164(8 inches.
     160

Here, the gore on the stay per cloth is 1 foot 8 inches, or 20 inches.

Linings.—The tack-piece is cut three-quarters of a yard, the peak-piece one yard, and the clue-piece extends two yards up the leech.

Holes are made in the stay, three-quarters of a yard apart, and two holes in the clue and tack, for cringles.

In sewing on the bolt-rope, a regular *slack* should be taken up in the foot and stay, but none in the leech.

Iron thimbles are put in the cringles at the clue and tack, and in the earing at the peak.

COLLIER'S MAIN-STAYSAIL.

132. Among the *colliers* this sail is frequently cut with a bunt, and a gore is sometimes made on the foot, with a hollow. It has also a reef-band, at about 4 feet from the foot. The following is an example :—

	FT.	IN.			FT.	IN.	
Leech	22	0	21 feet tabled.		22	0	
Bunt	5	6	ditto.		5	6	Stay-gore.
Foot	-	-	15 cloths.				FT. IN.
Stay	-	-	14 ditto.	Divide by 14)16	6(1	2	

$$14$$
$$\overline{}$$
$$2$$
$$12$$
$$\overline{}$$
$$30$$
$$28$$
$$\overline{}$$

Foot-gores 2, 3, 4, 4 inches.

FORE-STAYSAIL.

133. This sail is made of canvass No. 1 or 2, and is in the form of a right-angled triangle. It is extended on the forestay, between the fore-mast and bowsprit.

Referring to Rule at page 26 :—Suppose the head of the fore-course 28 cloths, Then $\frac{1}{2}$)28 cloths.

$$\overline{}$$
$$14$$
Add 2
$$\overline{}$$
16 cloths in the foot.

Leech.—Depth of the middle of the fore-course, 27 feet.

Stay-gore.— 16)27(1 foot 8 inches.
$$16$$
$$\overline{}$$
$$11$$
$$12$$
$$\overline{}$$
132(8 inches.
$$128$$
$$\overline{}$$

Linings.—The tack and peak pieces are half a yard each, and the clue-piece extends two yards up the leech.

K

Holes on the stay are 27 inches apart, and two holes in the clue and tack, for the cringles.

In sewing on the bolt rope, a regular *slack* should be taken in the foot and stay, but none in the leech.

Iron thimbles are stuck in the corners: the peak is an earing. (See last chapter, Art. 98.)

MIZEN-STAYSAIL.

134. This sail is made of canvass *No.* 1, and is extended on the mizen-stay (14 feet up the mainmast), between the main and mizen masts. It has a bunt or fore-leech one-third to two-thirds the depth of the after-leech. The foot drops to clear 6 or 7 feet of the deck, and is cut square.

Gores.—Two cloths are generally gored on the fore-leech; and the foot is equal to one-half the number of cloths in the head of the main-course. (See page 26.)

Rule to find the depth of each gore on the stay.—Subtract the depth of the bunt from the depth of the leech, and the remainder, divided by the number of cloths in the stay, gives the gore per cloth. Thus—

  Leech - - - 24 feet.
  Bunt - - 8
      —

  Divide by 16 cloths)16(1 foot gore.
      16
      —

The bunt or fore-leech is lined with half a breadth of No. 4 or 5 canvass. The clue piece is two yards up the leech, and the peak-piece three-quarters of a yard in length.

Holes are made in the stay, three-quarters of a yard apart; and two holes in the clue, tack, and nock, for sticking cringles through.

In sewing on the bolt-rope, a regular *slack* should be taken in with the rope, in the foot, bunt, and stay, but none in the leech.

Iron thimbles are stuck in all the corners. One or two holes are made in the after-leech for the brails, and a large hole, with a thimble in it, in the middle of the sail, to lead them fair through. These are generally left to be done by the seamen or sailmaker on board.

MAIN-TOPMAST-STAYSAIL.

135. This sail is made of canvass No. 4 or 5. It is extended on the main-topmast-stay, between the main and fore topmasts. The standing-jib is occasionally substituted for a main-topmast-staysail, when the main-topmast-stay reaches to the stem.

The leech is 5 or 6 yards deeper than the main-topsail, but, in small vessels, the depth of the fore-topsail; and there are as many cloths in the foot as the leech is yards in depth. The bunt is two-fifths to one-half the depth of the after-leech.

Gores.—Two or three cloths are usually gored on the fore-leech; and the stay-gore is found similar to that of the mizen-staysail. A gore of 6 or 7 inches is sometimes made on each cloth of the foot.

This sail is finished in every respect the same as the preceding one.

CHAPTER IV.

RULES FOR FINDING THE QUANTITY OF YARDS OF
CANVASS CONTAINED IN THE DIFFERENT SAILS.

136. The general practice is, amongst sailmakers, first to take an account of the canvass intended for the sail; and the canvass left over the sail which is cut, measured and deducted from the whole, leaves the quantity of yards in the sail.

137. It is desirable, however, to know, in making out estimates, the number of yards contained in sails for new ships, having their dimensions to go by, for which the following rules will be particularly useful.

RULES.

I. To find the quantity of yards in main and fore courses, main, fore, and mizen topsails, topgallantsails, royals, skysails, lower-studdingsails, topmast-studdingsails, topgallant-studdingsails, awnings, &c.

138. Add the number of cloths in the head and foot, and half the sum for the mean width; then multiply by the depth of the middle-cloth, and add the quantity contained in the foot-gores for the yards in the sail; to this sum add the respective linings, which gives the total quantity of yards.

To find the quantity of yards in the foot-gores.—Multiply the whole gore of the foot, by the number of cloths gored on one side of the sail, and bring it into yards.

EXAMPLES :——MAIN-TOPSAIL.

```
24  cloths in the head.
36  cloths in the foot.
   —
2)60  sum.
   —
   30  half the sum.
13⅓  yards deep.                To find the quantity in the foot-gores?
   —                                 12 gores on each side.
   90                                  2 feet gore.
   30                                  —
   10                             3)24 feet.
   —                                  —
 400  the product.
   8  yards in the foot-gores      8 yards.
   —
 408  yards in the sail.
  29      "      two leech-linings.
  34½     "      four double-reef bands.
  10      "      middle-band.
   7      "      reef-tackle pieces.
   8      "      foot-band.
   6½     "      two buntline-pieces.
  58      "      top-lining.
   —
Total, 561  yards.
```

MAIN-COURSE.

34 cloths in the head.
38 cloths in the foot.
___

½)72 sum.
___

36 half the sum.	To find the quantity in the
12⅔ yards deep.	foot-gores ?
	7½ cloths gored on each side.
432	3 feet gore.
24	___
___	3)21½
456 the product.	___
7½ yards in the foot-gores - 7½ yards.

___

463½ yards in the sail.
28   "   two leech-linings.
24   "   four buntline-cloths.
7   "   reef-band—one-third of a cloth.
11   "   middle-band.
12   "   foot-band.

Total, 545½ yards for a ship of 1,000 tons.

MIZEN-TOPGALLANTSAIL.

13¼ cloths in the head.
19 cloths in the foot.
___

½)32¼ sum.
___

16⅛ square cloths.	To find the quantity in the
5⅛ yards deep.	foot-gores ?
	6 feet the foot-gores.
80⅝	9 cloths gored on one side.
1⅔	___
___	3)54
82¼ the product.	___
18 yards in the foot-gores - 18 yards.

___

100¼ yards in the sail.
7¼   "   two leech-linings.
4   "   foot-band.
11   "   top-lining.
___

Total, 122¾ yards.

TOPMAST-STUDDINGSAIL.

To find the quantity in the gores ?

Foot-gore, 5 inches.

11 cloths in the head. Head-gore, 4 inches.
15 cloths in the foot. ————

½)26 sum. Diff. - 1
  —— Foot, - 15 cloths.
  ——

13 square cloths. 15 inches.
14⅙ yards deep. 7½ half the cloths in the foot.

52 105
13 7½
2 ——
—— 36)112¼ the product.
184 the product. ——
3 yards in the gores - 3 yards.
——
187 yards in the sail.
1¾ " reef-band.
3 " pieces.
——
Total, 191¾ yards.

FORECASTLE-AWNING (PAGE 47).

FT. IN. Cathead - 20 feet.
Breadth at foremast - 27 6 End - - 3
  25 6 ——
Cathead to cathead 20 0 2)23
—— ——
3)73 0 11½ feet.
—— 12 cloths.
24 4 = 8⅓ yards. ——
—— 3)138
73 yards. ——
46 yards - 46
——
119 yards.

WINDSAIL.

4 number of cloths.
8 yards in length.
——
32
Sub. 1½ the opening.
——
30½ yards the tube.
3 " the two wings.
¾ " the top.
1¾ " the bands.
——
Total 36 yards.

II. To find the quantity of yards contained in jibs, fore-topmast-staysails, jib-gaff-topsails, and all triangular sails with curved edges.

Set down the depths of the stay and foot gores; find the lengths of the cloths by adding the stay-gores. Take the sum of the first stay-gore at the tack, and the length of the leech, with the amount of foot-gore added; then the sum of the second, fourth, sixth, or even lengths of the cloths, and multiply it by four; and then take the sum of the remaining odd lengths, as third, fifth, &c., and multiply it by two. To the sum of these two products, add the sum of the extreme lengths. Subtract the quantity in the foot-gores, found by a similar way, and the remainder gives the number of yards.

EXAMPLE:—STANDING-JIB.

Add the depths of the stay and foot gores of the jib (see page 53), thus:—1st gore, 10 feet; 1st and 2d, 10 + 6 = 16 feet; 16 added to 3d, or 16 + 5 = 21, &c., and set them down as the following, viz:—

	The Stay Gores added. FT. IN.	Even Lengths of the Cloths. FT. IN.	Odd Lengths. FT. IN.	The Foot Gores added. IN.	Even Lengths. IN.	Odd Lengths. IN.
1st	10 0.	- -	- -	2		
2d	16 0	16 0	- -	0	0	
3d	21 0	- -	21 0	2	-	2
4th	25 9	25 9	- -	5	5	
5th	29 9	- -	29 9	9	-	9
6th	33 9	33 9	- -	14	14	
7th	37 3	- -	37 3	20	-	20
8th	40 9	40 9	- -	28	28	
9th	43 9	- -	43 9	38	-	38
10th	46 9	46 9	- -	51	51	
11th	49 6	- -	49 6	66	-	66
12th	52 3	52 3	- -	83	83	
13th	54 9	- -	54 9	103	-	103
14th	57 3	57 3	236 0	125	125	238
15th	59 9		2	149		2
		272 6			306	
		4	472 0		4	476

```
              1090  0          1224
               472  0           476
                10  0  1st.       2  1st.
                59  9  15th.    149  15th.

            9)1631  9         12)1851

                                9)154
               181  yards.
Subtract        17  - -          17  yards.

    Total,     164  yards.
```

⁎ This is a very correct method for finding the quantity of yards in any jib cut with a round stay and foot.

Some find the quantity of yards in a jib by the following rule:—

<pre>
                                   To find the quantity in the foot-gores
                              147 inches gore in the foot.
                               7½ half the number of cloths.
                              ─────
                              1029
   16 yards, depth of the leech.   73
    7½ half the number of cloths.   ─────
   ─────   36)1102 the product.
  120 yards.   ─────
   30½ "   in the foot-gores   30½ yards.
  ─────
</pre>

Total, 150½ yards.
        164   "   per the above.

Diff.   13½

Hence, by the latter rule, there is a deficiency of 13½ yards, by the want of the round on the stay.

III. To find the quantity of canvass contained in main and fore staysails.

Multiply half the number of cloths by the depth of the leech, and add the quantity in the pieces.

EXAMPLE:—MAIN-STAYSAIL.

<pre>
   10 half the number of cloths.
   11 yards, depth of the leech.
  ─────
  110 yards in the sail.
    4   "   "   pieces.
  ─────
</pre>

Total, 114 yards.

IV. To find the quantity of canvass contained in drivers, mizens, main-trysails, fore-trysails, brigs' mainsails, schooners' mainsails, sloops' mainsails, &c.

Add the number of cloths in the head and foot, and half the sum to make it square. Add together the depth of the mast-gores; then multiply the number of square cloths by the depth of the mast. To this product add the quantity contained in the head and foot gores, and the slack cloth held in the sail for the yards in the sail. The quantity of yards contained in the foot, head, and slack cloth, is found thus:—Add the gores in the foot, from the tack to the square cloth near the clue, and multiply half the sum by the number of cloths in the foot; then add together the gores from the clue to the square, and multiply half the sum by the number of cloths gored up the clue, which, subtracted from the product of the gores to the tack, gives the quantity in the foot-gores. In a similar way, find the quantity in the head-gores. Add together the inches of slack cloth there are in the seams, and multiply by half the number of cloths: the whole of these added will give the answer.

EXAMPLE :—BARQUE'S MIZEN.

IN.
¼)102 gores to the tack.
——
51
17 cloths in the foot.
——
357
51
——
867
Sub. 9
——
36)858 inches.
——
23¾ yards

12½ cloths in the head.
17 cloths in the foot.
——
½)29½
——
14¾ square cloths.
8¾ yards the mast.
——
118
10½
——
128½ yards.
23¾ "   foot-gores.

IN.
½)6 gores to the clue.
——
3
3 cloths gored.
——
9 inches.

IN.
½)33 slack in the seams.
——
16½
6 cloths which have slack.
——
36)99 inches.
——
2¾ yards.

2¾   of slack.

IN.
¼)45 gores to the peak.
——
22½
12¼ cloths in the head.
——
270
11
——
36)281 inches.
——
7¾ yards

7¾   head-gores.

Total, 162¾ yards in the sail.

V. To find the quantity of canvass contained in mizen and main-topmast staysails.

Add the number of cloths in the stay and foot together, and half the sum to make them square ; add the depth of the bunt or fore-leech to the depth of the after-leech, and half them for a medium depth ; then multiply the number of square cloths by the mean depth, and add the quantity in the linings and pieces.

EXAMPLE :—MIZEN-STAYSAIL.

Cloths in the stay - 16
Cloths in the foot - 18

8 yards, depth of the leech.
2¾ " " " bunt.

½)34

½)10¾

17 square cloths.

5¼ - - - 5¼ mean depth.

85
4¼

89¼ yards in the sail.
5 " lining and pieces.

Total, 94¼ yards.

V. To find the quantity of canvass in boats' lugsails.

Add together the number of cloths in the head and foot, and half the sum to make it square; add the depth of the two leeches, and half the sum for a medium depth; then multiply the number of square cloths by the medium depth. To this product add the quantity in the foot-gore and pieces.

EXAMPLE.

	FT.	IN.
Fore-leech -	9	6
After-leech -	14	6

5 cloths in the head.
7 cloths in the foot.

½)24 0

½)12 sum.

3)12 0 feet.

6 square cloths.
4 yards, medium depth -

4 yards.

24 yards, the product.
3 " in the gores and pieces.

Total, 27 yards.

SECTION THIRD.

CHAPTER I.

ON DETERMINING THE SIZE, DIMENSIONS FOR CUT-
TING-OUT, AND QUANTITY OF CANVASS CONTAINED IN EVERY
PART OF EACH SAIL, FOR A BARQUE OF 300 TONS.

139. The determining the sizes of the sails for a barque are subject
to the same rules as for a full-rigged ship, which rules are given in
chapter 3, page 14. The dimensions are these :—

MAIN-COURSE.

	FT. IN.	FT. IN.		FT. IN.
Mainmast	61 0	9 0 head.	Mainyard	47 0
"		4 0 sling.	" two arms	6 0
"		16 0 housing.		——
"		1 3 chess-tree.	" hounded	41 0
		——	Subtract - -	3 0
	30 3			——
	——		Head	38 0
	30 9			6
Stretching	1 0			——
	——		11)228 0	
Leech -	29 9			
			20¾ cloths.	

Dimensions for Cutting-out.

	FT. IN.	
Head	38 0	equal to 20¾ cloths.
Foot	51 0	equal to 25 cloths.
Leech	29 9	tabled.
Gore	3 0	
Middle - -	27 0	cut.

For the number of squares - - 25 cloths.

    (Art. 37)   Multiply by 3

Leech-gores.

FT. IN.
1 9
14 0
14 0
——
29 9

            Divide by 5)75
                —
                15 squares,
    and gores 2, 4, 7—10, 13 inches.

Quantity of Canvass.

(By Rule I., page 73.)

20¾ cloths in the head.
25 cloths in the foot.

½)45¾

23 square cloths.
9 yards deep.

207 the product.
5 yards in the foot-gores

3 feet gore.
5 cloths gored.

3)15 feet.

5 yards.

(No. 3.) 212 yards in the sail.
21 " " two leech-linings.
12 " " four buntline-cloths.
4½ " " reef-band.
8¼ " " middle-band.
8¼ " " foot-band.

Total, 266 yards.

This sail has one *reef-band*, at 5 feet 6 inches down from the head, of one-quarter to one-third the breadth of a cloth. The *reef-tackle cringle* is 3 feet below the reef.

A *middle-band*, of half a breadth of canvass, extends from leech to leech under the linings : often none at all.

Linings on the leeches are of one breadth of cloth, extending from the clue to the earing ; and on the *foot*, one-third to one-half of a breadth from clue to clue.

Four *buntline-cloths*, at equal distances, or the foot divided into five parts, are carried up to the lower side of the middle-band. The outer ones are put on one and a half cloths, inclining at an angle inwards, and the middle two straight up and down.

Reef-cringles are made on each leech, one at each reef-band, stuck through holes ; *reef-tackle cringles* at 3 feet below ; and three *bowlines*, the upper one at 3 feet above half-way of the leech, and the other two equally divided between it and the clue.

Holes are made on the foot, in the middle of each buntline cloth.

Cringles are made in lieu of turned clues, and a *hole* for the clue-garnet block-strop to reeve through

Becket for *bunt-jigger*, worked in the bunt, so that it may be furled with a peak. Thus :—A diamond-piece of canvass is stitched on at 3 feet below the centre of the head, and two holes worked in it for splicing the strop. The particulars are fully given at pages 61-2.

FORE-COURSE.

	FT.	IN.	FT.	IN.				FT.	IN.
Foremast	57	0	8	6	head.	Foreyard - -		45	3
"			4	0	sling.	" two arms		5	6
"			16	0	housing.				
"			4	0	height of cathead.	hounded		39	9
						Subtract -		3	0
	32	6							
Leech -	24	6				Head -		36	9
									6
						Divide by 11)220			6
						20 cloths.			

Dimensions for Cutting-out.

		FT.	IN.	
Head		36	9	equal to 20 cloths.
Leech		24	6	tabled.
Gore -	-	2	6	
Middle - - - -		22	6	cut.

8 squares, and the gores 2, 3, 4, 5, 7, 9 inches.

Quantity of Canvass.

20 cloths.
7½ yards deep.   To find the quantity in the foot-gores?
———   6 cloths, gored on each side.
140   2½ feet gore.
10   ——
——   3)15 feet.
150 the product.
5 yards in the foot-gores - 5 yards.

(No. 2.)	155	sail.
	17	two leech-linings.
	6	half-breadth middle-band.
	6	half-breadth foot-band
	4	one-third of a breadth reef-band.
	5½	two buntline-cloths.

Total, 193½ yards.

The depth of the reef is 5 feet 6 inches from the head. The linings, &c , for a fore-course, are fully given at page 62.

(By Rule, page 15.)   MAIN-TOPSAIL.

	FT.	IN.			FT.	IN.
Topmast -	33	6	Mainyard, hounded - -		41	0
" head	4	6	Subtract		1	4

	29	0 hoist.	pin and pin	39	8 foot.
					4

Divide by 7)158 8

22 cloths.

	FT.	IN.
Main-topsail-yard - - -	36	0
" " two arms	5	6

	FT.	IN.
hounded - - - - -	30	6
within the cleats the earings	5	0

	Head	25	6
			6

Divide by 11)153 0

14 cloths.

Close-reef, at one foot above half-way of the leech, 32 feet.
To find the hollow on each leech?

	FT.		Head -	14	cloths.
Here, reef	32		Foot	22	ditto.
Multiply by -	6				

(Art. 32.)   ½)36

Divide by 11)192

18 cloths the mean.

17½ cloths   Reef   17½   ditto.

Diff. -   ½ cloth = 12in.
Hollow on each leech = 6in.

Dimensions for Cutting-out.

	FT.	IN.		Foot-gores.
Head	25	6	equal to 14 cloths.	IN.
Reef	32	0		1
Foot	39	8	equal to 22 cloths.	1
Hoist -	29	0		2 Leech-gores.
Gore -	1	9		2 (Art. 49)
Middle	27	3	cut—5 squares. (Art. 52.)	—

*** It will be observed that there are *four* gores in each leech; that is, half a cloth at each earing, and half a cloth at the clues.

	FT. DEC.		FT.	IN.
3 — 4·63	=	4	7
3 — 8·10	=	8	1
4 — 7·04	=	7	1
4 — 6·30	=	6	3
2 — 2·93	=	3	0

22   29·00 = 29   0

Quantity of Canvass.

```
14   cloths in the head
17½  cloths in the low reef.
22   cloths in the foot.
     ───
3)53½  sum.
```

```
18   square cloths.
9 1/12  yards deep.
     ───
162
  1½
     ───
163½  the product.
  5   yards in the foot-gores -
```

To find the quantity in the
foot-gores?

```
8½  cloths, gored on one side.
1¾  feet gore.
     ───
3)15  feet.
     ───
5 yards.
```

```
(No. 2.)  168½      sail.
          10        two leech-linings, half breadths.
          10½       three reef-bands, one-third of a cloth.
          6         middle-band
          3         reef-tackle pieces.
          5         foot band.
          23½       top-lining.
```

Total, 226½ yards.

MEMORANDUM.—It has *three bands*, put on at one foot above the half-way of the leech, the close-reef: the others are divided equally between the head and the lower-reef, and they extend from leech to leech underneath the leech-linings. They are one third of a breadth of canvass, put on single: the first edge is stuck long-work, and turned down and tabled close-work.

A *middle-band* is sometimes put on, which is between the lower reef-band and foot, and is made and put on in the same way as that of the main-course.

Linings.—The leeches are lined from the clue to the earing with half of a breadth of cloth; and the foot is lined from the clue under the leech-lining to the buntline-hole with a third or a half-breadth.

The *reef-tackle cringle* is 3 feet below the lower reef. The reef-tackle pieces are put on the fore-side of the sail, when the sail has a middle-band; but on the aft-side, when it has none.

Also, a *top-lining* on the aft-side, which for this sail is 8 cloths; and the cloths are cut 2¼ yards, so as to sew the top-edge to the centre of the middle band; and two cloths run up to the lower-reef band, covering the centre cloths of the sail that distance, or 5 yards.

Two *bowlines*, divided equally distant from each other, between the reef-tackle cringle and the clue. One *buntline-hole* is made at one-third of the foot, on each side of the top-lining, and to take the foot-band end.

The *thickness* of *bolt-rope* on the leeches and along the foot is 3½ inches, and for 18 inches to 2 feet up each leech and along the foot is parcelled and served; and before it is marled to the sail, the foot-rope should be well stretched, and the length of the foot of the sail set off.

Cringles, 3¾ inches thick, of bolt-rope, are made in lieu of turned clues; as also on the leeches, at the end of each reef-band. The hole for the clue-garnet is worked close to the clue-cringle holes.

FORE-TOPSAIL.

(By Rule, page 15.)

	FT.	IN.			FT.	IN.
Topmast -	32	6		Foreyard, hounded -	39	9
" head	4	3		Subtract	1	4
	28	3 hoist.		pin and pin	39	5 foot.
						4
				Divide by 7)153	8	
					21½	cloths.

		FT.	IN.
Fore-topsail-yard - -		34	3
" " two arms		5	6
hounded - - - - - -		28	9
within the cleats the earings		5	0
Head		23	9
			6
Divide by 11)142		6	
		13	cloths.

Close-reef, at one foot above half-way of the leech, 30ft. 3in.

To find the hollow on each leech?

	FT.	IN.			
Here, reef -	30	3	Head -	13	cloths.
Multiply by -		6	Foot -	21½	ditto.
Divide by 11)181		6	½)34½		
	16½	cloths	17¼	cloths the mean.	
			Reef	16½	ditto.
			Diff. -	¼ cloth = 18in.	
			Hollow on each leech = 9in.		

Dimensions for Cutting-out.

	FT.	IN.		Foot-gores.
Head	23	9	equal to 13 cloths.	IN.
Reef	30	3		1
Foot	38	5	equal to 21¼ cloths.	1
Hoist	28	3		2 Leech-gores.
Gore	1	9		2 (Art. 49.)
Middle	26	6	out—5 squares.	

	FT. DEC.	FT.	IN.
3 —	8·84 =	8	10
3 —	6·97 =	7	0
4 —	5·93 =	6	0
4 —	5·21 =	5	2
1 —	1·30 =	1	3
21	28·25 =	28	3

Quantity of Canvass.

13   cloths in the head.
16½ cloths in the close reef.
21¼ cloths in the foot.
—
3)51   sum.
—
17   square cloths.
8½ yards deep.
—
136
14
—
150   product.
4¾ yards in the foot-gores

To find the quantity in the foot-gores?

	FT.	IN.
	1	9
	8¼ cloths gored.	
	—	
	14	0
	0	5
	—	
3)14	5	product.
	—	
	4¾ yards.	

(No. 2.)	154¾	sail.
	10	two leech-linings, half breadths.
	10	three reef-bands, one-third breadth.
	5¾	middle-band.
	3	reef-tackle pieces.
	4¾	foot-band.
	23½	top-lining.

Total, 211¾ yards.

MEMORANDUM.—It has the same number of *reefs* in it as those of the main-topsail; and the *linings*, &c., are exactly the same.

MAIN-TOPGALLANTSAIL.

(By Rule, page 19.)

	FT.		Main-topsail-yard, hounded -	FT.	IN.
Topgallantmast -	18			30	6
Add - - -	1		Subtract - -	1	0
	——			——	
	19	hoist.	pin and pin	29	6 foot.
				4	
				——	
			Divide by 7)118	0	
				——	
			16	cloths.	

		FT.	IN.
Main-topgallant-yard - - -		25	6
" " two arms -		2	6
		——	
hounded - - - - - -		23	0
within the cleats the earings		1	0
		——	
Head		22	0
		6	
		——	
Divide by 11)132	0	
	——	
12 cloths.	

Dimensions for Cutting-out.

	FT.	IN.		Foot-gores.
				IN.
Head -	22	0	equal to 12 cloths.	2
Foot -	29	6	equal to 16 cloths.	3
Hoist -	19	0		4
Gore -	3	0		5 Leech-
Middle	16	0	cut—2 squares.	6 gores.
				— FT. IN.
				7 — 9 6
				8 — 9 6
				———
				35 19 0

M

Quantity of Canvass.

12   cloths in the head.
16   cloths in the foot.
————
$\frac{1}{2}$)28   sum.
————
14   square cloths.
5$\frac{1}{3}$ yards deep.
————
70
4$\frac{3}{4}$
————
74$\frac{3}{4}$ product.
7   yards in the foot-gores

To find the quantity in the foot-gores?

7 cloths, gored one side.
3 feet gore.
————
3)21 feet.
————
7 yards.

(No. 4.)   81$\frac{1}{4}$ "   sail.
6$\frac{1}{2}$ "   two leech-linings.
3$\frac{1}{4}$ "   foot-band.
11$\frac{3}{4}$ "   top-lining.
————
Total, 103$\frac{1}{2}$ yards.

MEMORANDUM.—*Linings* on the *leeches* are of half a breadth, and extend from the clue to the earing; and the *foot-band*, of the same breadth, extends from the clue to one-third the cloths along the foot. Also, a *top-lining* on the aft-side of the sail, which covers one-third of the cloths in the foot, or 6 cloths, and runs up 1$\frac{1}{4}$ yard from the foot. One *mast-cloth*, 4$\frac{1}{4}$ yards, is laced on to the top of the top-lining, covering the middle of the sail on the aft-side, between the top-lining and head.

Cringles are made in lieu of turned clues, and a *hole* for the clue-garnet.

The whole length of the *foot-rope*, from clue to clue and 15 inches up each leech, is served with small spunyarn; and before it is marled to the sail, the foot-rope should be well stretched, and the length of the foot of the sail measured off.

Iron thimbles are put in the clue-cringles, and the earings served with houseline.

FORE-TOPGALLANTSAIL.

(By Rule, page 19.)

	FT.		FT.	IN.
Topgallantmast	18	Fore-topsail-yard, hounded -	28	9
Add - - -	1	Subtract - -	1	0
	——		——	——
	19 hoist.	pin and pin	27	9 foot.
				4
		Divide by 7)111	0
			——
		15$\frac{1}{4}$ cloths.

	FT.	IN.
Fore-topgallant-yard - - -	23	6
" " two arms	2	4
hounded - - - - -	21	2
within the cleats the earings	1	0
Head	20	2
		6
Divide by 11)121	0	

Dimensions for Cutting-out.

11 cloths.

	FT.	IN.	
Head	20	2	equal to 11 cloths.
Foot	27	9	equal to 15¼ cloths.
Hoist -	19	0	
Gore -	3	0	
Middle	16	0	out—1 square.

Foot-gores.
IN.
2
3
4
5   Leech-
6   gores.
—   FT. IN.
7 — 8 11
8 — 8 11
1 — 1   2
—   —— —
36   19   0

Quantity of Canvass.

11 cloths in the head.
15 cloths in the foot.
—
½)26 sum.
—
13 square cloths.
 5⅓ yards deep.
—
65
 4½
—
69⅓ the product.
 7 yards in the foot-gores

To find the quantity in the
foot-gores?
7 cloths, gored on one side.
3 feet gore.
—
3)21 feet.
—
7 yards.

(No. 4.) 76⅓   sail.
          6¼   two leech-linings.
          3¼   foot band.
         11¾   top-lining.
         —
Total, 98 yards.

MEMORANDUM.—The *linings*, &c., are exactly similar to those of the main-topgallantsail. (See Art. 114.)

MAIN-ROYAL.

(By Rule, page 22.)

Royalmast	-	- 12 feet the hoist.

	FT.
Main-topgallantyard, hounded -	23
Subtract	1
	—
pin and pin	22 foot.
	7
	—

Divide by 13)154(12 cloths in the foot.
13
—
24
26
—

	FT.	IN.
Main-royal-yard - - - -	19	6
" " two arms	1	6
	—	
hounded -	18	0
		3
	—	

Divide by 15)144   0(9¼ cloths.
135
—
9
2
—
15)18(¼ cloth.
15
—
3
—

Dimensions for Cutting-out.

	FT.	IN.	
Head	18	0	equal to 9½ cloths.
Foot -	22	0	equal to 12 cloths.
Hoist -	12	0	
Gore -	0	6	
Middle	11	6	cut—4 squares.

Foot-gores.

IN.	Leech-
1	gores.
1	FT. IN.
2 —	2 5
2 —	9 7
—	—
6	12 0

Quantity of Canvass.

9¼ cloths in the head.
12 cloths in the foot.

―――

½)21¼ sum.

―――

10⅝ half the sum
4 yards.

―――

43 the product.
1 yard in the pieces.

―――

Total, 44 yards of No. 6.

MEMORANDUM.—Pieces are put on at all the corners, and the clues are formed of the bolt-rope, sewed home to the clues, and seized with houseline or marline.

FORE-ROYAL.

(By Rule, page 22.)

Royalmast   -   - 11ft. 6in. the hoist.

	FT.	IN.
Fore-topgallant-yard, hounded	21	2
Subtract	1	0

―――

pin and pin   20   2 foot.
7

―――

Divide by 13)141   2(11 cloths in the foot.
13

―――

11
13

―――

	FT.	IN.
Fore-royal-yard - - -	17	3
" " two arms -	1	6

―――

"   hounded   15   9
8

―――

Divide by 15)126   0(8¼ cloths.
120

―――

6

―――

Dimensions for Cutting-out.

	FT.	IN.				Foot-gores.	
Head	15	9	equal to 8½ cloths.			IN.	Leech-
Foot	20	2	equal to 11 cloths.			1	gores.
Hoist	11	6				1	FT. IN.
Gore	0	6				2 — 2	3
Middle	11	0	cut—3 squares.			2 — 9	3
						6	11 6

Quantity of Canvass.

8½ cloths in the head.
11 cloths in the foot.

¼)19½ sum.

9¾ half the sum.
3¾ yards deep.

29¼
7¼

36½ the product.
1 yard in the pieces.

Total, 37½ yards of No. 6.

This sail is finished precisely in the same way as the main-royal.

FORE-TOPMAST-STAYSAIL.

(By Rule, page 26.)

Fore-topmast, hounded, 28ft. 3in.; or leech, 10 yards, cut; foot, 9 cloths.

Dimensions for Cutting-out.

	FT.	IN.			FT.	IN.		Stay-gores.	
Leech	30	0	cut	-	28	3	tabled.	FT.	IN.
Stay	-	34	6	tabled.				6	4
Foot	-	16	6	equal to 9 cloths.				4	0
Foot-gores	-	0	4	per cloth.				3	8
								3	4
								3	0
								3	0
								3	0
								3	0
								32	4

Quantity of Canvass.

```
10  yards, depth of the leech.
4½ half the number of cloths.
──
40
 5
──
45  the product.
4½ yards in the foot-gores
──
```

To find the quantity in
the foot-gores?

$4 \times 9 = 36$ in. $= 1$ yard, the foot-gore.
4½ half the cloths.
──
4½ yards.

```
(No. 2.)  49½   "  sail.
           3    "  pieces.
          ──
```

Total, 52½ yards.

MEMORANDUM.—The clue-piece is two yards long, and the tack-piece one yard, so cut as to form the piece for that at the peak. (See Art. 119.)

STANDING-JIB.

The common size given to the jib at the foot is ⅙ the length of the jib-boom, and one cloth less for small ships. (See Art. 45, page 28.) Therefore,

```
                                       FT.
Jib-boom   -                           35
    "   end  -                          1
                                       ──
         hounded                        34
                                         5
                                       ──
                                     6)170
                                       ──
                                       28 the foot.
```

```
                              FT.
Then, per Rule III., page 12  -  -  -  28
                  Multiply by        19
                                    ──
                                    252
                                     28
                                    ──
         Divide by 36)532(    14 cloths.
                   36   Sub.  1
                   ──         ──
                  172          13 cloths.
                  144
                  ──
```

Dimensions for Cutting-out.

	FT.	IN.		FT.	
Leech -	42	6	cut	41	tabled.
Stay	59	6	out	58	tabled.
Foot	26	6	equal to 13 cloths.		

Cloths.	Stay-gores. FT.	IN.	Foot-gores. IN.
1	10	0	5
2	6	0	6
3	5	0	7
4	4	9	8
5	4	0	9
6	4	0	10
7	3	6	12
8	3	6	14
9	3	0	16
10	3	0	18
11	2	9	20
12	2	9	22
13	2	6	24

Quantity of Canvass.

126 yards, (No. 4).

MEMORANDUM.—The clue-piece is cut two yards.   (See Art. 120, page 66.)

FLYING-JIB.

	FT.	IN.	
Leech	31	0	tabled.
Stay -	41	0	tabled.
Foot -	17	6	equal to 9 cloths.

Cloths.	Stay-gores. FT.	IN.	Foot-gores. IN.
1	8	0	2
2	6	0	3
3	4	6	5
4	4	0	7
5	3	6	9
6	3	6	11
7	3	6	13
8	3	6	15
9	3	6	18

Quantity of Canvass.

72 yards, (No. 6).

MEMORANDUM.—The clue-piece is two yards out.   (See Art. 121, page 67.)

MIZEN.

	FT.	IN.	FT.	IN.	
(By Rule, page 24.)					
Mizenmast -	58	6	8	0	head.
"			4	6	cat-harpin.
"			17	0	housing.
	29	6	———		

	FT.	IN.	
	29	0	height of throat from the deck.
	5	8	height of the boom.
	23	4	
	1	4	for stretching.
Depth of mast	22	0	

	FT.	IN.		FT.	
Gaff - -	27	0	Boom -	33	
" end	5	0	Subtract	3	
" hounded -	22	0		30	the foot.
Subtract	1	6		24	
Head	20	6	Divide by 43)720(16 cloths.		
		5	43		
Divide by 9)102		6	290		
			258		

11 cloths.

To find the first foot-gore at the tack ?

The foot-gore (see Plate 9), is 9 feet ; the 4th cloth a square ; leaving 12 cloths.

FT.		FT.		FT. DEC.	
Therefore 24 = 12 cloths.		24 = 12 cloths.		36·5	
24		2 = 1 cloth.		36·5	
96		22		1825	
48		22		2190	
9)576		44		1095	
64		44		1332·25	
9		484		484	
½)73				848·25(29·1	
				4	27·5
36·5 feet, the radius.					
9·0 feet, the foot-gore.				49)448	1·6
				441	or 19in.
27·5					
				581) 725	

Hence, the first foot-gore at the tack is 19 inches. (See page 38.)

Dimensions for Cutting-out.

	FT.	IN.	
Head	20	6	equal to 11 cloths.
Foot -	30	0	equal to 16 cloths.
Leech	33	0	tabled.
Mast -	22	0	tabled.

Cloths.	Foot-gores.	Mast-gores.		Head-gores.	Slack-seams.
	IN.	FT.	IN.	IN.	IN.
1	19	5	0		
2	17	4	6		
3	15	4	6		
4	13	4	0		
5	11	3	6		
6	9	-	-	8	
7	8			7	
8	6			6	
9	4			5	
10	3			4	2
11	2			3	3
12	1			2	4
13	0			1	5
14	1			0	6
15	2			2	7
16	3			3	8

Quantity of Canvass.

140 yards, (No. 3).

MEMORANDUM.—Two reefs, 5 feet 6 inches and 5 feet, parallel to the foot, which have holes made in every seam of the sail.

Linings.—The after-leech is lined with one breadth of cloth, from the clue to one yard above the upper-reef, or 5 yards long. The *peak-piece* is one and a quarter yard in length; and the fore-leech or mast is lined with half a breadth of cloth, from the tack to the nock.

Holes are made for the reefs, clue, and tack-cringles.

Bolt-ropes.—The thickness and sewing them on are described at page 67, Art 122.

Iron thimbles are put in the cringles stuck at the tack, nock, clue, and reefs. The peak-earing is generally served.

Cringles, for the lacing, are made above the upper-reef on the mast-leech, 27 inches asunder, except the one next the nock, which is one yard from the nock. A luff cringle is made on the mast-leech, between the lower-reef and the foot, which has also a thimble.

MAIN-TRYSAIL.

	FT.	FT.		FT.	IN.
Mainmast	61	9 head.	Trysail, gaff	16	6
"		4 cat-harpin.	" end	0	6
"		16 housing.		—	
		—		16	0
	29		Subtract	1	0
		—		—	
	32	the throat of the gaff	Head -	15	
		from the main-deck.		5	
		10 the tack to stand above the deck.		—	
		—		9)75	
Depth of mast,	22	tabled.			

8⅜ cloths.

	FT.
Distance between the main and mizen masts -	24
Subtract	3
	—
	21 the foot.
	24
	—
	84
	42
	—

Divide by 43)504(11⅜ cloths.

```
                43
                —
                74
                43
                —
                31
                —
```

• The after-leech of the main-trysail, to look well,
ought to be parallel to the leech of the mizen.

Dimensions for Cutting-out.

Head	- - - -	15 feet, equal to 8⅜ cloths.
Foot	- -	21 feet, equal to 11⅜ cloths.
Leech		30 feet, tabled.
Mast	- - -	22 feet, tabled.

Cloths.	Mast-gores.		Foot-gores.	Head-gores.	Slack-seams.
	FT.	IN.	IN.	IN.	IN.
½	2	4	4		
1	7	4	12		
2	7	4	10		
3	5	0	8	4	
4	-	-	7	6	
5			6	6	
6			5	5	
7			4	5	2
8			3	4	3
9			2	3	4
10			1	2	5
11			0	1	6

Quantity of Canvass.

90 yards, (No. 2).

MEMORANDUM.—This sail has no reefs. The clue-lining is out two-yards. The *peak-piece* is one and a quarter yard in length; and the fore-leech is lined with half a breadth of cloth. from the tack to the nock.

Iron thimbles are stuck in the cringles at the clue, tack, and nock, the peak-earing being served.

Cringles, two high, are stuck in the bolt-rope on the mast-leech, at three-quarters of a yard apart, for the lacing of the mast.

Holes on the head, in the middle of each cloth, for seizing the hanks, in lieu of being laced to the gaff.

FORE-TRYSAIL.

	FT.	IN.	FT.	IN.			FT.
Foremast	57	0	8	6	head.	Fore-gaff -	22
"			4	0	cat-harpin.	Subtract	2
"			16	0	housing.		—
						Head	20
	28	6					5
	—						—
	28	6					9)100
Subtract	7	6	tack to stand above the deck.				—
	—						11 cloths.

Depth of mast 21 0 tabled.

Distance of mainstay, where it crosses the foremast, FT. IN.
   to the fore-part of gangway, (see page 8) - - 33 6
                                Subtract   3 6

                                     30 0 the foot.
                                   24

Divide by 43)720(16 cloths.
                   43
                   —
                 290
                 258
                 —
                 32

Dimensions for Cutting-out.

Head	20 feet, equal to 11 cloths.
Foot	30 feet 6 inches, equal to 16 cloths.
Leech	34 feet 6 inches, tabled.
Mast - -	21 feet, tabled.

Cross-gore, from the throat to the clue, 35 feet 6 inches.

Cloths.	Mast-gores.		Foot-gores.	Head-gores.	Slack-seams.
	FT.	IN.	IN.	IN.	IN.
1	4	6	26		
2	4	0	23		
3	4	0	19		
4	4	0	16		
5	3	6	14		
6	-	-	12	8	
7			10	6	
8			8	6	
9			7	5	
10			6	5	1
11			5	4	2
12			4	4	3
13			3	3	4
14			2	2	5
15			1	1	6
16			0	0	8

Quantity of Canvass.

145 yards, (No. 2).

MEMORANDUM.—This sail has *one* reef of 5 feet from the foot.

Linings.—The after-leech is lined with one breadth of cloth, 3 yards in length, from the clue. A *strengthening-band* at the clue, which ought to be in a line with the tack, is taken over four cloths; and the mast is lined with half a breadth. It is similarly finished as the preceding.

GAFF-TOPSAIL.

	FT.	IN.		FT.	IN.
Mizen-topmast	29	6	Yard for the head	10	6
Add	4	6	Subtract	1	0
Depth of fore-leech	34	0	Head -	9	6
					6
			Divide by 11)57	0	
				5 cloths.	

Head of the mizen, 11 cloths, equal to the foot of the gaffsail.

Dimensions for Cutting-out.

	FT.	IN.	
Head	9	6	equal to 5 cloths.
Foot	20	0	equal to 11 cloths.
Leech - -	29	0	out, 28 feet tabled.
Mast -	33	0	out, 32 feet tabled.

Mast-gores.	Foot-gores.	Head-gores.	Slack-seams.
FT.	IN.	IN.	IN.
7	0		
6	1		
5	2		
5	3	6	
5	5	5	2
5	7	3	3
	9	2	4
	12	1	5
	15		
	18		

Quantity of Canvass.

102 yards, (No. 6).

MEMORANDUM.—Pieces on the four corners, and holes in the head. The head is bent to a yard, similar to a lugsail, by which it is hoisted to the topgallantmast-head, and the foot spreads the gaff of the mizen. This sail is only used in light winds.

LOWER-STUDDINGSAIL.

(By rule, page 26.)

Foresail, 21 cloths, and $21 \times \frac{2}{3} = 14$ cloths, the *head;* and the depth of the sail, ·25 feet 6 inches, cut.

Quantity of Canvass.

14   cloths.
8$\frac{1}{2}$ yards deep.
———
112
7
———
119   the product.
2$\frac{1}{2}$ yards in the pieces.
———

Total, 121$\frac{1}{2}$ yards of No. 5.

MEMORANDUM.—Pieces at all the corners, and a piece, half a yard long, on one-third of the head.

Holes are made in only *one-third* of the cloths in the head, and two in each clue, and in the third of the head, for the cringles. (See Art. 123, page 68.)

TOPMAST-STUDDINGSAILS.

140. A regular *gore* is made on the head and foot, decreasing to the outer-earing, and increasing in depth from the inner-leech. The gore is given on account of the studdingsail inclining at an angle inwards, or spreading beyond the leeches of the topsails. Hence, the gore on the studdingsail-head is governed by the number of goring cloths in the leeches of the topsail. The greater the number of goring cloths in the topsail leech, the stronger will be the head-gore of the studdingsail; and the less cloths in the topsail leeches, the lesser gore on the head of the studdingsail; and when there are no goring cloths in the leeches, (that is, a foresail,) the heads are cut square.

RULE.—To find the *gore* on the head and foot of *topmast* and *topgallant-studdingsails?* Divide the number of cloths in the leech of the topsail by one and a half times the depth in yards of the leech of the topmast studdingsail, and the quotient will give the gore at the head in terms of a cloth. Thus—Suppose the number of cloths in the leech of the topsail is *four*, and the length of the leech of the studdingsail, or hoist of the topsail, 10 yards. Then, 10 yards × 1½ times = 15, and 4 cloths = 8 feet = 96 inches.

Therefore 15)96

6 inches gore for the head of the studdingsail.

MAIN AND FORE-TOPMAST STUDDINGSAILS.

(By rule, page 26.) The outer-leech is gored 3 cloths.

Dimensions for Cutting-out.

Head	6 cloths.
Foot	9 cloths.
Leech - - - - - - - -	29 feet 9 inches.

Head and *foot gores*, 6 inches per cloth.

Quantity of Canvass.

77 yards, (No. 5).

MAIN AND FORE-TOPGALLANT STUDDINGSAILS.

Head	5 cloths.
Foot	7 cloths.
Leech - - - - - - - --	19 feet 6 inches.

(By Art. 140.) *Head* and *foot gores*, 6½ yards × 1½ = 9½, and *two* cloths = 4 feet = 48 inches. Therefore 9½) 48

4   4

39)192

5 inches per cloth

Quantity of Canvass.

5 cloths in the head.
7 cloths in the foot.
———
¼)12 sum.
———
6 square cloths.
6¼ yards deep.
———
39 yards, the product.
1 yard in the pieces.
———
Total, 40 yards of No. 6.

———

SUMMARY OF THE QUANTITY AND QUALITY OF CANVASS, WITH THE USUAL PRICE PER YARD GIVEN FOR THE BEST CANVASS, AND THE POUNDS WEIGHT OF EACH BOLT OF COKER-CANVASS, 40 YARDS TO THE BOLT, FOR MAKING A SUIT OF SAILS FOR A BARQUE OF 300 TONS.

Species of Sails.	Total Quantity.	No. 2. 1s. 2¼d. 41℔.	No. 3. 1s. 2d. 38℔.	No 4. 1s. 1½d. 35℔.	No. 5. 1s. 1d. 32℔.	No. 6. 1s. 0¼d. 29℔.
	Yards.	Yards.	Yards.	Yards.	Yards.	Yards.
1 Main-course	266	..	212	..	54	..
2 Main-topsails............	453	337	..	..	116	..
2 Main-topgallantsails	207	..	..	163½	..	43½
1 Main-royal...............	44	..	..	..	..	44
2 Fore-courses	367	310	..	..	77	..
2 Fore-topsails	423½	309½	..	..	114	..
1 Fore-topgallantsail	98	..	..	76½	.	21½
1 Fore-royal	37½	..	..	..	..	37½
2 Fore-topmast-staysails ...	105	99	..	..	6	..
2 Jibs	252	..	..	252	..	..
1 Flying-jib	72	..	..	..	..	72
2 Lower-studdingsails	248	..	..	..	248	..
2 M.-topmast-studdingsails ..	154	..	..	..	154	..
2 M.-topgall.-studdingsails ..	80	..	..	..	..	80
1 Fore-topmast-studdingsail	77	..	..	..	77	..
1 F.-topgallant-studdingsail	40	..	..	..	..	40
1 Main-trysail	90	82	..	..	8	..
1 Mizen	140	..	130½	..	9½	..
1 Fore-trysail	145	..	137	..	8	..
1 Gaff-topsail	102	..	..	..	..	102
Total	3416	1137½	479½	492	866½	440½

When a suit of sails is made of the best canvass, with the best materials, and estimated, when finished, one with another, at *nineteenpence halfpenny* a yard, the value will e obtained as nearly as possible. But single sails vary in price, according to the uality of canvass, fixing on the bolt-rope and thimbles, and pointing the reefs. It is ather singular that *ten yards* of canvass is nearly the average rate for every *ton* the hip is burthened.

Tons. Yards.
Thus:—300 = 3,000 in the sails.
400 = 4,000 "
1,000 = 10,000 "

CHAPTER II.

RULES FOR DETERMINING THE SIZE, DIMENSIONS
FOR CUTTING-OUT, AND QUANTITY AND QUALITY OF CANVASS CONTAINED IN EACH SAIL, FOR A BRIG OF 18 KEELS.*

141. The close-reef of the topsail, and the length of the foot, govern the length of the head of the sail; and it is to be observed, that the close-reef must never extend beyond the *lifts* of the topsail-yard. Hence, the method of fixing the length on the head of the topsail, or the distance of the head of the sail from the topsail-lifts, will cause the hollow given to the leeches of the topsails always to be more or less, according as the lengths of the lower yards at the sheaves exceed the lengths of the topsail-yards at the lifts, or place of the low-reef, which, in colliers, is invariable, and gives the leeches a very considerable hollow. Thus—Suppose a topsail has 18 cloths in the foot, 14 cloths in the close-reef, and the leeches require a hollow of half a cloth on each side, what number of cloths ought there to be in the head?

Here - -	14 cloths in the close-reef.
Add	1 cloth, the hollow of the two leeches.
	15 cloths in the reef, when straight.
	2 times.
	30
Subtract	18 cloths in the foot.
	12 cloths in the head.

Again—If we suppose 19 cloths in the foot, and the rest the same as before, it will be seen that the cloths in the head are less.

Thus - -	14 cloths in the reef.
Add	1 cloth, the hollow.
	15 cloths in the reef, straight leeches.
	2 times.
	30
Subtract	19 cloths in the foot.
	11 cloths in the head.

Showing that the head is entirely regulated by the reef and foot; consequently, the cloths in the foot and close-reef must be determined first, and then see whether the leeches will require much or little hollow for the head to extend well out on the topsail-yard, which is generally from 2 to 2¼ feet on each side, from the topsail-lifts.

* *Keel* is a name given to a low, flat, interior vessel, used to bring coals down the river Tyne for loading the colliers. Hence, a collier is said to carry so many "keels of coals."

TOPSAIL.

Measurements.

	FT.	IN.
Topsail-yard, from lift to lift -	27	0
Subtract -	1	6

Topmast, from the pin of the sheave-hole down to the heel, 27ft. 9in.

	FT.	IN.
Reef - -	25	6
		6

Divide by 11)153 0

14 cloths in the reef.

	FT.	IN.
Mainyard, pin and pin - -	35	6
Subtract	1	6

	FT.	IN.
	34	0 the foot.
		7

Divide by 13)238 0(18 cloths.
13

108
104

$\frac{4}{13} = \frac{1}{2}$ cloth.

Head.—To make the leeches straight in this sail, there must be only 10 cloths in the *head*, which will measure 18 feet 6 inches; that is, bringing the earings 4 feet on each side from the hauling-out to the cleats, which is a great deal too much. Hence, we must hollow the leeches to get a squarer head—generally half a cloth on each side. The cloths in the head are obtained as shown in the preceding article (141).

Dimensions for Cutting-out.

	FT.	IN.	
Head	22	0	equal to 12 cloths.
Reef	25	6	equal to 14 cloths.
Foot	34	0	equal to 18 cloths.
Hoist	27	9	
Gore	2	6	
Middle -	25	3	cut—4 squares, (Art. 52.)

Foot-gores.

IN.	
1	
2	Leech-
3	gores.
4	(Art. 49.)

	FT.	IN.
5 —	14	0
7 —	7	9
9 —	6	0
31	27	9

To find the leech-gores?

(Plate I.) Here 3 cloths = 6 feet, and ½ cloth hollow = 1 foot, and 27ft. 9in. = 27ft. 75dec.

FT. DEC.

Therefore 27·75 AB.
27·75

27·75 AB.
14·19 AI.

13875	24975
19425	2775
19425	11100
3 cloths = 6 5550	2775
6	
— 770·0625	6)393·7725
36 - 36·	
	65·628 IG.
806·0625(¼)28·39 AC.	1· IN.
4	66·628
— 14·19 AI.	
48)406 14·19	101·178 ON.
384	7 3 OF.
— 12771	
563)2206 1419	108·478
1689 5676	93·878
— 1419	
5669)51725	867824
51021 201·3561	759346
1· ½ cloth hol-	867824
— low.	325434
¼)202·3561	976302
101·178 ON, rad.	—————
66·628	10183·697684(100·9 AF.
— 1 2	
34·55 OG.	—
6 CB. 2009)18369 98.9	
— 18081	
28·39)207·30(7·3 OF.	
198·73 298	
—————	
8570	
8517	
———	
53	

To find the leech-gores (*continued*) ?

101·178	101·178
98·9	96·9

200·078	198·078
2·278	4·278

1600624	1584624
1400546	1386546
400156	396156
400156	792312

455·777684(21·3   847·877684(29·1
4   7·3   4   7·8

41)55   14 ft., 1st gore.   49)447   21·8
41   441   14

423)1477   581)637   7·8 2d gore.
1269   581

208   27·75   56
         21·8

      5·95 3d gore.
      7·8 2d gore.
      14· 1st gore.

Proof   27·75

BOOM-FORESAIL.

Measurements.

	FT.	IN.
Foreyard, from cleat to cleat on the yard-arms	35	6
Subtract	2	0
	32	6
		6
Divide by 11)195		0

17¾ cloths.

Depth.—The height of the centre of the yard from the mainstay, 17ft.

	FT.	IN.
Boom, between the two auger-holes	29	6
		6
Divide by 11)177		0

16 cloths.

Dimensions for Cutting-out.

	FT.	IN.	
Head	32	6	equal to 18 cloths.
Foot	29	6	equal to 16 cloths.
Depth	17	0	cut—square on the foot.

Quantity of Canvass.

```
  18   cloths in the head.
  16   cloths in the foot.
  ──
¼)34   sum.
  ──
  17   square cloths.
  17   feet, the depth.
  ──
 119
  17
  ──
3)289
  ──
```

(No. 2.)	96¼	yards in the sail.
	12	" the two leech-linings.
	3½	" one-third the reef-band.
	2	" the two buntline-cloths.

Total, 113¾ yards.

MEMORANDUM.—*Linings* on the leeches are of one breadth, and extend from the clue to the earing.

No *foot-band.* A *reef-band,* one-fourth to one-third of a breadth, is put on at 5 feet below the head.

Two *buntline-cloths* run about one yard up from the foot; and small *cringles* are stuck in the bolt-rope, in lieu of buntline-holes.

Two *bowlines,* the upper bowline-cringle being made in the middle of the leech, and the lower one equally distant from the upper one and the clue.

Cringles are made in the two lower corners or clues.

Bolt-rope.—The bolt-rope is sewed round the sail.

PART II.

SECTION FIRST.

ON DRAUGHTING AND CENTRE OF EFFORT OF THE SAILS.

DRAWING PLANS OF SAILS.

142. Plans of sails are drawn to a scale of reduced proportion to the real dimensions, as the 8th or 4th of an inch to the foot, as may be convenient for the drawing. This sort of drawing is called *geometrical*, because it has no reference to a spectator, and is not designed to give the appearances of the sails *perspectively*, but only purposes to exhibit the form and measurement of the surfaces of the sails in height and breadth, and also for rightly ascertaining the dimensions of the leeches, stays, and total amount of the sweep-gores on the head and foot, &c., of particular sails, as jibs, drivers, &c.

The whole of these operations are performed by means of a rule containing a scale of equal parts, a compass, a parallel ruler, and a square.

To draw the plan of sails for a new ship, it is requisite to have the *dimensions of the hull*, as :—

The distance between the foreside of the stem to the centre of the foremast.

The distance between the centre of the foremast to the centre of the mainmast.

The distance between the centre of the mainmast to the centre of the mizenmast.

The distance between the centre of the mizenmast to the outside of the taffrail.

The housing of the foremast.
      "   "   mainmast.
      "   "   mizenmast.

The step of the foremast above a straight line from the step of the mainmast.

The step of the mizenmast above a straight line from the step of the mainmast.

The number of inches the foremast rakes to the foot.

    "   "   "   mainmast   "   "

    "   "   "   mizenmast   "   "

    "   "   "   bowsprit rises to the foot.

The height of the rail or gunwale.

    "   "   topgallant forecastle.

    "   "   poop.

    "   "   cathead or bumkins.

Also, the *dimensions of masts, yards, gaffs, &c.*, as shown in the form, page 14.

As the surface of the sail, when the yards are braced up, is somewhat before the mast, it will be necessary to determine, as nearly as possible, the line or axis upon which the sails revolve. This line will be more or less forward, according as the topmasts or topgallantmasts project before the lower masts; and, as regards the lower yards, it will be according to the angle of the stay and shrouds, or as the trusses are eased off, and will be found to vary in different ships of the same class—some rather forward, and in others a little aft.

The rake of this line, or axis of the sails, will be somewhat less than the intended rake of the mast, since the plane of the sails, when the yards are braced sharp up, will be about the diameter of the yard before the topgallantmast, at the tie, and will be well with the lower side of the lower yard. When these lines are determined, set upon them the heights for the heads of the royalsails, topgallantsails, topsails, and courses; and also the height of the lower part of the courses at the middle, which is determined by the height of the boats for the main, and by the mainstay, when it is carried to the stem, for the fore. Draw lines perpendicular to the axis of the sails upon the lower one, which is the head of the course, when set off at its breadth; the next above at its breadth, which is the head of the topsail; and so on, setting off likewise upon the corresponding lines on the fore and mizen the breadths of the sails on these masts. Before the form of the leeches of the topsails, topgallantsails, &c., can be determined, it will be requisite to set off the lengths of the yards, and the cleats on the yard-arms; and the lines at first drawn are intended to give the breadths on the heads of the courses, topsails, and topgallantsails, within the cleats on the yard-arms, to the allowance made for stretching, which, according to the present custom, is 18 inches for the topsails and courses, and 9 inches for topgallantsails, within the cleats, to give the earings. The clues, however, are drawn to the pin of the sheave-hole within the hounds of the yards. When the correct lines for the heads and depths of the sails are drawn, the leeches of the topgallantsails and topsails may be completed; but, as the leeches of the topsails are commonly hollowed for taking in the lower reef, it will be requisite to determine the spread of the sail at the lowest reef; or, as the most common way is, to allow 18 inches within the outer end of the yard, from each end, for the spread of the sail at the lowest reef. Set down from the head half the depth of the topsail, for the place of the lowest reef, and below it 3 feet, for the reef-tackle or pendant : when the breadth of the outer part of the sheave is set off at this distance down, it will give the spread of the sail at the lowest reef, or breadth of the sail at this place.   Then, through the breadth of the sail at the head, the breadth at the lowest reef, and the breadth of the clues, pass a curve, which may be the arc of a circle, and the leeches of the topsails are thus obtained by the common method of hollowing them.   (See calculation of hollow topsail leeches, page 30.)

For the leeches of the courses, draw a line from the breadth given at the head to the breadth they are intended to be at the foot.   The mainsail has, in general, a greater spread of from 3 to 6 feet.   The foresail is sometimes narrowed at the foot, for bringing the tack to the cathead—formerly, about 3 feet 9 inches, and, in general, about 2 feet; but the foresail will, generally, stand better with parallel leeches.   This is the case with ships which have boomkins to bring the tack properly down. (See Art. 39, page 27.)

CHAPTER I.

ON THE PRINCIPLES OF DRAWING PLANS OF SAILS.

143. In order to have a right understanding of draughting sails, geometry ought to be learned. To prepare the mind for this, the most useful problems are herein briefly illustrated, and those who have leisure and opportunity will find themselves amply rewarded by a deeper study, whether it can be brought into immediate use or not; for the art of draughting presents difficulties to persons ignorant of it, which to the geometrician are easily surmounted. The following problems, being the most useful, have been selected.

I. *To bisect a given line, AB, that is, to divide it into two equal parts.*
(Fig. 1., Plate 16.)

From the centres A and B, with any radius, describe two arcs intersecting each other in C and D, and draw the line CD, which will bisect the line AB in the point E, as required.

The two ends of the line AB are called centres, being made so to draw the arcs, the intersections of which being equally distant from the two ends, a line from C to D must pass through the centre of the line, and divide it equally.

II. *At a given point, C, in a given line, AB, to erect a perpendicular.*
(Fig. 2, Plate 16.)

From the given point, C, cut off equal parts, CD, CE, on the given line; then, making D and E centres, describe arcs intersecting in F; then join CF, which will be perpendicular, as required.

Otherwise.— When the point C is near the end of the line. *(Fig. 3, Plate 16.)*

Draw the line AB, and mark a point, C, near the end of the line. From a point, D, assumed above the line for a centre, describe a circle passing through C, and cutting the line at E.

Draw a line from E through the centre D, and cutting the circle at F. Join CF, which will be a perpendicular.

III. *From a point, A, to let fall a perpendicular on a line, BC.*
(Fig. 4, Plate 16.)

Draw the line BC, and choose a point, A, above it. From the point A, with a convenient radius, describe an arc, cutting the given line at the two points, D, E. Then, with any radius, describe two arcs, intersecting at F, and draw AF through G, which will be the perpendicular required.

Otherwise.—When the point is nearly opposite to the end of the line.
(Fig. 5, Plate 16.)

Draw the line BC, and fix the point A near the end of the line.
From any point, D, in the line BC, as a centre, describe the arc of a circle through the point A, cutting BC in E.
Now, from the centre, E, with the length, EA, describe another arc below the line, cutting the first arc at F.
Draw AGF, which will be the perpendicular to BC, as required.

IV. *To describe the circumference of a circle through three given points,*
A, B, C. (Fig. 6, Plate 16.)

Make three points, in any position, and mark them A, B, C.
From the middle point B, draw to each of the other points, A and C.
Bisect these lines, BA, BC, perpendicularly by lines meeting in O, which will be the centre.
Then from the centre O, with the distance of any one of the points, as OA, describe a circle through the two other points, B and C.

V. *Upon a straight line, AC, as a chord to describe the arc of a circle,*
the height of the middle of the arc being given. (See Fig. 7, Plate 16.)

Bisect AC by a perpendicular BE, intersecting AC in D; make DB equal to the height of the arc; draw the chord AB of the half arc; bisect AB by a perpendicular, meeting BE in E; from E, with the distance EB, describe the arc ABC, and ABC is the arc required.

PRACTICAL METHODS OF CONSTRUCTING SAILS.

MAIN-COURSE.

144. *To draw the plan.*—Given the widths of the head and foot, the depth of the middle, the length of the leech, and the roach of the foot.
(Plate 9.) *Head.*—Set off half the breadth of the head, from the centre of the mainyard, both ways.
Depth.—Set down, from the centre of the yard, the depth of the middle perpendicularly, and produce it to the given roach of the foot.
Foot.—Draw a line perpendicular to the depth, or depth and roach on the same line, and set off from the middle, half the width of the foot both ways.
Leeches.—Join the places which are set off for the earings and clues.

Roach of the foot.—Through the depth of the middle of the foot draw a line parallel to the head, and set off both ways, from the middle, half of three-fifths of the breadth of the foot, from which places the roach is carried down to the clues.

MAIN-TOPSAIL.

145. *To draw the plan.*—Given the widths of the head and foot, the height of the middle, and the roach of the foot.

(Plate 9.) *Mast or hoist.*—Set down the depth, from the centre of the topsail-yard to the centre of the mainyard, at right angles to both.

Head and foot.—Set off half the widths of the head and foot, from the centre of the yards, both ways.

Leeches.—Join the places set off for the earings and clues.

Roach of the foot.—Draw the arc of a circle through the roach set above the centre of the mainyard and the clues. (See Prob. V. page 112.)

Close-reef.—Set down from the head half the hoist of the topsail, and between it and the head the other reefs. (See Art. 110, page 64.)

Hollow on the leeches.—Through the breadth of the sail at the head, the breadth at the lowest reef, and the breadth at the clues, pass the arc of a circle. (See Art. 49, page 30, and Prob. IV., page 112.)

Middle-band.—Set down from the lower-reef half the distance between the reef and middle of the foot.

Reef-tackle pendant.—Set down three feet (from a scale of equal parts) below the close-reef on the leeches.

Buntlines.—At one-third the breadth of the foot.

Bowlines.—At one-third the distance between the clue and reef-tackle. The references to the other parts are obviously seen on Plate 13.

MAIN-TOPGALLANTSAIL.

146. *To draw the plan.*—Given the widths of the head and foot, the height of the middle, and the roach of the foot.

(Plate 9.) Set down the *hoist*, from the centre of the topgallantyard, to the centre of the topsailyard, at right angles to both.

Head and foot.—Set off half the widths of the head and foot, from the centre of each of the yards.

Leeches.—Join the places set off for the earings and clues.

Roach of the foot.—Draw the arc of a circle through the height of the roach set up on the mast, above the topsail-yard and the clues. (See Prob. V., page 112.)

MAIN-ROYAL.

147. *To draw the plan.*—Given the widths of the head and foot, the height of the middle, and the roach of the foot.

It is precisely the same way drawn as that of the preceding, excepting the roach, which is a deal less.

148. The sails on the fore and mizen masts are likewise drawn in a similar manner to those on the mainmast.

149. *To draw the plan.*—Given the length of the leech, the gore of the foot, and the number of cloths, or width of the foot.

(Plate 16, fig. 8.) Make AB equal the given length of the leech, BD the gore of the foot, and at right angles to AD draw CD equal the number of cloths (in feet), the width of the foot. Join AC, and from B draw BI perpendicular to AC; produce BI to the roach, or greatest round on the stay; through the points A, N, C, pass a curve, which is nearly the arc of a circle, and ANC is the curved stay.

For the round of the foot.—Join BC, and in the middle of which, set without, a perpendicular equal to the roach; and through the clue, roach, and tack, pass the arc of a circle.

150. *To draw the plan.*—Given the length of the head, the length of the foot, the length of the fore-leech, and the length of the cross-gore. (See page 8.)

(Plate 1.) Make AB equal the length of the fore-leech. On AB, with the length of BC and AC, construct the triangle ABC.* Draw AD equal the length of the head; or, if the length of the leech is determined in the proportion of the fore-leech, (see page 29, Art. 47,) construct a triangle ACD, with the lengths of CD and AD, and ABCD is the driver.

For the foot.—Draw the arc of a circle through BIC. (See page 38.)

* It is clear that the four sides will not be sufficient for drawing the figure of this sail, as the figure may be moved out of its position; we must, therefore, take the cross-gore, that is, one of the diagonals also, and this being done, will resolve the figure into two triangles, which is comprehended in the above construction.

CHAPTER II.

ON THE CENTRE OF EFFORT.

Definition.—The point of sail or place in which the whole effort of the wind is supposed to be collected, is commonly called the CENTRE OF EFFORT of the sails; and is the point in which, if a single force were applied equally, and directly opposed to the force of the wind, it would destroy its effect, or produce the same result as when uniformly distributed; or as if in this point, the centre of a single sail were placed with a surface equal to the sum of the surfaces of all the sails.

151. It is found in a manner similar to that by which we find the common centre of gravity of several bodies, only that we in this case consider the surface in place of the weight or magnitude of the body.

152. Before the centre of effort of the sails can be obtained, it is necessary to make a plan of the sails (see plate 8), and find the centre of gravity of each sail to obtain the moments.*

153. The sails that are in general placed in the plan of the sails, are those which are most frequently used; in square-rigged vessels, the fore and main courses, fore, main, and mizen topsails, fore, main, and mizen topgallant sails, driver, jib, and sometimes fore-topmast-staysail; and in fore and aft rigged vessels, as cutters, the mainsail, foresail, and jib (the second or third jib is commonly taken, as it is seldom that the first jib is set on a wind.) The whole of these sails may not always be set; nor is the pressure of the wind, when it acts obliquely and as the sail becomes more pressed, the same on both leeches; but since we obtain the moment of the sails, with a view only to compare with ships in which the quantity of sail is well proportioned to the stability, and in which the position of the point of sail is correct as to length, the unequal effect of the wind, and the number of the sails used (and these the principal sails), being the same in each case, will not affect the comparison.

154. If sails were rectangular, the centre of gravity of each sail would evidently be in the point where its diagonals intersect each other. But since most sails are either trapeziums or triangles, their centre of gravity must be found differently. If two sides of a triangular sail, as the jib, be bisected, and lines drawn from these points to the opposite angles, the intersection of the two lines will be the centre of gravity. The sails that are trapeziums with two equal sides, as the topsails, are formed into two triangles gqz and gqv, by drawing the diagonal gq; the centre of gravity of each triangle is found, as for the jib; a line, ba, is drawn through the two centres of gravity, and the point in which it cuts the middle line of the sail, c, is its centre of gravity.

155. When the sail is a trapezium, as the driver, not having two equal surfaces on each side of the middle, it is first divided into two triangles, azd and azg, by drawing the diagonal az; the centres of gravity are found as before, and a line, hl, is drawn to pass through them; this figure is then formed again into two triangles, dga and dgz, by drawing the diagonal dg, from the two other angles d and g, the centre of gravity of these is found, and a line, of, drawn to pass through them; the intersection m, of the two lines of and hl, is the centre of gravity of the sail.

156. The areas of all the sails that are triangular are found by multiplying the base by half the height, as in obtaining the area of a common triangle; and the area of a trapezium, by forming it into two triangles, obtaining the area of each, and taking the sum of the two. The mo-

* Thus, by the nature of the lever, when two bodies are in equilibria about a fixed point O, they are reciprocally as their distances from that point;

As $A : B :: CB : CA$,

or $CA . A = CB . B$, that is, the two products are equal,

which are made by multiplying each body by its distance from the centre of gravity. It is frequently necessary to refer to this power of a force to produce rotation, and, accordingly, the product just mentioned, has received a particular denomination. It is called the *Moment* of the force round the axis. The moment is therefore meant the product of the force and leverage.

ment, as to height, is obtained by multiplying the height of the centre of gravity of each sail into the area ; the sum of the moments of all the sails, divided by the sum of the areas, gives the height of the centre of effort (151.)   To obtain the distance of the centre of effort from the middle of the length of the water-line, multiply the distances of the centres of those sails that are before it into their areas, for the sum of the moments before ; and the distance of the centres of those that are abaft into their areas, for the sum of those abaft ; when, if the difference between the sums of the two moments be divided by the sum of the areas, it will give the place of the centre of effort, either before or abaft the middle, according to which the moments has the excess.*

AREAS AND MOMENTS OF SAILS.

157. The area of the sails is the measure of their surface, or the space contained within the boundaries of that surface, and is estimated by the number of squares contained therein.

The area of a triangle and trapezium is found according to rules in books on mensuration.   Thus :—

I. *For the area of a triangle.*—Multiply the base by the perpendicular height, and half the product will be the area.

II. *For the area of a trapezium.*—Let two perpendiculars be drawn from the opposite angles to the diagonal.   Multiply the sum of these perpendiculars by the diagonal, and half the product will give the area.

(By rule I.)   JIB.

Perp.   24·0   937·0 area.
Stay -   76   46 height of centre of gravity.

       1480   56240
       17260   374933

    2)1874·0   43117·0 moment.

Area   937·0 square feet.
           937·0 area.
           77·5 distance of centre of gravity from the middle.

       46866
      656133
      6561333

   72643·30 moment before.

* See Treatise on Masting Ships, and Mast Making, by Mr. John Fincham, Master Shipwright of Her Majesty's Dockyard, late at Chatham, p. 6.

(By rule II.)   FORE-COURSE.

Perps. - { 20·5
         { 20·5

                    994·25 area.
                    26·∅ height of centre of gravity.

Sum   41·0   9)596550
Diag.   48·5

                      662833
         2050   596550
         3280   198850
         1640

                  26513·33∅ moment.
      2)1988·50

Area   994·25 square feet.

               994·25 area.
               40·5 distance of centre of gravity from the middle.

             497125
             397700

           40267·125 moment before.

(By rule II.)   FORE-TOPSAIL.

Perps. { 28   49·5 diagonal.   1188 area.
        { 20   48   56·∅ height of centre of gravity.

Sum -   48   3960   9)3564
            1980

                    3960
         2)2376·0   7128
                    5940

Area -   1188· square feet.
                   66924·0 moment.

               1188 area.
               40·∅ distance of centre of gravity from the middle.

            9)3564

              3960
             4752

           47916·0 moment before.

(By rule II.)   FORE-TOPGALLANTSAIL.

Perps. $\begin{cases} 13 \\ 17 \end{cases}$ 510 area.
                        85·5 height of centre of gravity.

Sum   - 30   2550
Diag.   - 34   2550
                         4080

2)1020

                         43605·0 moment.

Area   510 square feet.
          40·1∅ distance of centre of gravity from the middle.
          510 area.

          40166
          2008333

          20485·00 moment before.

(By rule II.)   MAIN-COURSE.

Perps. - $\begin{cases} 24 \\ 27 \end{cases}$ 1530 area.
                          29·∅ height of centre of gravity.

Sum - - 51   9)4590
Diag. -   60
                         5100
2)3060   13770
                         3060

Area   1530 square feet.
                         44880·0 moment.

          1530 area.
          9 distance of centre of gravity from the middle.

          13770 moment abaft.

(By rule II.)   MAIN-TOPSAIL.

Perps. $\begin{cases} 22\cdot5 & 55\cdot\emptyset \\ 31\cdot5 & 54 \end{cases}$ diagonal.   1494 area.
                          62·5 height of centre of gravity.

Sum   54·   2213   7470
             27666   2988
                             8964
2)2988·0
                             93375·0 moment.

Area - 1494 square feet.
          1494 area.
          10·5 distance of centre of gravity from the middle.

          7470
          1494

          15687·0 moment abaft.

(By rule II.)   **MAIN-TOPGALLANTSAIL.**

Perps. - $\begin{cases} 14 \\ 18 \end{cases}$ 592 area.
            94·5 height of centre of gravity.

Sum   32   2960
Diag.   37   2368
             5328

       224
        96   55944·0 moment.

   2)1184

Area   592 square feet.
         592 area.
         12 distance of centre of gravity from the middle.

     7104 moment abaft.

(By rule II.)   **DRIVER.**

Perps. $\begin{cases} 26 \\ 20 \end{cases}$ 42 ∅ diagonal.   981·∅ area.
       46   30·5 height of centre of gravity.

Sum - 46 2560   49066
         17066   2944000

   2)1962·∅   29930·6∅ moment.

Area   981·∅ square feet.
      981·∅ area.
       52 distance of centre of gravity from the middle.

    19626
   490666

   51029·∅ moment abaft.

(By rule II.)   **MIZEN-TOPSAIL.**

Perps. $\begin{cases} 15·3∅ \\ 22·5 \end{cases}$ 728·291∅ area.
         55·∅ height of centre of gravity.
             728·291∅

Sum 37·8∅ 9)43697500   44·∅ distance.
Diag. 38·5

         48552777   9)21848750
   18916   364145833
  302666   3641458333   24276388
 1135000   291316666
        40541·5694∅ mom. 2913166666

  2)1456·58∅
              32287·5972∅ moment abaft.

Area 728·291∅ square feet.

(By rule II.)   MIZEN-TOPGALLANTSAIL.

Perps. $\begin{cases} 10 & 25\cdot5 \text{ diagonal.} \\ 13 & 23 \end{cases}$ 293·25 area.
                         79·ø height of centre of gravity.

Sum   23   765   9)87975
               510   ————
            ————   97750
        2)586·5   263925
        ————   205275
Area   293·25 sq. feet. ————
                      23264·500 moment.

        293·25 area.
         46 distance of centre of gravity from the middle.
        ————
       175950
       117300
      ————
    13489·50 moment abaft.

CENTRE OF EFFORT.

Species of Sails.	Areas.	Moments.	Moments before.	Moments abaft.
Jib - - -	937·333ø	43117·333ø	72643·333ø	
Fore-course - -	994·25	26513·333ø	40267·1250	
Fore-topsail - -	1188·	66924·0000	47916·0000	
F.-topgallantsail	510·	43605·0000	20485·0000	
Main-course	1530·	44980·0000	- -	13770·
Main-topsail -	1494·	93375·0000	-	15687·
M.-topgallantsail	592·	55944·0000		7104·
Driver - - -	981·333ø	29930·666ø	-	51029·3ø
Mizen-topsail -	728·291ø	40541·569ø	- -	32287·597
M.-topgallantsail	293·25	23264·5000	- -	13489·5
Sum - -	9248·458ø	468095·4027	181311·458ø	133367·43

Height of centre of effort above the water-line, $\dfrac{468095\cdot40\emptyset}{9248\cdot458\emptyset} = 50\cdot61$ feet.

Centre of effort before the middle of water-line, taken from the fore-part of the stem to the after-part of the stern-post, $\dfrac{181311\cdot4583 - 133367\cdot43}{9248\cdot4583} = 5\cdot1.$

Relative proportion of the fore as to the after moments, $\dfrac{133367\cdot43}{181311\cdot4583} =$ ·73, or 1 : ·73.

158. The determination of the position of the centre of effort by the foregoing rule, is made under the supposition that the sails are plane surfaces; while by the pressure of the wind the whole assume a curved surface, by which the centre of effort is carried further aft, which in a degree causes the ardency to increase with the force of the wind; and the helm, which may have been a-lee in light winds, may be carried a-weather as the wind increases. The inclination of the ship, by the same cause, will increase the ardency; but these effects are not necessary to be considered in making the calculations, as, when the causes are known, the ardency may be corrected by trimming the sails. The centre of effort of the sails, to produce the *best effect*, must be higher or lower according as the ship is more or less full at the load water-line, compared with the fulness of the body at the extremities below the water. Ships that are full at the load water-line, and clean below, at the extremities, require the higher masts.

159. The situation of the point of sail, as to height, affects the ship more or less according as the wind is aft; and, to determine its place, the direct and vertical resistances on the fore and after bodies are calculated. These results, however, cannot be obtained without considerable labour, owing to the extent of the calculation required; and for this reason they are seldom made by constructors, who, in general, rest satisfied with making a comparison with other ships, and placing the point of sail according to their judgment of the form of the body.

160. If the correct place of the point of the sail were determined with the sails that are commonly taken into the account for obtaining the moments, it would seldom be the point of sail when the wind is abaft the beam, for the studding and other sails are frequently set according to circumstances; and, when the wind is right aft, it acts with full effect only on part of the sails; consequently, it would be impossible to adjust this point by the sails commonly taken into this account, so as to produce the best effect in propelling the ship under all circumstances. The variable sails ought therefore to be adjusted when they are set, according to the judgment of the officer; and it will be found that a greater rate of sailing will sometimes be obtained by taking in the top-gallant or top-studding sails. The effect produced, however, would be best determined by experiments made on the ship in smooth water, by an instrument that would indicate the trim, and show if either extremity was depressed from it.

161. The centre of effort of the sails, as to length, requires to be more or less forward, (before the common centre of gravity of the ship,) according as the ship is less or more full forward, compared with the fulness of the body aft, and likewise according as she is less or more by the stern. Those ships that are cleanest at the foremost extremity, and the least by the stern, will require the masts the furthest forward. It is therefore desirable for ships that are sharp at the foremost extremity to have a greater difference of draught of water; with the excess aft to avoid, when the centre of effort is in its right position, having the masts further forward than the position in which the pressure of the water on the body can afford adequate support.

162. The following rule will always give the place of the centre of effort of the sails, for the ship to answer well; and though it will not agree in all cases with the table from which the several results are selected, yet it will fall within the limits in which ships are found to answer, and will vary with the elements that must affect the mean result, as will be seen by the following

RULE.

Add three-quarters of the distance that the centre of gravity of the vertical longitudinal section is abaft the middle of the water-line, to two-thirds of the distance that the centre of gravity of displacement is before the said middle; by the sum of which, divide the distance that the centre of gravity of displacement and centre of gravity of the vertical longitudinal section are apart, and the result will give a divisor for dividing one-tenth the length of the load water-line, taken from the fore-part of the stem to the after-part of the stern-post: this last result will give the distance, nearly, that the centre of effort of the sails should be before the centre of gravity of the vertical longitudinal section. In cutters, and in vessels with the fore-and-aft rigging, the effect of the sails is different, and will require an alteration in the rule; in which case, one-tenth the length of the water-line should be divided by the distance between the centre of gravity of displacement and centre of gravity of the vertical longitudinal section, for the distance that the centre of effort is before the latter centre.

EXAMPLE 1:—MERCHANT SHIPS.

Length of the water-line   - - -   165 $\frac{165}{10}$ = 16·5

Centre of gravity of displacement before the middle,   2·1 feet.
     "   "   vertical longitudinal section abaft
the middle - - - - - - - - - - - - - 3·

$\frac{2}{3}$ of 2·1 = 1·4. $\frac{3}{4}$ of 3 = 2·25.   2·25 + 1·4 = 3·65.

$\frac{2·1 + 3}{3·65}$ = 1·39. $\frac{16·5}{1·39}$ = 11 = what the centre of effort of the sails should be before the centre of gravity of the vertical longitudinal section, according to the rule.   3 + 8·3 = 11·3 = what the centre of effort should be according to the table before-mentioned, giving a very small error.

EXAMPLE 2.

Length of the water-line -   - 124·75 $\frac{124·75}{10}$ = 12·475

Centre of gravity of displacement before the middle,   1·8 feet.
     "   "   vertical longitudinal section
abaft the middle - - - - - - - - - - 3

$\frac{2}{3}$ of 1·8 = 1·2. $\frac{3}{4}$ of 3 = 2·25.   2·25 + 1·2 = 3·45.

$\frac{1·8 + 3}{3·45}$ = 1·39. $\frac{12·475}{1·39}$ = 8·97 = what the centre of effort should be before the centre of gravity of the vertical longitudinal section, according to the rule.   3 + 5·6 = 8·6 = what the centre of effort should be, according to the table, giving a very small error.

EXAMPLE 3 :—BRIG.

Length of the water-line -   - $76 \frac{76}{10} = 7\cdot6$

Centre of gravity of displacement before the middle,   1·5 feet.
     "   "   vertical longitudinal section abaft
     the middle - - - - - - - - - - - - - 1·6

$\frac{2}{3}$ of 1·5 = 1. $\frac{3}{4}$ of 1·6 = 1·2.   1·2 + 1 = 2·2.

$\frac{1\cdot5 + \cdot1\cdot6}{2\cdot2} = 1\cdot4.$ $\frac{7\cdot6}{1\cdot4} = 5\cdot4 =$ what the centre of effort of the sails should be before the centre of gravity of the vertical longitudinal section, according to the rule.   1·6 + 3·6 = 5·2 = what the centre of effort should be, according to the table, giving a very small error.

163. By attending to the position of the centre of effort of the sails, we may, by modifying their arrangement, if necessary, succeed in balancing the ship in a wind; but to produce such a disposition of the sails as may conduce to facilitate the working of the ship, there must be a correct relation between the moment of sail before and abaft the centre of gravity of the ship, or axis of rotation, which may not be the case, though the ship may be properly balanced when by the wind.

164. When the ship is in stays, a certain and reciprocal effect should be produced by the sails forward and aft, as the quality of working depends, in a great measure, on properly proportioning the fore and after sails. If the moment of sail be too powerful forward, and the sails be not worked quickly, the mean result of the water will pass to the lee quarter, the ship will fall off before she has recovered her way through the water, and considerable time will be lost before she can be brought by the wind; or, if not powerful enough, the ship will not pay off, but remain head to wind, and get stern away. If, on the contrary, the after-movement be too powerful, the ship may come to before head-way is obtained, and the head sails are brought to act. These inconveniences in working the ship may be prevented, to a certain extent, when there is not too great an influence produced by the excess of either of the moments, by an attention to the trim of the ship, and to the bracing of the yards. This, however, must not be depended on, since, to produce this, the ship may be brought out of her proper trim, and may be made uneasy; but we must attain, as near as possible, the correct proportions, by an attentive comparison of the fore and after moments of ships that work well, with other elements upon which the placing of the sails depends.

165. The relation which the fore and after moments should bear to each other, can be determined only by examining their relation in a number of ships. In a ship that had a strong tendency to come to in stays, the fore moment, from the middle of the length of the water-line, was found to the after moment as 1 : ·84; while, in a ship that was found to fall off in stays, the fore moment was to the after moment as 1 : ·66. The comparative moments of several other ships that were found to work well, according to the reports given by experienced officers on board of them, varied from 1 : ·72 to 1 : ·77.

166. It would appear, therefore, according to the experience we have

obtained by the working of good ships, that the relation of the moments should be somewhere between the two limits ; and, having determined this, which may be done with more certainty by examining the moments of a greater number of ships, any little disposition to come to, or fall off, may always be corrected by an attention to the trim, and that without affecting any other quality of the ship.*

167. For determining the height of the sail, the area of the load-water section, and the depth of the centre of gravity of displacement, are the elements most proper to be compared together, as both the direct and vertical resistances are chiefly affected by them ; and the following rule will give very nearly the truth, as it regards the proper height of the centre of effort.

RULE.

Divide $\frac{8}{100}$ of the area of the load-water line, by the depth of the centre of gravity.

EXAMPLE 1.

Area of load-water section - 6276 $\frac{6276 \times 8}{100} = 502 \cdot 08$

Distance of the centre of gravity of displacement below
the load-water line - - - - - - - - 9·2

And, therefore, $\frac{502 \cdot 08}{9 \cdot 2} = 54$, the height of the centre of effort.

N.B.—Breadth on the water-line - - - - - 42 feet.
Head of the main-topgallantsail above the water-line 150 "
    "   fore   "   "   "   135 "
    "   mizen   "   "   "   114 "
Height of gaff at the mast - - - - - - - 58 "
Relative proportion of sail the main as to fore, 1 : ·77.
    "   "   "   main as to mizen, 1 : ·53.
Fore as to after momentum of the sails, - - 1 : ·72.

EXAMPLE 2.

Area of the load-water section - 3516 $\frac{3516 \times 8}{100} = 281 \cdot 28$

Distance of the centre of gravity of displacement below
the load-water line - - - - - - - - 7·4

And, therefore, $\frac{281 \cdot 28}{7 \cdot 4} = 38$, the height of the centre of effort.

N.B.—Breadth on the water-line - - - - - - 32 feet.
Head of the main-topgallantsail above the water-line, 112 "
    "   fore   "   "   "   101 "
    "   mizen   "   "   "   81 "
Height of gaff at the mast - - - - - - - 40 "
Relative proportion of sail the main as to fore, 1 : ·76.
    "   "   "   main as to mizen, 1 : ·48.
Fore as to after momentum of the sails, - - 1 : ·76.

* See Fincham's work on Masting Ships ; in reference to which, I have much pleasure in acknowledging the use I have here made of several articles in his valuable work.

EXAMPLE 3 :—BRIG.

Area of the load-water section $1553 \cdot 8 \ \dfrac{1553 \cdot 8 \times 8}{100} = 124 \cdot 304$

Distance of the centre of gravity of displacement below
   the load-water line - - - - - - - -   5·2

And, therefore, $\dfrac{124 \cdot 304}{5 \cdot 2} = 24$, the height of the centre of effort.

N.B.—Breadth on the water-line - - - - - 23 feet.
Head of the main-topgallantsail above the water-line, 70 "
    "   fore   "   "   "   67 "
Height of gaff at the mast - - - - - - - - 32 "
Relative proportion of sail the main as to fore, 1 : ·72.
Fore as to after momentum of the sails, - - 1 : ·80.

168. In determining the quantity of sail, the length and breadth of ships are the elements commonly used :—the *length* for the length of the yards, or spread of the sails; and the *breadth* for the height of the masts, or depth of the sails. The using of these two elements alone, in determining the quantity of canvass for a ship, may appear to show a want of system, since the form of the body, and the place of the common centre of gravity, may cause the stability of ships of the same length and breadth to be different; but while the relative length and breadth of the ship may make it desirable at times to vary the proportions of the masts to the yards, still the *length* and *breadth* are the *best* elements for obtaining them.

169. From the masts and yards, determined by the length and breadth of the vessel, we obtain the quantity of canvass, or area of sail, from which the moment of sail is obtained, and compare it with the moment of stability. When these are defined, we have only to bring the moment of sail to the given terms of stability, so that the ship may not exceed a determined inclination, under certain circumstances; or to estimate the moment of stability at the inclination, under the given circumstances, and make the moment of the power of the wind on the sails equal to it.

170. The Swedish author, Chapman, in his invaluable little treatise on the "Area of Sails," gives an example, in which, in a "reef-topsail gale," which would be classed by our seamen as a moderate gale, with two reefs in the main and fore topsails, one in the mizen-topsail, main and fore courses, and with the staysails that are commonly set in their service, the inclination was not more than $7\frac{1}{2}$ degrees; and in another case, with a "topsail gale," equal to our strong breeze, with men at their quarters on the lee side, the inclination did not exceed 7 degrees. That ships may be found sufficiently stiff under all circumstances, we have only to discover what power of wind would give a momentum of sail equal to their stabilities, or, what would be the same, to determine their moment of sail in terms of the stability.

EXAMPLE 1 :—MERCHANT SHIPS.

Moment of sails, 1475304 : moment of stability at 10° inclination, 1547. Therefore, moment of sails in terms of stability, $\dfrac{1475304}{1547} = 953.$

EXAMPLE 2.

Moment of sails, 607809 : moment of stability at 10° inclination, 864. Therefore, moment of sails in terms of stability, $\frac{607809}{864} = 703$.

EXAMPLE 3 :—BRIG.

Moment of sails, 214132 : moment of stability at 10° inclination, 209. Therefore, moment of sails in terms of stability, $\frac{214132}{209} = 1024$.

171. The inclination produced by the force of the wind on the sails, may be determined very nearly, under different circumstances, by having the force of the wind and moment of sail, which may be brought into such terms as to compare them with the stability at different angles of inclination.

172. From the experiments made by Lynn, Smeaton, and others, we are able to compare, by the following table, the power of the wind on the surface of a square foot, according as the winds are commonly distinguished by the seamen in our service; and having this, with the quantity and moment of sails, we can easily obtain the effect that is produced, and what degrees of inclination the ship will make under the different powers of the wind.

ON THE POWER OF THE WIND, WITH DIFFERENT BREEZES.

Winds, as commonly Distinguished.	Power of Winds on a Square Foot.		Sails commonly set by the Wind.
Winds.	From	To	Species of Sails.
	℔.	℔.	
Light airs.........	·006	·05	Courses, topsails, topgallantsails, royals, spanker, jib, flying-jib, and all light sails.
Light winds........	·09	·14	Ditto ditto ditto ditto.
Light breezes	·20	·27	Ditto ditto ditto ditto.
Moderate breezes ..	·36	·45	Ditto ditto ditto ditto.
Fresh breezes	·56	1·27	Royals and flying-jib, taken in, in a seaway, to two reefs in the topsails.
Strong breezes	1·45	2·27	Single-reefed topsails and topgallantsails; in much sea, two reefs in the topsails to taking in topgallantsails.
Moderate gales .. .	2·5	3·54	Double-reefed topsails to treble-reefed topsails, reefed spanker and jib.
Fresh gales	3·8	5·10	Close-reefed topsails, reefed courses, to taking in spanker, jib, fore and mizen topsails.
Strong gales	5·44	6·94	Reefed courses, close-reefed main-topsail, fore-staysail, mizen-trysail, to taking in the mainsail.
Heavy gales........	7·34	9·0	Close-reefed main-topsail, storm-staysails, to storm-staysails or close-reefed main-topsails only.
Storms	9·53	13·6	

173. The quantity of sail set, and the power of the wind being known, the product of this power into the moment of sail set, shows the inclining force acting upon a ship under any circumstances whatever;

and a comparison of this force with the degrees of stability of the body, will show nearly the angle of inclination which will be produced. When, therefore, it is required to ascertain the quantity of sail which will be necessary and sufficient for any ship, without exceeding the stability of the body, all that is requisite to be done is, to compare the moment of sails in terms of the stability of the ship, with the amount of sails in terms of the stability, as found in Art. 169; it will then be seen whether the amount of sail is sufficient to propel the ship, without producing any undue inclination.

EXAMPLE

FOR OBTAINING THE INCLINATION THAT WILL BE PRODUCED WITH A CERTAIN WIND AND GIVEN QUANTITY OF SAIL.

Let AB be the longitudinal axis of the ship, CD the yard, and EF the direction of the wind and its force: EF is equivalent to EP and PF, of which EP = the effective force of the wind acting on the sail. Resolve EP into EO and OP respectively, perpendicular and parallel to AB: OP is the force that moves the ship ahead, and EO that which inclines her. If the ship is sailing $5\frac{1}{4}$ points (which has been found by experience that vessels make most way to windward,) near the wind, with the yards braced 21° with the line of the keel; or, making the angle AFP = 21°, and angle AFE = 62°, the wind will then strike the sails at an angle EFP = 41°. The force of the wind, in a strong breeze, will be 2lbs. on a square foot; and, according to the experiment of the Academy of Sciences at Paris, the oblique impulsion at 41° would be to the direct force as ·533 is to 1; but, as the whole of this force will not be exerted to incline the ship (only the part that acts perpendicularly to the longitudinal axis), it will be reduced in the ratio of the sine of the angle which the sail makes with the longitudinal axis; and assuming the mast to be raked 7°, whilst the ship has an inclination of 5°, the plane of the sails would become nearly vertical, and therefore the inclination of the ship may be disregarded as to its effect on the calculations. Now, the cosine of 21° = ·93358, and the moment of sail = 1475304, we have, therefore, ·533 × 2lbs. × ·93358 × 1475304 = 1468217lbs. = 655 tons = the pressure of the wind on the sails to produce the inclination. The wind on the hull will likewise have an effect to incline the ship. Assuming the moment of the surface of the hull, that is, the surface of the top-side above the water, multiplied by the height of the centre of gravity of the top-side above the water = 31185, angle formed by the wind and hull, sailing $5\frac{1}{4}$ points, nearly 62°, not considering the form of the side, pressure on a square foot about 2lbs., oblique impulsion, according to experiments made, ·85 to 1; we have, therefore, ·85 × 2lbs. × 31185 = 53014·5lbs. = 23·65 tons; and the whole pressure to incline the ship will be 655 tons + 23·67 tons = 678·67; so that, in a strong breeze, with single-reefed topsails and top-gallantsails set, our large merchant ships would incline from about 6° to 7°.

IN ESTIMATING THE POWER OF A SAIL TO RAISE OR DEPRESS A SHIP'S HEAD, ACCORDING TO THE POSITION OF THE CENTRE OF GRAVITY OF THE SAIL.

174. Let AS, the jib (Plate 8), be a line passing through the centre of gravity C. Suppose a plumb-line drawn through the centre of gravity of the section of the ship and water, intersecting the water-line, taken from the fore-part of the stem to the after-part of the sternpost in O. Through C, the centre of gravity of the sail, draw DC perpendicular to the sail, CB perpendicular to the water-line, and AS in the plane of the triangle CBD.

Then, if DC be the force of the wind against the sail AS, then DB is the force generating her progressive motion, and BC is the force lifting the ship upwards. Now, the force DB, acting at C, in direction DB, endeavours to turn the ship round an axis passing through O, with a force which is equal to the absolute force BD $\times$ by the distance CB, or CB $\times$ BD; and this is the force by which her head is depressed. Likewise, the force BC, in direction BC, endeavours to turn the ship round an axis at O, on the contrary way, and that with the force BC $\times$ distance BO, or BC $\times$ BO; and this is the force that raises her head. Therefore, the force to raise her head is to the force to depress it as CB $\times$ BO to CB $\times$ BD, or as BO to BD.

Hence, if the point D fall before O, then the sail endeavours to raise the ship's head; if it be behind O, it endeavours to sink it; if it be in O, it will keep her steady. The height of the sail, AS, contributes nothing to her progressive motion; and the same ratio of the absolute to the progressive force remains still as CD to DB.

175. After the explanation that has been given of the area, power, and position of the sails, it only remains to obtain their forms, and approximate to their quantities, that the moment and centre of effort may be obtained and compared with the data that has been furnished.

176. In fixing the proportions of different sails to each other, as the depth of the topsails to that of the courses, of topgallantsails to topsails, the depth of the topgallantsails to that of the courses, or the proportions of the sails on the fore and mizen masts to those on the mainmast, we shall be guided best by our observations as to the proportions that have been given to different ships, without any disadvantageous consequence in their application; for in every case in which the proportion of different sails to each other has been carried to an extreme either way, experience has soon discovered the error, and determined the limits. Thus, making the sails too nearly equal, on the main and fore masts, cannot be done without pressing the ship too much forward, or by carrying the foremast back, which not only obstructs the proper working of the yards, but prevents the wind having its full effect on all the sails. If the topsails are too deep, in relation to the courses, there is a difficulty in shifting a topmast; if the topgallantsails are too square, it is difficult to support the superincumbent masts; or if too narrow, the proper area of sail cannot be obtained without making the sail too taunt, or increasing the moment in a greater proportion to the area than is necessary to bring the centre of effort to its proper height.

177. In the following examples the limits are given, as taken from ships of each class, with differently-proportioned sails ; and from them may be determined, according to the idea of the constructor, the proportions he may consider best, without the danger of exceeding the proper limits. If deep topsails are considered desirable, it is only requisite to take the proportions under that head, and multiply the whole depth from the head of the topgallantsail to the bottom of the course at the middle by them separately, when the depth of each sail is obtained. According, likewise, as the form requires a square or taunt sail, or proportionally so, it may be regulated by the proportions given for the height of the head of the main-topgallantsail, and breadth of the main-course at the head ; and so on, for the proportions of the fore and mizen sails to the mainsails.

EXAMPLE 1 :—DEEP-TOPSAIL MERCHANT SHIP.

Height from the foot of the course at the middle, to the head of the topgallant-sail = 116 feet.

$$116 \times .36 = 41\ 76 \text{ feet} = \text{depth of the course.}$$
$$116 \times .43 = 49.88 \text{ `` } = \text{ `` } \text{ `` } \text{ topsail.}$$
$$116 \times .21 = 24.36 \text{ `` } = \text{ `` } \text{ `` } \text{ topgallant-sail.}$$

Proof 116.00 or 116 feet.

EXAMPLE 2 :—DEEP TOPSAIL MERCHANT SHIP.

Height from the foot of the course at the middle, to the head of the topgallant-sail = 112.5 feet.

$$112.5 \times .36 = 40.5 \text{ feet} = \text{depth of the course.}$$
$$112.5 \times .43 = 48.375 \text{ `` } = \text{ `` } \text{ `` } \text{ topsail.}$$
$$112.5 \times .21 = 23.625 \text{ `` } = \text{ `` } \text{ `` } \text{ topgallant-sail.}$$

Proof 112.500 or 112.5 feet.

The other proportions for a barque and a brig are respectively .35, .40, and .25 ; and .36, .40, and .24.

EXAMPLE 3 :—DEEP-TOPSAIL MERCHANT SHIP.

Height from the foot of the course at the middle, to the head of the topgallant-sail = 91 feet.

$$91 \times .36 = 32.76 \text{ feet} = \text{depth of the course.}$$
$$91 \times .43 = 39.13 \text{ `` } = \text{ `` } \text{ `` } \text{ topsail.}$$
$$91 \times .21 = 19.11 \text{ `` } = \text{ `` } \text{ `` } \text{ topgallant-sail.}$$

Proof 91.00 or 91 feet.

The relative proportion for deep-courses, and topgallant-sails are :— For deep courses, .33, .45, and .22 ; and for deep topgallant-sails, .32, .43, and .25. For deep-courses—barque, .42, .34, and .24 ; and deep topgallant-sails, .37, .37, and .26, respectively, for the depth of the courses, topsails, and topgallant-sails.

CHAPTER III.

PROPORTIONS GIVEN FOR MASTS, SAILS, &c., OF BOATS
DIFFERENTLY RIGGED, WITH THE MOMENTS AND AREAS OF SAILS, AND THE POSITION OF THE MASTS.

178. The sails of boats are subject to the same rules for placing the centre of effort, as those of vessels of the largest magnitude ; but as the effect of the wind on a boat's sails is very considerable, in comparison with its stability, and as they can be more easily taken in, the centre of effort must be so situated that the boat may have a strong tendency to fly up in the wind, and so diminish its effect on the sails. It is, however, of little importance that the form of the boat should be such as would ensure their being ardent, since the quality of being ardent may be so easily procured by varying the position of the stowage or sitters.

179. The proportions in the following examples for the sizes of the sails in relation to the masts, yards, &c., are all taken as they were actually found in boats considered to be properly rigged, and with well proportioned sails ; but those in general given are for

BOATS' SPRITSAILS.

180. These sails are quadrilateral, and made of canvass No. 6 or 7 ; the fore-leeches are attached to their respective masts by lacings, reeved through holes made in them, and the heads are elevated and extended by sprits, or small poles, that cross the sail diagonally, in a wreath or collar of rope called a snotter, which encircles the mast at the foot of the sail.

The fore-leeches of the main and fore-spritsails are 12 inches less than the depth from the sheave at the mast-head to the gunwale, with one or two gore cloths. The heads of them have an even gore of 12 to 14 inches to each cloth.

The fore leech of the mizen spritsail is the depth from the sheave at the mast head, so as to clear the gunwale, and has no goring cloths. The head of it has seldom more than a gore of 11 inches to each cloth.

BOATS' LUGSAILS.

181. These sails are quadrilateral, and made of canvass No. 6 or 7. The head is bent to a yard, which hangs obliquely to the mast at one-third of its length, and spreads the yard to about 4 inches of the cleats.

The fore leech is as deep as the length of the head, with two or three gored cloths. The head has about a six-inch gore to each cloth ; the foot is gored to have a small sweep ; and the after leech is longer by one half the depth of the fore leech, or the fore leech is generally two-thirds the length of the after leech.

SETTEE SAILS.

182. These sails are quadrilateral, and made of canvass No. 7 or 8. The head is bent to a lateen yard, which hangs obliquely to the mast at one-third of its length, and spreads the yard to about six inches of the cleats. The leech is commonly five-sixths of the length of the head, and the luff one-fifth of the depth of the leech, or to the reef with the first cloth gored to the neck. The length of the head, divided by the number of cloths in it, gives the length of each gore. The foot is gored to have a circular sweep.

LATEEN SAILS.

183. The sails are triangular, and made of canvass No. 6 or 7. The head has the same spread in relation to the yard as settees; the heads of these sails commonly gore the breadth of the cloth, and the foot is cut square.

184. The lateen rig seems to have been preferred by the Greeks and Romans, and by most of the ancients who frequented the Mediterranean, where it is now in use, though much more common in the Levant. This mode of rigging does not present so great a surface of sail in relation to the moment as the lug, but possesses advantages in light winds, when close hauled. When sailing before the wind, and in a rough sea, it is the most disadvantageous of all sails; and when by the wind, it is more liable to be taken aback than the common lug, which, likewise, requires the most delicate management, and, under the same points of sailing, the greatest care and attention. The most complete rig of the lugger description is that of the

XEBEC.

185. It has in general three sails, with a foremast raking forward, and the mizenmast aft, in order to extend the sail as much as possible. With the lateen is sometimes combined the square sail, which is used when it is blowing hard, or whilst the vessel is scudding, at which time a square main-topsail is frequently set.

The Spanish xebec has in general a lateen fore, with a square mainsail and mizen; the foremast, as is common in these vessels, raking forward.

Xebecs have sometimes three sets of sails: for moderate weather, when the wind is aft, an extensive square sail for the main, and sometimes for the foresail; and when by the wind, large lateen sails; and for bad weather, small lateen sails.

The fore and mainmasts of these vessels are sometimes called block-masts from their being short and square at the head. In the square of the mast-head are commonly fixed sheaves for the halyards. The shrouds of these vessels are set up as runners to cutters, that they may be shifted when the vessel goes about, and the yards are worked round the masts by parallels fixed to the yard, about one-third the length of the yard from the weather arm. The lee-yard-arm is worked by braces, and supported by vangs near the mast, and the weather-arm by bowlines, and the clue of the sails is extended by a sheet, as common to square sails.

DIMENSIONS OF MASTS AND GEAR, IN TERMS OF KNOWN QUANTITIES.

SLIDING GUNTER SAILS (PLATE 14).

Length of boat, 32 feet ; breadth, 8 feet 6 inches, or 8·5 feet.

Species of Masts and Gear.		Known Quantities.		Proportions.	Length.
Mainmast		Breadth	8·5	2·2	= 18·7 feet.
Foremast		Mainmast ..	18·7	·93	= 17·5 "
Mizenmast		Ditto	18·7	·53	= 10·0 "
Main-slide...................	Is equal the	Ditto	18·7	1·0	= 18·7 "
Fore-slide		Foremast ..	17·5	1·	= 17·5 "
Mizen-slide		Mizenmast ..	10·0	1·	= 10·0 "
Bowsprit		Length	32·0	·25	= 8·0 "
Outrigger		Ditto	32·0	·34	= 11·0 "
Mainmast from the middle		Ditto	32·0	·053	= 1·7 before.
Foremast ditto ditto		Ditto	32·0	·328	= 10·5 "

Mainmast to rake, in a foot, 1½ inches.
Foremast ditto ditto 1 inch.
Mizenmast ditto ditto, as the transom.

SIZE AND POSITIONS OF THE SAILS.

Species of Sails.	Dimensions.				Surfaces.	In Relation to the Water-line.			In Relation to the Middle of the Length.			
	Foot	Mast or Bend.	Leech.	Area.	Area	Height of Centre.	Moment.	Area.	Distance from Middle.	Moment Before.	Moment Abaft.
	Ft.	Ft.	Ft.	Sq. Ft.							
Jib..........	7·9	Stay. 15·2	12·3	47·0	47 × 7·5	= 353		47 × 13·5	= 634		
Foresail	14·2	24·4	26·8	169·0	169 × 11·2	=1893		169 × 5·2	= 879		
Main........	15·0	26·9	27·6	193·	193 × 12·1	=2335		193 × 4·5		= 868	
Mizen	9·0	14·2	15·0	61·	61 × 8·1	= 494		61 × 19·6		= 1196	
Total ...					470		5075	470		1513	2064

Centre of effort above the water-line .... $\dfrac{5075}{470}$ = 10·8 height.

Centre of effort before the middle of water-line .. $\dfrac{2064-1513}{470}$ = 1·17 abaft.

DIMENSIONS OF MASTS AND GEAR IN TERMS OF KNOWN QUANTITIES.

LATEEN OR SETTEE SAILS (PLATE 15).

Length of boat, 32 feet ; breadth, 8·5 feet.

Species of Masts and Gear.		Known Quantities.		Proportions.	Length.
Mainmast		Breadth	8·5	2·15	= 18·3 feet.
Foremast		Mainmast ..	18·3	·8	= 14·6 "
Mizenmast		Ditto	18·3	·43	= 8·0 "
Main-yard.....................	Is equal the	Length	32·0	·83	= 26·5 "
Foreyard		Mainyard ..	26·5	·95	= 25·0 "
Mizen-yard		Ditto	26·5	·56	= 15·0 "
Outrigger		Length	32·0	·38	= 12·2 "
Mainmast from the middle		Ditto	32·0	·037	= 1·2 abaft.
Foremast ditto ditto		Ditto	32·0	·312	= 10·0 before.

SIZE AND POSITIONS OF THE SAILS.

Species of Sails.	Dimensions.				Surfaces.	In Relation to the Water-line.			In Relation to the Middle of the Length.			
	Head or Bend.	Foot	Luff	Leech	Area.	Area.	Height of Centre.	Moment.	Area.	Distance from Middle.	Moment Before.	Moment Abaft.
	Ft.	Ft.	Ft.	Ft.	Sq. Ft.							
Foresail..	24·2	20·6	4·0	21·0	240	240	× 10·7	= 2568	240	× 3·7	= 888	
Main	25·6	20·6	4·6	22·2	254	254	× 11·1	= 2819	254	× 6·3		= 1600
Mizen ..	14·0	10·4	2·6	12·1	76	76	× 7·75	= 589	76	× 21·4		= 1626
Total..					570			5976	570		888	3226

Centre of effort above the water-line .... $\dfrac{5976}{570}$ = 10·48 height.

Centre of effort before the middle of water-line .. $\dfrac{3226 - 888}{570}$ = 4·1 abaft.

DIMENSIONS OF MASTS AND GEAR IN TERMS OF KNOWN QUANTITIES.

EXAMPLE 1.

CUTTER WITH THREE LUGSAILS, SQUARE AT THE HEADS (PLATE 12).

Length of boat, 26; breadth, 6·5 feet.

Species of Masts and Gear.		Known Quantities.		Proportions.		Length.
Mainmast		Breadth	6·5	2·4	=	15·6 feet.
Foremast		Mainmast ..	15·6	·92	=	14·3 "
Mizenmast		Ditto	15·6	·6	=	9·3 "
Main-yard	Is equal the	Length	26·0	·5	=	13·0 "
Fore-yard		Main-yard ..	13·0	·9	=	11·7 "
Mizen-yard		Ditto	13·0	·63	=	8·2 "
Mainmast from the middle		Length	26·0	·034	=	·8 before.
Foremast ditto ditto		Ditto	26·0	·287	=	7·4 "
Outrigger		Ditto	26·0	·4	=	10·4 feet.

EXAMPLE 2.

Length of boat, 32 feet; breadth, 8·5 feet.

Species of Mast and Gear.		Known Quantities.		Proportions.		Length.
Mainmast		Breadth	8·5	2·4	=	20·4 feet.
Foremast		Mainmast ..	20·4	·92	=	18·8 "
Mizenmast		Ditto	20·4	·6	=	12·2 "
Main-yard	Is equal the	Length	32·0	·5	=	16·0 "
Fore-yard		Main-yard ..	16·0	·9	=	14·4 "
Mizen-yard		Ditto	16·0	·63	=	10·2 "
Outrigger		Length	32·0	·4	=	12·8 "
Mainmast from the middle		Ditto	32·0	·034	=	1·0 before.
Foremast ditto ditto		Ditto	32·0	·287	=	9·2 "

SIZE AND POSITIONS OF THE SAILS.

Species of Sails.	Dimensions.				Surfaces.	In Relation to the Water-line.			In Relation to the Middle of the Length.			
	Head.	Foot	Luff	Leech.	Area.	Area.	Height of Centre.	Moment.	Area.	Distance from Middle.	Moment Before.	Moment Abaft.
	Ft.	Ft.	Ft.	Ft.	Sq. Ft.							
Foresail...	13·7	15 7	13·5	16 6	215	215 × 10·9		=2344	215 × 5·9		=1269	
Main	15·2	17·3	14·8	17·9	262	262 × 11·4		=2987	262 × 2·7			= 707
Mizen ..	9·5	10·3	10·3	12·1	108	108 × 9·4		=1015	108 × 19·5			=2100
Total..					585	585		6346	585		1269	2811

Centre of effort above the water-line........$\dfrac{6346}{585}$ = 10·84 height.

Centre of effort from the middle............$\dfrac{2813-1269}{585}$ = 2 64 abaft.

DIMENSIONS OF MASTS AND GEAR IN TERMS OF KNOWN QUANTITIES.

EXAMPLE 1.

CUTTER WITH THREE LUGSAILS, NARROW HEADS (PLATE 14).

Length of boat, 28 feet; breadth, 7 feet.

Species of Masts and Gear.		Known Quantities.		Proportions.		Length.
Mainmast		Breadth	7·0	2·7	=	18·9 feet.
Foremast		Mainmast ..	18·9	·9	=	17·0 "
Mizenmast....................		Ditto	18·9	·6	=	11·3 "
Main-yard	Is equal the	Length	28·0	·38	=	10·6 "
Fore-yard		Main-yard ..	10·6	·86	=	9·1 "
Mizen-yard		Ditto	10·6	·55	=	5·8 "
Outrigger		Length	28·0	·34	=	9·5 "
Mainmast from the middle		Ditto	28·0	·015	=	·4 abaft.
Foremast　ditto　ditto		Ditto	28·0	·281	=	7·8 before

Mainmast to rake, in a foot, 1 inch.
Foremast　ditto　ditto　⅓ ditto.
Mizenmast ditto　　ditto, as the transom.

EXAMPLE 2.

Length of boat, 32 feet; breadth, 8·5.

Species of Masts and Gear.		Known Quantities.		Proportions.		Length.
Mainmast		Breadth	8·5	2·7	=	22·8 feet.
Foremast		Mainmast ..	22·8	·9	=	20·5 "
Mizenmast....................		Ditto	22·8	·6	=	13·6 "
Main-yard	the	Length	32·0	·38	=	12·2 "
Fore-yard		Main-yard ..	12·2	·86	=	10·5 "
Mizen-yard	Is equal	Ditto	12·2	·55	=	6·7 "
Bowsprit		Length	32·0	·28	=	9·0 "
Outrigger		Ditto	32·0	·84	=	11·0 "
Mainmast from the middle		Ditto	32·0	·015	=	·5 abaft.
Foremast　ditto　ditto		Ditto	32·0	·281	=	9·1 before

SIZE AND POSITIONS OF THE SAILS.

Species of Sails.	Dimensions.				Surfaces.	In Relation to the Water-line.			In Relation to the Middle of the Length.			
	Head.	Foot	Luff	Leech.	Area.	Area	Height of Centre.	Moment	Area	Distance from Middle.	Moment Before.	Moment Abaft.
	Ft.	Ft.	Ft.	Ft.	Sq.Ft.							
			Stay									
Jib.......		8·6	17·6	13·7	55	55 × 8·1 = 445			55 × 16·7 = 919			
Foresail...	9·8	15·6	14·6	17·9	194	194 × 10·9 = 2115			194 × 6·5 = 1241			
Main	11·0	17·0	16·8	20·8	252	252 × 12·2 = 3074			252 × 3·6 =			907
Mizen ..	5·8	8·6	10·5	12·8	74	74 × 8·7 = 644			74 × 18·9 =			1399
Total..					575			6278	575		2160	2306

Centre of effort above the water-line........ $\frac{6278}{575}$ = 10·97 height.

Centre of effort from the middle .... $\frac{2306-2160}{575}$ = ·25 abaft.

GIG, WITH FORE AND MAIN LUGSAILS.

Length of boat, 28 feet; breadth, 6 feet.

Species of Masts and Gear.		Known Quantities.		Proportions.	Length.
Mainmast		Breadth	6·0	2·7	= 16·2 feet.
Foremast		Mainmast ..	16·2	·9	= 14·5 "
Main-yard	Is equal the	Length	28·0	·38	= 10·6 "
Fore-yard		Main-yard ..	10·6	·86	= 9·1 "
Mainmast from the middle		Length ..	28·0	·015	= ·4 abaft.
Foremast ditto ditto		Ditto	28·0	·281	= 7·8 before.
Mainmast to rake, in a foot, 1 inch.					
Foremast ditto ditto ½ ditto.					

GIG, WITH ONE LUGSAIL (PLATE 15).

Length of boat, 20 feet; breadth, 5ft. 6in., or 5·5 feet.

Mast is equal the breadth 5·5, multiplied by 2·7 = 14·85 feet long.
Yard is equal the length 20·0,   "   "   ·5 = 10·   feet long.
Mast from middle, length 20·0,   "   "   ·4 = 8·   feet before.

Size of the Sail.

	FT.	IN.	
Head	10	0	equal 5½ cloths.
Foot - -	13	0	" 7 "
Fore-leech - - - -	10	0	

Head-gores, 6 inches per cloth.
Foot-gores, 8, 6, 4, 2, 1, 0, 3 inches.

TABLES

OF THE

DIMENSIONS OF JIBS, MAINSAILS, &c., &c.,

READY FOR CUTTING-OUT.

I. DIMENSIONS OF STANDING JIBS.

No.	120 Tons. 9 Cloths. Stay-gores. FT. IN.	Foot-gores. IN.	150 Tons. 10 Cloths. Stay-gores. FT. IN.	Foot-gores. IN.	200 Tons. 11 Cloths. Stay-gores. FT. IN.	Foot-gores. IN.
1	8 0	0	9 0	8	10 0	6
2	6 0	2	7 0	10	7 0	7
3	5 0	4	5 0	10	5 0	8
4	4 0	6	4 0	12	4 0	9
5	3 0	8	3 0	12	3 6	10
6	3 0	10	3 0	14	3 6	12
7	3 0	14	3 0	16	3 2	14
8	3 0	18	3 0	16	3 2	16
9	3 0	20	3 0	20	3 0	18
10			3 0	24	3 0	21
11					3 0	24
	Leech, 31ft. 6in. Stay, 41ft.		Leech, 33ft. Stay, 45ft. 6in.		Leech, 36ft. Stay, 49ft.	

No.	250 Tons. 12 Cloths. Stay-gores. FT. IN.	Foot-gores. IN.	300 Tons. 13 Cloths. Stay-gores. FT. IN.	Foot-gores. IN.	300 Tons. 14 Cloths. Stay-gores. FT. IN.	Foot-gores. IN.	340 Tons. 15 Cloths. Stay-gores. FT. IN.	Foot-gores. IN.
1	11 0	6	11 0	0	11 0	0	10 0	2
2	6 4	7	6 4	3	6 4	3	6 0	0
3	4 9	9	4 9	5	4 9	5	5 0	2
4	4 6	10	4 6	7	4 9	7	4 9	3
5	4 3	12	4 3	8	4 0	8	4 0	4
6	4 3	13	4 3	9	4 0	9	4 0	5
7	4 0	14	4 0	11	3 9	11	3 6	6
8	4 0	16	4 0	12	3 9	12	3 6	8
9	3 9	18	3 9	14	3 6	13	3 0	10
10	3 9	20	3 9	16	3 6	14	3 0	13
11	3 6	22	3 6	18	3 0	16	2 9	15
12	3 0	24	3 3	20	3 0	17	2 9	17
13			3 0	22	3 0	20	2 6	20
14					3 0	22	2 6	22
15							2 6	24
	Leech, 43ft. 6in. Stay, 57ft.		Leech, 45ft. Stay, 60ft.		Leech, 48ft. Stay, 63ft.		Leech, 48ft. 6in. Stay, 64ft.	

DIMENSIONS OF STANDING JIBS (CONTINUED).

No.	500 Tons. 16 Cloths. Stay-gores. FT. IN.	Foot-gores. IN.	600 Tons. 17 Cloths. Stay-gores. FT. IN.	Foot-gores. IN.	700 Tons. 18 Cloths. Stay-gores. FT. IN.	Foot-gores. IN.	900 Tons. 19 Cloths. Stay-gores. FT. IN.	Foot-gores. IN.
1	11 0	0	11 0	0	11 0	2	11 0	3
2	6 4	3	6 4	3	6 4	0	6 4	2
3	4 9	5	4 9	4	4 9	3	4 9	0
4	4 9	7	4 9	5	4 9	4	4 9	1
5	4 3	8	4 3	6	4 0	5	4 0	2
6	4 3	9	4 0	7	4 0	6	4 0	3
7	4 0	11	3 9	8	3 6	7	3 6	4
8	3 9	12	3 6	8	3 6	8	3 6	5
9	3 6	13	3 3	9	3 3	8	3 2	6
10	3 6	14	3 0	9	3 3	9	2 10	7
11	3 3	16	3 0	10	3 0	9	2 8	8
12	3 3	17	3 0	10	3 0	11	2 8	9
13	3 0	20	2 10	11	3 0	11	2 6	10
14	3 0	22	2 10	13	3 0	12	2 6	11
15	3 0	24	2 9	15	3 0	12	2 6	13
16	3 0	26	2 9	18	3 0	14	2 6	15
17			2 6	20	3 0	16	2 6	17
18					3 0	19	2 6	19
19							2 6	22
	Leech, 51ft. Stay, 72ft.		Leech, 54ft. Stay, 72ft.		Leech, 59ft. Stay, 75ft.		Leech, 54ft. 6in. Stay, 75ft.	

No.	1,000 Tons. 20 Cloths. Stay-gores. FT. IN.	Foot-gores. IN.	1,300 Tons. 21 Cloths. Stay-gores. FT. IN.	Foot-gores. IN.	1,400 Tons. 22 Cloths. Stay-gores. FT. IN.	Foot-gores. IN.
1	11 0	3	11 0	3	11 0	4
2	6 4	2	6 4	2	6 4	3
3	4 9	0	4 9	1	4 9	2
4	4 9	1	4 9	0	4 9	1
5	4 0	2	4 0	1	4 0	0
6	4 0	3	4 0	2	4 0	1
7	3 6	4	3 6	3	3 6	1
8	3 6	5	3 6	4	3 6	2
9	3 2	6	3 2	5	3 2	2
10	3 2	7	3 2	6	3 0	3
11	3 0	8	3 0	7	3 0	3
12	3 0	9	3 0	8	3 0	4
13	2 10	10	2 10	9	2 10	4
14	2 10	11	2 10	10	2 10	5
15	2 8	13	2 8	11	2 8	5
16	2 8	15	2 8	13	2 8	6
17	2 6	17	2 6	15	2 6	7
18	2 6	19	2 6	17	2 6	8
19	2 6	21	2 6	19	2 6	9
20	2 6	24	2 6	21	2 6	10
21			2 6	24	2 6	12
22					2 6	14
	Leech, 59ft. 3in. Stay, 79ft.		Leech, 61ft. 9in. Stay, 81ft. 6in.		Leech, 70ft. Stay, 87ft. Breadth of seams on	

II. DIMENSIONS OF FLYING JIBS.

No.	250 Tons. 8 Cloths. Stay-gores FT. IN.	Foot-gores IN.	300 Tons. 9 Cloths. Stay-gores FT. IN.	Foot-gores IN.	340 Tons. 10 Cloths. Stay-gores FT. IN.	Foot-gores IN.	500 Tons. 11 Cloths. Stay-gores FT. IN.	Foot-gores IN.
1	9 0	9	8 0	0	8 0	0	9 0	0
2	7 0	10	6 0	3	6 0	2	7 0	3
3	6 0	14	4 6	5	4 6	3	6 0	5
4	5 0	18	4 0	7	4 0	5	5 0	7
5	4 0	22	3 6	9	3 6	7	4 6	9
6	4 0	24	3 6	11	3 6	9	4 6	11
7	3 8	26	3 6	13	3 6	11	4 0	13
8	3 4	28	3 6	15	3 6	13	4 0	15
9			3 6	18	3 6	15	3 6	17
10					3 6	18	3 6	20
11							3 0	24
	Leech, 29ft. Stay, 43ft.		Leech, 32ft. Stay, 40ft. 6in.		Leech, 35ft. 6in. Stay, 44ft.		Leech, 42ft. 6in. Stay, 54ft. 5in.	

No.	600 Tons. 12 Cloths. Stay-gores FT. IN.	Foot-gores IN.	800 Tons. 13 Cloths. Stay-gores FT. IN.	Foot-gores IN.	1,000 Tons. 14 Cloths. Stay-gores FT. IN.	Foot-gores IN.	1,100 Tons. 15 Cloths. Stay-gores FT. IN.	Foot-gores IN.
1	9 0	0	9 0	0	9 0	0	9 0	2
2	7 0	3	7 0	2	7 0	1	7 0	0
3	6 0	5	6 0	3	6 0	2	6 0	1
4	5 0	7	5 0	4	5 0	3	5 0	2
5	4 8	9	4 8	5	4 8	4	4 8	3
6	4 8	10	4 8	6	4 8	5	4 8	4
7	4 8	12	4 6	7	4 6	6	4 6	5
8	4 6	12	4 0	9	4 6	7	4 6	7
9	4 6	14	4 0	10	4 0	8	4 0	9
10	4 0	14	4 0	12	4 0	10	4 0	11
11	3 6	16	3 6	14	3 6	12	3 6	13
12	3 0	18	3 0	16	3 3	14	3 3	15
13			3 0	18	3 0	16	3 0	18
14					2 6	18	2 6	21
15							2 6	24
	Leech, 50ft. Stay, 51½ft.		Leech, 53ft. Stay, 64ft.		Leech, 54ft. Stay, 64ft.		Leech, 54ft. Stay, 67ft.	

1,300 Tons. 16 Cloths.

No.	Stay-gores FT. IN.	Foot-gores IN.	No.	Stay-gores FT. IN.	Foot-gores IN.
1	9 0	3	9	3 8	6
2	7 0	2	10	3 8	8
3	6 0	0	11	3 6	10
4	5 0	1	12	3 3	12
5	4 8	2	13	3 0	15
6	4 8	3	14	3 0	18
7	4 4	4	15	2 10	21
8	4 0	5	16	2 10	24

1,400 Tons. 17 Cloths.

No.	Stay-gores FT. IN.	Foot-gores IN.	No.	Foot-gores FT. IN.	Stay-gores IN.
1	9 0	3	10	4 0	7
2	7 0	2	11	3 8	8
3	6 0	0	12	3 8	10
4	5 0	1	13	3 6	12
5	4 8	2	14	3 0	15
6	4 4	3	15	3 0	18
7	4 4	4	16	3 0	21
8	4 4	5	17	3 0	24
9	4 0	6			

III. DIMENSIONS OF BRIGS' MAINSAILS.

Head, 20ft. 6in. equal 11½ Cloths. Foot, 25ft. 0in. ditto 14 ditto.

Cloths. No.	Mast Gores. FT. IN.	Foot do. IN.	Foot do. IN.	Head do. IN.	Slack Seams. IN.
1	10 0	15			
2	9 0	14			
3	4 0	12	½ cloth.	5	
4			10	9	
5			8	7	
6			6	7	
7			4	6	
8			3	6	1
9			2	5	1
10			1	5	2
11			0	4	3
12			1	3	4
13			2	2	6
14			3	1	8
15					

Mast .... 23 feet.
Leech .. 34½ do.

Head, 20ft. 0in. equal 11 Cloths. Foot, 27ft. 0in. ditto 15 ditto.

Cloths. No.	Mast Gores. FT. IN.	Foot do. IN.	Foot do. IN.	Head do. IN.	Slack Seams. IN.
1	5 6	16			
2	5 0	13			
3	4 6	11			
4	4 6	9			
5			7	6	
6			6	6	
7			5	5	
8			4	5	
9			3	4	
10			2	4	2
11			1	3	3
12			0	2	4
13			1	1	5
14			2	0	6
15			3	2	7

Mast .... 20 feet.
Leech .. 32 do.

Head, 20ft. equal 11 Cloths. Foot, 29ft. ditto 16 ditto.

Cloths. No.	Mast Gores. FT. IN.	Foot do. IN.	Foot do. IN.	Head do. IN.	Slack Seams. IN.
1	5 0	16			
2	4 6	14			
3	4 6	13			
4	4 0	12			
5	4 0	10			
6			9	8	
7			8	7	
8			6	6	
9			4	5	
10			3	4	2
11			2	3	3
12			1	2	4
13			0	1	5
14			1	0	6
15			2	2	7
16			3	3	8

Mast .... 22ft. 6in.
Leech .. 34ft. 0in.

Head, 21ft. 6in. equal 12 Cloths. Foot, 31ft. 6in. ditto 16 ditto.

Cloths. No.	Mast Gores. FT. IN.	Foot do. IN.	Foot do. IN.	Head do. IN.	Slack Seams. IN.
1	5 0	18			
2	5 0	16			
3	5 0	13			
4	5 0	11			
5			9	6	
6			7	6	
7			6	5	
8			5	5	
9			4	4	
10			3	4	
11			2	3	2
12			1	3	3
13			0	2	4
14			1	0	6
15			2	2	6
16			3	3	8

Mast .... 21 feet.
Leech .. 33 do.

DIMENSIONS OF BRIGS' MAINSAILS (CONTINUED).

Cloths. — Head, 22ft. equal 12 Cloths. Foot, 32ft. ditto 17 ditto.

No.	Mast Gores FT. IN.	Foot do. IN.	Foot do. IN.	Head do. IN.	Slack Seams. IN.
1	5 6	22	..	..	..
2	5 0	18	..	..	..
3	4 0	15	..	..	..
4	4 0	13	..	..	..
5	3 6	12	..	..	..
6			10	6	..
7			9	6	..
8			7	5	..
9			6	5	..
10			5	4	..
11			4	4	2
12			3	3	3
13			2	3	4
14			0	2	5
15			1	0	6
16			2	2	7
17			3	3	8

Mast .... 23ft. 0in.
Leech .. 37ft. 6in.

Head, 24ft. equal 13 Cloths. Foot, 32ft. ditto 17 ditto.

No.	Mast Gores FT. IN.	Foot do. IN.	Foot do. IN.	Head do. IN.	Slack Seams. IN.
1	6 0	20	..	..	..
2	6 0	17	..	..	..
3	5 6	15	..	..	..
4	5 0	13	..	..	..
5			12	8	..
6			10	6	..
7			9	6	..
8			7	5	..
9			6	5	..
10			5	4	1
11			4	4	2
12			3	3	3
13			2	3	4
14			0	2	5
15			1	2	6
16			2	1	7
17			3	0	8

Mast .... 22ft. 6in.
Leech .. 38ft. 0in.

Cloths. — Head, 24ft. equal 18 cloths.* Foot, 33ft. ditto 18 ditto.

No.	Mast Gores FT. IN.	Foot do. IN.	Foot do. IN.	Head do. IN.	Slack Seams. IN.
1	4 6	15	..	..	..
2	5 0	14	..	..	..
3	4 6	12	..	..	..
4	3 6	10	..	..	..
5	3 0	9	..	..	..
6			8	8	..
7			7	6	..
8			6	6	..
9			5	5	..
10			4	5	..
11			3	4	1
12			2	4	2
13			1	3	3
14			0	2	4
15			1	1	5
16			2	0	6
17			3	2	7
18			4	3	8

Mast .... 20ft. 6in.
Leech .. 32f. 0in.

Head, 24ft. equal 13 Cloths. Foot, 33ft. ditto 18 ditto.

No.	Mast Gores FT. IN.	Foot do. IN.	Foot do. IN.	Head do. IN.	Slack Seams. IN.
1	5 0	20	..	..	..
2	4 6	17	..	..	..
3	4 6	15	..	..	..
4	4 0	13	..	..	..
5	4 0	12	..	..	..
6			10	8	..
7			9	7	..
8			7	6	..
9			6	5	..
10			5	4	1
11			4	3	2
12			3	2	3
13			2	1	3
14			1	0	4
15			0	0	6
16			1	0	6
17			2	2	7
18			3	3	8

Mast .... 22ft. 6in.
Leech .. 38ft. 0in.

DIMENSIONS OF BRIGS' MAINSAILS (CONTINUED).

Head, 25ft. equal 14 Cloths. Foot, 33ft. ditto 18 ditto.

Cloths. No.	Mast Gores. FT. IN.	Foot do. IN.	Foot do. IN.	Head do. IN.	Slack Seams. IN.
1	6 0	20			
2	5 6	17			
3	5 6	15			
4	5 0	13			
5			12	8	
6			10	6	
7			9	6	
8			7	5	
9			6	5	
10			5	4	
11			4	4	1
12			3	3	2
13			2	2	3
14			1	1	4
15			0	0	5
16			1	1	6
17			2	2	7
18			3	3	8
19					

Mast .... 23ft. 6in.
Leech .. 33ft, 0in.
No. 2, 184 yards.

Head, 25ft. equal 14 Cloths. Foot, 36ft. ditto 19 ditto.

Cloths. No.	Mast Gores. FT. IN.	Foot do. IN.	Foot do. IN.	Head do. IN.	Slack Seams. IN.
1	5 0	22			
2	5 0	20			
3	4 0	17			
4	4 0	15			
5	3 0	13			
6			12	8	
7			10	6	
8			9	6	
9			7	5	
10			6	5	
11			5	4	
12			4	4	1
13			3	3	2
14			2	2	3
15			1	1	4
16			0	0	5
17			1	1	6
18			2	2	7
19			3	3	8

Mast .... 22ft.
Leech .. 36ft.

Head, 24ft. 6in. equal 14 Cloths. Foot, 37ft. 6in. ditto 20 ditto.

Cloths. No.	Mast Gores. FT. IN.	Foot do. IN.	Foot do. IN.	Head do. IN.	Slack Seams. IN.
1	3 9	22			
2	4 0	20			
3	4 0	18			
4	3 9	16			
5	3 6	16			
6	3 0	14			
7			14	8	
8			12	6	
9			10	6	
10			8	5	
11			7	5	
12			6	4	
13			5	4	1
14			4	3	2
15			3	2	3
16			2	1	4
17			0	0	5
18			1	0	6
19			2	2	7
20			3	3	8
21					
22					

Mast .... 24ft. 6in.
Leech .. 40ft. 0in.

Head, 25ft. equal 14½ Cloths. Foot, 41ft. ditto 22 ditto.

Cloths. No.	Mast Gores. FT. IN.	Foot do. IN.	Foot do. IN.	Head do. IN.	Slack Seams. IN.
1	3 4	22			
2	3 9	20			
3	3 9	18			
4	3 6	16			
5	3 6	14			
6	3 0	12			
7	3 0	10			
8	2 6	10		3	
9			9	5	
10			9	4	
11			8	4	
12			8	3	
13			7	3	
14			5	2	
15			4	1	3
16			2	0	4
17			1	1	5
18			0	2	6
19			1	3	7
20			2	3	8
21			3	4	9
22			4	4	10

Mast .... 23ft. 6in.
Leech .. 42ft. 0in.

IV. DIMENSIONS OF BRIGS' STORM MAINSAILS.

Head, 11ft. 0in. equal 6 Cloths. Foot, 25ft. 6in. ditto 12 ditto.

No.	Mast Gores. FT. IN.	Foot do. IN.	Foot do. IN.	Head do. IN.	Slack Seams. IN.
1	3 0	32	..	..	..
2	3 0	30	..	..	..
3	2 6	28	..	..	..
4	2 6	26	..	..	..
5	2 0	24	..	..	..
6	2 0	22	..	..	..
7			18	9	..
8			14	7	..
9			10	5	2
10			6	3	4
11			4	2	6
12			2	0	8

Mast .... 17ft. 6in.
Leech .. 32ft. 6in.

Head, 11ft. 6in. equal 7 Cloths. Foot, 24ft. 6in. ditto 12 ditto.

No.	Mast Gores. FT. IN.	Foot do. IN.	Foot do. IN.	Head do. IN.	Slack Seams. IN.
1	5 0	26	..	..	..
2	5 0	23	..	..	..
3	5 0	19	..	..	..
4	5 0	16	..	..	..
5	5 0	13	..	..	..
6			10	6	..
7			8	5	..
8			6	5	..
9			4	4	2
10			3	4	4
11			2	2	6
12			1	1	8

Mast .... 25ft.

Head, 16ft. equal 8½ Cloths. Foot, 26ft. ditto 14 ditto.

No.	Mast Gores. FT. IN.	Foot do. IN.	Foot do. IN.	Head do. IN.	Slack Seams. IN.
1	4 6	26	..	..	..
2	4 6	23	..	..	..
3	3 0	19	..	..	..
4	3 0	16	..	..	..
5	2 6	14	..	..	..
6	1 6	12	..	8	..
7			10	6	..
8			8	5	..
9			6	5	..
10			5	4	1
11			4	4	2
12			3	3	3
13			2	3	4
14			1	2	6
15					
16					

Mast .... 21ft. 6in.
Leech .. 32ft. 0in.

Head, 19ft. equal 10½ Cloths. Foot, 31ft. ditto 16 ditto.

No.	Mast Gores. FT. IN.	Foot do. IN.	Foot do. IN.	Head do. IN.	Slack Seams. IN.
1	4 6	26	..	..	..
2	4 6	23	..	..	..
3	3 6	19	..	..	..
4	3 6	16	..	..	..
5	2 6	14	..	..	..
6	1 6	12	..	6	..
7			10	9	..
8			9	7	..
9			8	6	..
10			7	6	..
11			6	5	..
12			5	5	1
13			4	4	2
14			3	3	3
15			2	2	4
16			1	2	6

Mast .... 22ft. 6in.
Leech .. 37ft. 0in.

V.—DIMENSIONS OF BRIGS' FORE TRYSAILS.

Cloths.	Head, 16ft. equal 9 Cloths. Foot, 26ft. ditto 13 ditto.					Head, 16ft. 6in. equal 9 Cloths. Foot, 27ft. 0in. ditto 13 ditto.				
	Mast Gores.	Foot do.	Foot do.	Head do.	Slack Seams.	Mast Gores.	Foot do.	Foot do.	Head do.	Slack Seams.
No.	FT. IN.	IN.	IN.	IN.	IN.	FT. IN.	IN.	IN.	IN.	IN.
1	4 0	24				4 0	24			
2	4 0	22				4 0	22			
3	3 0	20				3 6	20			
4	2 0	18				2 6	18			
5			16	6				16	6	
6			14	6				14	6	
7			11	5				11	5	
8			9	5	1			9	5	1
9			7	3	2			7	3	2
10			5	3	3			5	3	3
11			3	2	4			3	2	4
12			2	2	5			2	2	5
13			1	1	6			1	1	6

Mast .... 14ft. 0in.
Leech .. 28ft. 6in.

Mast .... 16 feet.
Leech .. 30ft. 6in.

Cloths.	Head, 18ft. 0in. equal 10 Cloths. Foot, 28ft. 0in. ditto 15 ditto.					Head, 20ft. 0in. equal 11 Cloths. Foot, 31ft. 6in. ditto 16½ ditto.				
	Mast Gores.	Foot do.	Foot do.	Head do.	Slack Seams.	Mast Gores.	Foot do.	Foot do.	Head do.	Slack Seams.
No.	FT. IN.	IN.	IN.	IN.	IN.	FT. IN.	IN.	IN.	IN.	IN.
1	4 6	26				2 0	13			
2	4 0	23				4 6	26			
3	3 6	19				4 0	23			
4	3 6	16				3 6	19			
5	2 6	14				3 6	16			
6			12	8		2 6	14			
7			10	6				12	8	
8			8	6				10	6	
9			7	5				9	6	
10			6	5	1			8	5	
11			5	4	2			7	5	
12			4	4	3			6	4	1
13			3	3	4			5	4	2
14			2	2	5			3	3	3
15			1	1	6			3	2	4
16								2	1	5
17								1	0	6

Mast .....19 feet.
Leech .. 33 do.

Mast .... 20ft. 0in.
Leech .. 33ft. 6in.

VI.—DIMENSIONS OF BARQUES' MIZENS.

**Head, 19ft. 6in. equal 11 Cloths.
Foot, 27ft. 0in. ditto 15 ditto.**

No.	Mast Gores. FT. IN.		Foot do. IN.	Foot do. IN.	Head do. IN.	Slack Seams. IN.
1	5	6 ..	19 ..	..	..	..
2	5	6 ..	17 ..	..	..	..
3	5	0 ..	15 ..	..	..	..
4	4	6 ..	13 ..	..	..	..
5				11 ..	12 ..	..
6				9 ..	10 ..	..
7				7 ..	10 ..	..
8				5 ..	9 ..	..
9				3 ..	9 ..	..
10				2 ..	8 ..	3
11				1 ..	6 ..	4
12				0 ..	4 ..	5
13				1 ..	3 ..	6
14				2 ..	2 ..	7
15				3 ..	0 ..	8
16						

Mast .... 21 feet.
Leech .. 39 feet.

**Head, 20ft. equal 11 cloths.
Foot, 29ft. ditto 16 ditto.**

No.	Mast Gores. FT. IN.		Foot do. IN.	Foot do. IN.	Head do. IN.	Slack Seams. IN.
1	4	6 ..	16 ..	..	..	..
2	4	6 ..	14 ..	..	..	..
3	5	0 ..	13 ..	..	..	..
4	4	0 ..	12 ..	..	..	..
5	3	0 ..	10 ..	..	..	..
6				9 ..	8	..
7				8 ..	7	..
8				6 ..	6	..
9				4 ..	5	..
10				3 ..	4 ..	2
11				2 ..	3 ..	3
12				1 ..	2 ..	4
13				0 ..	1 ..	5
14				1 ..	0 ..	6
15				2 ..	1 ..	7
16				3 ..	2 ..	8

Mast .... 22ft. 0in.
Leech .. 33ft. 6in.

**Head, 21ft. equal 11½ Cloths.
Foot, 29ft. ditto 15½ ditto.**

No.	Mast Gores. FT. IN.		Foot do. IN.	Foot do. IN.	Head do. IN.	Slack Seams. IN.
½	2	6 ..	9 ..	..	..	..
1	5	6 ..	19 ..	..	..	..
2	5	6 ..	16 ..	..	..	..
3	5	0 ..	13 ..	..	..	..
4	2	0 ..	10 ..	..	6	..
5				8 ..	12	..
6				6 ..	10	..
7				5 ..	8	..
8				4 ..	6	..
9				3 ..	5 ..	..
10				2 ..	3 ..	1
11				1 ..	2 ..	2
12				0 ..	1 ..	3
13				1 ..	0 ..	4
14				2 ..	2 ..	6
15				3 ..	3 ..	8

Mast .... 21 feet.
Leech 33 feet.

**Head, 21ft. equal 11½ Cloths.
Foot, 27ft. ditto 15 ditto.**

No.	Mast Gores. FT. IN.		Foot do. IN.	Foot do. IN.	Head do. IN.	Slack Seams. IN.
½	..	..	18 ..	..	..	..
1	7	0 ..	18 ..	..	..	..
2	7	0 ..	16 ..	..	..	..
3	6	0 ..	13 ..	..	..	..
4	3	0 ..	..	10 ..	5	..
5				9 ..	9 ..	..
6				8 ..	7 ..	..
7				6 ..	6 ..	..
8				4 ..	5 ..	..
9				3 ..	4 ..	2
10				2 ..	3 ..	3
11				1 ..	2 ..	4
12				0 ..	1 ..	5
13				1 ..	0 ..	6
14				2 ..	1 ..	7
15				3 ..	2 ..	8

Mast .... 22ft. 6in.
Leech .. 33ft. 0in.

DIMENSIONS OF BARQUES' MIZENS (CONTINUED).

Cloths.	Head, 22ft. equal 12 Cloths. Foot 32ft. ditto 17 ditto.					Head, 22ft. 6in. equal 12½ Cloths. Foot, 30ft. 6in. ditto 17 ditto.				
	Mast Gores.	Foot do.	Foot do.	Head do.	Slack Seams.	Mast Gores.	Foot do.	Foot do.	Head do.	Slack Seams.
No.	FT. IN.	IN.	IN.	IN.	IN.	FT. IN.	IN.	IN.	IN.	IN.
1	6 0	18	..	..	..	6 6	16	..	..	..
2	5 0	16	..	..	..	6 0	14	..	..	..
3	5 0	14	..	..	..	6 0	13	..	..	..
4	4 0	13	..	..	..	5 6	12	..	..	..
5	3 0	12	..	9	..	2 6	10	..	5	..
6		10	9	..	..		9	9	..	..
7		9	8	..	..		7	8	..	..
8		8	7	..	..		6	7	..	..
9		6	6	..	..		5	6	..	..
10		4	5	..	..		4	5	..	..
11		3	4	2			3	4	..	
12		2	3	3			2	3	..	3
13		1	2	4			1	2	..	4
14		0	1	5			0	1	..	6
15		1	0	6			1	0		6
16		2	2	7			2	1		7
17		3	3	8			3	2		8
	Mast .... 25ft 6in. Leech .. 37ft. 6in.					Mast .... 26ft. Leech .. 39ft.				

VII. DIMENSIONS OF BARQUES' MAIN-TRYSAILS.

Cloths.	Head, 15ft. 0in. equal 8½ Cloths. Foot, 22ft. 0in. ditto 11½ ditto.					Head, 18ft. 0in. equal 10 Cloths. Foot, 22ft. 0in. ditto 11½ ditto.				
	Mast Gores.	Foot do.	Foot do.	Head do.	Slack Seams.	Mast Gores.	Foot do.	Foot do.	Head do.	Slack Seams.
No.	FT. IN.	IN.	IN.	IN.	IN.	FT. IN.	IN.	IN.	IN.	IN.
½	4 0	8	..	..	..	7 4	5	..	..	..
1	8 0	16	..	..	..	14 8	10	..	..	..
2	8 0	14	..	..	..		8	12	..	..
3	4 0	10	..	3	..		7	10	..	..
4		8	6	..	..		6	9	..	..
5		6	5	..	..		5	8	..	..
6		4	4	..	..		4	6	..	..
7		3	3	..	3		3	4	..	1
8		2	2	..	5		2	3	..	2
9		1	1	6			1	2	..	3
10		0	0	7			0	1	..	4
11		2	2	8			2	0	..	6
	Mast .... 24ft. 0in. Leech .. 31ft. 0in.					Mast .... 21ft. 6in. Leech .. 30ft. 6in.				

DIMENSIONS OF BARQUES' MAIN-TRYSAILS (CONTINUED).

Cloths. No.	Head, 15ft. 6in. equal 9 Cloths. Foot, 22ft. 0in. ditto 12 ditto.					Head, 19ft. 0in. equal 11 Cloths. Foot, 28ft. 6in. ditto 16 ditto.				
	Mast Gores. FT. IN.	Foot do. IN.	Foot do. IN.	Head do. IN.	Slack Seams. IN.	Mast Gores. FT. IN.	Foot do. IN.	Foot do. IN.	Head do. IN.	Slack Seams. IN.
1	8 0	9				5 6	16			
2	8 0	8				5 6	14½			
3	8 0	7				5 0	13			
4			6	6		5 0	12			
5			5	4		4 6	10			
6			4	4				9	8	
7			3	3				8	7	
8			2	3	3			6	6	
9			1	2	5			4	5	
10			0	2	6			3	4	2
11			1	0	7			2	3	3
12			2	1	8			1	2	4
13								0	1	5
14								1	0	6
15								2	2	7
16								3	3	8
	Mast .... 24ft. Leech .. 31ft.					Mast .... 26ft. 0in. Leech .. 37ft. 6in.				

VIII. DIMENSIONS OF BARQUES' FORE-TRYSAILS.

Cloths. No.	Head, 15ft. 6in. equal 8¾ Cloths. Foot, 24ft. 0in. ditto 13 ditto.					Head, 20ft. equal 11 Cloths. Foot, 30ft. ditto 16 ditto.				
	Mast Gores. FT. IN.	Foot do. IN.	Foot do. IN.	Head do. IN.	Slack Seams. IN.	Mast Gores. FT. IN.	Foot do. IN.	Foot do. IN.	Head do. IN.	Slack Seams. IN.
1	6 0	19				4 6	26			
2	5 6	16				4 6	23			
3	4 6	14				3 6	19			
4	4 6	12				3 6	16			
5			10	6		3 0	14			
6			8	8				12	8	
7			7	7				10	6	
8			6	6				8	6	
9			5	5				7	5	
10			4	4	3			6	5	1
11			3	3	4			5	4	2
12			2	2	5			4	4	3
13			1	1	6			3	3	4
14								2	2	5
15								1	1	6
16								0	0	8
	Mast .... 21ft. 10in. Leech .. 33ft. 0in.					Mast .... 21ft. 10in. Leech .. 34ft. 6in.				

IX. DIMENSIONS OF BARQUES' GAFF-TOPSAILS.

Cloths. — Head, 2ft. 0in. equal 1 Cloth. Foot, 21ft. 6in. ditto 10½ ditto.

No.	Mast Gores FT. IN.	Foot do. IN.	Foot do. IN.	Head do. IN.
1	3 0	0	..	..
2	6 0	1	..	..
3	5 0	2	..	..
4	4 0	3	..	..
5	3 6	4	..	..
6	3 0	5	..	..
7	2 6	7	..	..
8	2 6	9	..	..
9	2 3	12	..	..
10	2 3	15	..	..
11	...	...	18	0
12	...	...	...	...

Mast .... 37ft. 0in.
Leech .. 27ft. 6in.

Cloths. — Foot, 22ft. equal 12 Cloths.

No.	Mast Gores FT. IN.	Foot Gores IN.
1	6 0	2
2	5 0	0
3	4 0	2
4	3 0	3
5	2 6	4
6	2 6	5
7	2 3	7
8	2 0	9
9	2 0	12
10	1 9	15
11	1 9	18
12	1 9	20

Mast .... 40ft. 0in.
Leech .. 26ft. 6in.

Cloths. — Head, 3 Cloths. Foot, 12 ditto.

No.	Mast Gores FT. IN.	Foot do. IN.	Foot do. IN.	Head do. IN.
1	6 0	2	..	..
2	5 0	1	..	..
3	4 0	0	..	..
4	3 0	1	..	..
5	2 6	2	..	..
6	2 6	3	..	..
7	2 6	4	..	..
8	2 6	5	..	..
9	2 0	6	..	..
10	...	...	8	0
11	...	...	10	0
12	...	...	12	

Mast .... 33ft. 0in.
Leech .. 25ft. 6in.

Cloths. — Head, 9ft. 6in. equal 5 Cloths. Foot, 22ft. 0in. ditto 12 ditto.

No.	Mast Gores FT. IN.	Foot do. IN.	Foot do. IN.	Head do. IN.
1	7 0	2	..	..
2	5 6	0	..	..
3	4 0	1	..	..
4	4 0	2	..	..
5	4 0	3	..	..
6	4 0	4	..	..
7	4 0	5	..	..
8	...	...	7	10
9	...	...	9	9
10	...	...	12	8
11	...	...	15	7
12	...	...	18	6

Mast .... 34ft.
Leech .. 29ft.

X. DIMENSIONS OF SHIPS' DRIVERS.

Cloths. Head, 22ft. equal 12 Cloths. Foot, 31ft. ditto 16 ditto.

No.	Mast Gores FT. IN.	Foot do. IN.	Foot do. IN.	Head do. IN.	Slack Seams IN.
1	5 6	19	..	..	..
2	5 0	17	..	..	..
3	4 6	15	..	..	..
4	4 0	13	..	..	..
5			11	12	..
6			9	10	..
7			7	9	..
8			5	8	..
9			4	7	..
10			3	6	1
11			2	5	2
12			1	4	3
13			0	3	4
14			1	2	5
15			2	1	6
16			3	0	8
17					

Mast .... 19ft. 4in.
Leech .. 35ft. 6in.

Cloths. Head, 28ft. 6in. equal 18 Cloths. Foot, 32ft. 0in. ditto 17 ditto.

No.	Mast Gores FT. IN.	Foot do. IN.	Foot do. IN.	Head do. IN.	Slack Seams IN.
1	5 6	19	..	..	..
2	5 6	17	..	..	..
3	5 0	15	..	..	..
4	4 6	13	..	..	..
5			11	12	..
6			10	12	..
7			9	10	..
8			8	9	..
9			6	8	..
10			4	8	2
11			3	7	3
12			2	6	4
13			1	5	5
14			0	4	6
15			1	3	7
16			2	2	8
17			3	1	9

Mast .... 20ft. 6in.
Leech .. 37ft. 6in.

Cloths. Head, 27ft. 0in. equal 15 Cloths. Foot, 36ft. 6in. ditto 19½ ditto.

No.	Mast Gores FT. IN.	Foot do. IN.	Foot do. IN.	Head do. IN.	Slack Seams IN.
	2 6	12	..	..	..
1	5 0	20	..	..	..
2	5 0	18	..	..	..
3	5 0	15	..	..	..
4	4 0	12	..	..	..
5			10	12	..
6			9	9	..
7			8	8	..
8			7	8	..
9			6	6	..
10			5	6	..
11			4	4	..
12			3	3	1
13			2	3	2
14			2	2	3
15			1	1	4
16			0	0	5
17			1	1	6
18			2	2	7
19			3	3	8
20					

Mast .... 22 feet.
Leech .. 38 feet.

Cloths. Head, 27ft. 0in. equal 15 Cloths. Foot, 37ft. 6in. ditto 20 ditto.

No.	Mast Gores FT. IN.	Foot do. IN.	Foot do. IN.	Head do. IN.	Slack Seams IN.
	.. ..	..	..	..	..
1	5 0	22	..	..	..
2	5 0	20	..	..	..
3	4 0	18	..	..	..
4	4 0	16	..	..	..
5	3 0	16	..	..	..
6			14	8	..
7			14	6	..
8			12	6	..
9			10	5	..
10			8	5	..
11			6	4	..
12			5	4	..
13			4	3	1
14			3	3	2
15			2	2	3
16			1	1	4
17			0	0	5
18			1	1	6
19			2	2	7
20			3	2	8

Mast .... 22 feet.
Leech .. 41 feet.

DIMENSIONS OF SHIPS' DRIVERS (CONTINUED).

Head, 29ft. equal 16 Cloths. Foot,* 36ft. ditto 20 ditto.

Cloths. No.	Mast Gores. FT. IN.	Foot do. IN.	Foot do. FT.	Head do. FT.	Slack Seams. FT.
½					
1	5 6 .. 4				
2	5 6 .. 4				
3	5 0 .. 8				
4	5 0 .. 3				
5		2½ In. {	5 ..	12 ..	
6			12 ..	12 ..	
7		2½ In.	18 ..	10 ..	
8			18 ..	10 ..	
9			16 ..	9 ..	
10			14 ..	9 ..	
11			12 ..	8 ..	
12		4 In.	10 ..	8 ..	
13			8 ..	6 ..	1
14			6 ..	6 ..	2
15			5 ..	4 ..	3
16			4 ..	4 ..	4
17			3 ..	3 ..	6
18		3 In. {	2 ..	2 ..	8
19			1 ..	1 ..	9
20			0 ..	0 ..	10
21					

Mast .... 21ft. 6in.
Leech .. 41ft. 0in.
* The foot out to clear the wheel.

Head, 30ft. equal 17 Cloths. Foot, 39ft. ditto 21½ ditto.

Cloths. No.	Mast Gores. FT. IN.	Foot do. IN.	Foot do. IN.	Head do. IN.	Slack Seams. IN.
½	2 6 .. 12				
1	5 0 .. 20				
2	5 6 .. 18				
3	5 0 .. 15				
4	4 6 .. 12				
5		10 ..	12 ..		
6		9 ..	9 ..		
7		8 ..	8 ..		
8		7 ..	8 ..		
9		6 ..	7 ..		
10		5 ..	7 ..		
11		4 ..	6 ..		
12		3 ..	6 ..		
13		3 ..	5 ..	1	
14		2 ..	5 ..	2	
15		1 ..	4 ..	3	
16		0 ..	3 ..	4	
17		1 ..	3 ..	6	
18		2 ..	1 ..	7	
19		3 ..	0 ..	8	
20		4 ..	2 ..	9	
21		5 ..	3 ..	10	

Mast ... 23 feet.
Leech .. 39 feet.

Head, 31ft. 0in. equal 17½ Cloths. Foot, 42ft. 6in. ditto 23 ditto.

Cloths. No.	Mast Gores. FT. IN.	Foot do. IN.	Foot do. IN.	Head do. IN.	Slack Seams. IN.
1	5 0 .. 24				
2	5 0 .. 22				
3	5 0 .. 20				
4	4 0 .. 18				
5	4 0 .. 16				
6	2 0 .. 14			6	
7		12 ..	10 ..		
8		10 ..	8 ..		
9		9 ..	7 ..		
10		9 ..	7 ..		
11		7 ..	6 ..		
12		7 ..	6 ..		
13		5 ..	5 ..		
14		5 ..	5 ..	1	
15		4 ..	3 ..	2	
16		3 ..	2 ..	3	
17		2 ..	1 ..	4	
18		1 ..	0 ..	5	
19		0 ..	1 ..	6	
20		1 ..	2 ..	7	
21		2 ..	3 ..	8	
22		3 ..	4 ..	9	
23		4 ..	5 ..	10	
24					

Mast ... 25ft. 6in.

Head, 33ft. equal 18½ Cloths. Foot, 45ft. ditto 24 ditto.

Cloths. No.	Mast Gores. FT. IN.	Foot do. IN.	Foot do. IN.	Head do. IN.	Slack Seams. IN.
1	5 6 .. 23				
2	5 0 .. 21				
3	5 0 .. 19				
4	4 6 .. 16				
5	4 0 .. 14				
6	2 0 .. 12			6	
7		10 ..	10 ..		
8		10 ..	8 ..		
9		9 ..	8 ..		
10		9 ..	6 ..		
11		8 ..	5 ..		
12		8 ..	4 ..		
13		7 ..	3 ..		
14		7 ..	2 ..		
15		5 ..	1 ..		
16		4 ..	0 ..	1	
17		3 ..	0 ..	3	
18		2 ..	1 ..	3	
19		1 ..	2 ..	4	
20		0 ..	2 ..	5	
21		1 ..	3 ..	6	
22		2 ..	3 ..	7	
23		3 ..	4 ..	8	
24		4 ..	4 ..	10	

Mast .... 26ft. 9in.

DIMENSIONS OF SHIPS' DRIVERS (CONTINUED).

Cloths.	Head, 39ft. equal 30 Cloths. Foot, 54ft. ditto 40 ditto. 18 inches wide Canvass.					Head, 39ft. equal 22 Cloths. Foot, 54ft. ditto 30 ditto.				
No.	Mast Gores. FT. IN.	Foot do. IN.	Foot do. IN.	Head do. IN.	Slack Seams. IN.	Mast Gores. FT. IN.	Foot do. IN.	Foot do. IN.	Head do. IN.	Slack Seams. IN.
1	4 0	16	..	..	..	4 0	18	..	..	..
2	4 0	14	..	..	..	4 0	17	..	..	..
3	3 6	12	..	..	..	3 10	16	..	..	..
4	3 6	10	..	..	..	3 10	15	..	..	..
5	3 3	10	..	..	..	3 8	14	..	..	..
6	3 3	9	..	..	..	3 8	13	..	..	..
7	3 0	9	..	..	..	3 6	12	..	..	..
8	3 0	8	..	..	..	3 6	11	..	..	..
9	2 6	8	..	..	..		10	6	..	..
10	2 6	8	..	..	..		9	6	..	..
11		8	..	4	..		8	5	..	..
12		6½	..	4	..		8	5	..	..
13		5¾	..	4	..		7	4	..	..
14		5½	..	4	..		7	4	..	..
15		5½	..	3	..		6	3	..	..
16		5½	..	3	..		6	3	..	..
17		5¼	..	3	..		5	2	..	1
18		5½	..	3	..		4	2	..	2
19		5	..	2	..		3	1	..	3
20		5	..	2	..		3	1	..	4
21		5	..	2	.. 1		2	0	..	5
22		4½	..	2	.. 1		2	0	..	6
23		4	..	1	.. 2		1	1	..	7
24		4	..	1	.. 2		1	1	..	8
25		3½	..	1	.. 3		0	2	..	9
26		2¾	..	1	.. 3		1	2	..	10
27		2	..	½	.. 4		2	3	..	11
28		1½	..	½	.. 4		3	3	..	12
29		1	..	0	.. 5		4	4	..	13
30		½	..	0	.. 5		5	4	..	14
31		0	..	1	.. 6					
32		1½	..	1	.. 6					
33		2¼	..	2	.. 7					
34		2¼	..	2	.. 7					
35		3	..	3	.. 8					
36		3	..	3	.. 8					
37		4	..	4	.. 9					
38		4	..	4	.. 9					
39		4½	..	5	.. 10					
40		4½	..	5	.. 12					

Mast .... 34ft. 0in.   Mast .... 32ft.
Leech .. 55f. 6in.   Leech .. 53ft.

XI. DIMENSIONS OF A CLIPPER SCHOONER (PLATE XVII.)

MASTS, ETC.	Extreme Length.	Headed length.	YARDS, ETC.	Extreme Length.	Yard-arms.
	FT. IN.	FT. IN.		FT. IN.	FT. IN
Mainmast	69 7	8 3	Fore yard	55 0	2 10
Foremast	66 4	7 10	Topsail yard	41 0	2 8
Fore-topmast, hoist	21 0	Royal	Top-gallant yard	29 6	1 6
Fore-topgallantmast, hoist	12 0	8 6	Main boom	59 0	Pole
Main-topmast, hoist	35 0	Pole	Ditto gaff	29 0	4 0
Bowsprit, outside	..	6 0	Fore gaff	23 3	
Jib-boom, outside of cap..	16 0		Gaff-topsail yard	7 0	
Flying jib-boom	10 6		Distance from forestay to		
Lower masts, house each..	13 6		centre of foremast......	29 6	
Rake of the foremast to the			From centre of foremast to		
foot	0 1¾		mainmast	24 0	
Ditto mainmast	0 2⅜		Centre of mainmast to taff-		
Steave of Bowsprit	0 3½		rail	46 0	
Rise of the Deck	1 0		Height of rail............	3 6	

	MAINSAIL.	FORESAIL.
Cloths.	Head, 23ft. 6in. equal 13 Cloths. Foot, 53ft. 0in. ditto 29 ditto.	Head, 21ft. equal 11½ Cloths. Foot, 28ft. ditto 15 ditto.

No.	Mast Gores. FT. IN.	Foot do. IN.	Foot do. IN.	Head do. IN.	Slack Seams. IN.	Mast Gores. FT. IN.	Foot do. IN.	Foot do. IN.	Head do. IN.	Slack Seams. IN.
1	1 ·5	.. 30	.. ..	.. ..	.. ..	10 6	.. 11	.. ..	.. ..	.. ..
2	1 5	.. 27	.. ..	.. ..	.. ..	10 0	.. 10	.. ..	.. ..	.. ..
3	1 4	.. 24	.. ..	.. ..	.. ..	9 6	.. 9	.. ..	.. ..	.. ..
4	1 4	.. 24	.. ..	.. ..	.. ..	4 6	.. 8	.. ..	.. 4	.. ..
5	1 3	.. 23	.. ..	.. ..	.. ..	....	.. 7	.. 8	.. ..	.. ..
6	1 3	.. 19	.. ..	.. ..	.. ..	....	.. 6	.. 6	.. ..	.. ..
7	1 2	.. 17	.. ..	.. ..	.. ..	....	.. 5	.. 5	.. ..	.. ..
8	1 2	.. 16	.. ..	.. ..	.. ..	....	.. 4	.. 5	.. ..	.. ..
9	1 1	.. 15	.. ..	.. ..	.. ..	....	.. 3	.. 4	.. 2	
10	1 1	.. 13	.. ..	.. ..	.. ..	....	.. 2	.. 3	.. 3	
11	1 1	.. 12	.. ..	.. ..	.. ..	....	.. 1	.. 2	.. 4	
12	1 1	.. 11	.. ..	.. ..	.. ..	....	.. 0	.. 1	.. 6	
13	1 0	.. 10	.. ..	.. ..	.. ..	....	.. 1	.. 0	.. 8	
14	1 0	.. 9	.. ..	.. ..	.. ..	....	.. 2	.. 1	.. 10	
15	1 0	.. 8	.. ..	.. ..	.. ..	....	.. 3	.. 2	.. 12	
16	1 0	.. 7	.. ..	.. ..	.. ..					
17	....		6	.. 12	.. 1					
18	....		5	.. 10	.. 2					
19	....		4	.. 8	.. 3					
20	....		3	.. 6	.. 4					
21	....		2	.. 5	.. 5					
22	....		2	.. 4	.. 6					
23	....		1	.. 3	.. 7					
24	....		0	.. 2	.. 8					
25	....		1	.. 1	.. 10					
26	....		2	.. 0	.. 12					
27	....		2	.. 1	.. 14					
28	....		3	.. 2	.. 16					
29	....		4	.. 3	.. 18					

Mast .... 35ft. 6in.
Leech .. 56ft. 0in.

Mast .... 34ft. 6in.
Leech .. 45ft. 0in.

DIMENSIONS OF A CLI. PER SCHOONER (CONTINUED).

Cloths.	Jib Foresail, 15 Cloths. Leech, 32ft. 6in. Stay, 44ft. 0in.		Second Jib, 13 Cloths. Leech, 38ft. 0in. Stay, 53ft. 0in.		Jib, 12 Cloths. Leech, 44ft. 6in. Stay, 65ft. 0in.		Flying Jib, 8 Cloths. Leech, 36ft. 0in. Stay, 50ft. 0in.	
	Stay Gores.	Foot Gores.	Stay Gores.	Foot Gores.	Stay Gores.	Foot Gores.	Stay Gores.	Foot Gores
No.	FT. IN.	IN.	FT. IN.	IN.	FT. IN.	IN.	FT. IN.	IN.
1	2 8	3	8 0	0	10 0	2	11 0	2
2	2 6	2	6 0	1	7 0	3	8 0	4
3	2 4	1	4 6	2	6 0	5	6 0	7
4	2 4	1	4 0	4	5 0	7	5 0	11
5	2 4	0	3 6	5	4 8	10	5 0	15
6	2 4	1	3 6	7	4 8	12	5 0	20
7	2 4	1	3 3	9	4 6	15	5 0	28
8	2 4	2	3 3	10	4 6	18	5 0	45
9	2 4	3	3 0	13	4 6	22		
10	2 4	3	3 0	14	4 6	28		
11	2 4	4	3 0	17	4 6	37		
12	2 4	4	2 9	20	4 6	58		
13	2 4	5	2 9	24				
14	2 4	6						
15	2 4	7						

FORESAILS.—The foot of the foresail is commonly ·9, the distance between the stay and the fore part of the mast; the luff from ·8 to ·87, the length of the stay, and the leech ·8 of the luff. SECOND JIB.—The length of the foot of the second jib is the distance from the tack to the fore part of the stem, the luff ·8 to ·85, the length of the stay, and the leech of such a length that the clue may be a proper height for the sheets to bring an equal strain on the foot and leech ropes.

Cloths.	Gaff-topsail. Head, 3½ Cloths. Foot, 13 ditto.				Topsail. Head, 17 Cloths. Reef, 36ft. 6in. Foot, 26 Cloths.			Top-gallantsail. Head, 13½ Cloths. Foot, 20 ditto.		
	Fore-leech Gores.	Foot Gores.			Foot Gores.			Foot Gores.	Leech Gores.	
No.	FT. IN.	IN.			IN.			IN.	FT. IN.	
1	5 6	3			1			0	1 0	
2	4 6	2			2			1	4 0	
3	3 6	1			2			2	4 0	
4	3 6	0			3	Leech.		3	4 0	
5	3 0	1			3	Gores.				
6	3 0	2			4	FT. IN.		Hoist 13 0		
7	3 0	3	Head	Slack	4 .. 5	1 = ½ cloth.		Mid. 12 6 cut,		
8	3 0	4	Gores.	Seams.	5 .. 6	1		14 squares.		
9	3 0	5	.. IN.	IN.	6 .. 4	4				
10	2 0	6	.. 2	2	8 .. 3	5				
11	....	7	.. 3	4	10 .. 3	1				
12	....	8	.. 2	6						
13	....	9	.. 1	8	Hoist 22 0					
					Mid. 18 0 cut					
					4 squares.					

A DICTIONARY OF TECHNICAL TERMS
RELATIVE TO SAILS.

Awning.—A cover of canvass stretched flat over a ship above the deck, for protection from the rays of the sun in hot climates.

Balance Reef.—A reef that crosses a sail diagonally—that is, from the nock to the upper reef-cringle on the after leech—and is used to contract it in case of a storm.

Bands.—Pieces of canvass, from one-sixth to two-thirds of a breadth, strongly sewed or tabled across the sail to strengthen it.

Bark or Barque.—A general name given to vessels with three masts, with the mizen-mast and a pole-mast above, instead of a regular top-mast and top-gallant-mast; and if with a square topsail it is commonly set flying; but instead of this sail, it is more general to have a gaff-topsail.

Barca-longa.—A vessel common to the Mediterranean, as the large Spanish fishing-boat, carrying two or three masts with lug-sails.

Belly, or Bag Part.—The part of a sail that swells out into a larger capacity, by the seams being made broader on the head and foot than the remaining part. This forms what is called the belly part of the sail, which is restrained by the slack after-leech. (See *Slack.*)

Becket for Bunt-Jigger.—A strop spliced through two holes worked in the bunt of a sail, so that it may be furled with a peak. (See p. 81.)

Bolt-Rope.—The rope sewed on the edges of sails, to prevent their rending.

Bonnet.—The additional part of a sail, made to fasten with latchings to the foot of the sail it is intended for. It is exactly similar to the foot of the sail it is made for.

Boom.—A long pole run out from different places in the ship, to extend the bottoms of particular sails, as, jib-boom, flying-jib-boom, studdingsail-boom, driver or spanker-boom, ringtail-boom, main-boom, squaresail-boom, &c.

Booming.—Amongst seamen, denotes the application of a boom to the sails. Booming of the sails is never used but in quarter winds, or before a wind. When a ship is said to come booming towards us, it signifies that she comes with all the sail she can make.

Bowline.—A rope attached by the bridles to the bowline-cringles, on the leeches of topsails, courses, &c., to keep tight the windward or weather leech of the sail, when on a wind.

Brails.—Ropes to draw up the foot, leech, and other parts of fore and aft sails for furling, or when tacking.

Bridles of the Bowlins.—Short ropes, or legs, fastened to the bowline-cringles on the leeches of sails.

Brig.—A vessel having two masts, rigged similarly to the fore and main masts of ships, and fore and aft main-sail.

Bumkin, or Boomkin.—A short boom, or beam of timber, projecting from each side of the bow of a ship, to extend the clue or lower-corner of the foresail to windward; for which purpose there is a large block fixed on its outer end, through which the tack is passed, which being drawn tight down, the tack is said to be aboard.

Bunt.—The middle part of a sail stowed, and the foremost leech of staysails out with a nock.

Buntlines.—The ropes fastened to the foot rope on the bottom of the square-sails, to draw them up to the yards: they are inserted through certain blocks under the top, or on the upper part of the yard, whence passing downwards on the fore part of the sail, they are fastened below to the lower edge through holes in the foot of the sails, of which there are either two or four, called buntline-holes.

Buntline-Cloth.—The lining sewed up the sail, in the direction of the bunt-line, to prevent that rope from chafing the sail.

Canvass.—A strong kind of cloth of which the sails are made. (See p. 55.)

Cat-Harpins.—The rigging which spreads underneath the top, down below the hounds of the lower masts, and as far as the centre of the yard, or heads of the courses. The cat-harpins are in general one-eighth the hoist of the topsail.

Centre of Effort.—When the ship is under sail, there are two forces acting on it; the one, the force of the wind on the sails, to propel the ship; and the other, the resistance the water opposes to her motion. These forces, immediately the ship has acquired the velocity due to the strength of the wind, as is the case with all forces, may each be reasoned on as if acting on only one point of the surface over which its effect is diffused. This point is that in which, if the whole force were to be concentrated, its effect would be the same as when dispersed over the whole area: it is usual to call these, "resultant of forces," and the points on which they are supposed to act, "centres of effort." (See p. 114.)

Centre of Gravity of the Sails.—That point, about which, if supported, all the parts of the sail (acted upon only by the force of gravity) would balance each other in any position.

Chess-Tree.—A piece of timber with a sheave in, secured to the sides of a ship, to extend the tack of the main-course to windward:—the sheet is then hauled aft to leeward.

Cleats.—Pieces of wood nailed on the yard-arms, for preventing the earings sliding inwards; but it is now common, instead of having cleats, to have stops, formed out of the yards.

Cleat and Cleat.—The distance between the cleats or stops on the yard arms.

Close Reef.—The fourth or lowest reef of a topsail, and uppermost reef of a fore-and-aft mainsail.

Close-Hauled.—Is the arrangement or trim of a ship's sails when she endeavours to make a progress in the nearest direction possible towards that point of the compass from which the wind blows. In this manner of sailing, the keel of square rigged vessels commonly makes an angle of six points with the line of the wind, but cutters, luggers, and other fore-and-aft rigged vessels, will sail much nearer. All vessels, indeed, are supposed to make nearly a point of lee-way, when close hauled, even when they have the advantage of a good breeze and smooth water. The angle of the lee-way, however, enlarges in proportion to the increase of the wind and sea. In this disposition of the sails they are all extended sideways on the ship, so that the wind, as it crosses the ship obliquely towards the stern from forward, may fill their cavities. But as the current of wind also unites the cavities of the sails in an oblique direction, the effort of it to make the ship advance is considerably diminished: she will, therefore, make the least progress when sailing in this manner. The ship is said to be close-hauled, because at this time her tacks, or lower corners of the principal sails, are drawn close down to her side to windward; the sheets hauled close aft, and all the bowlines drawn to their greatest extension, in order to keep the sails steady.

Cloths.—The breadths or pieces of which a sail is composed.

Clue.—The lower corner of a sail, where a block is fixed in or shackled to, in courses, to receive a thick rope from aft, which is termed the sheet.

Clue Rope.—A short rope, larger than the bolt-rope on the sail, into which it is spliced at the after corners of stay-sails, jibs, and boom-sails. In the corner is stuck a cringle through two holes, to which the sheets are fastened.

Clue-Garnets.—A sort of tackle attached to the clues of square sails, to haul the clues up to the yards.

Concentrated or Convergent Sails.—Sails in which all the cloths and seams tend to one point, or to the clue. (See Plate 5.)

Cot.—A particular sort of bed-frame, suspended from the beams of a ship, for the officers to sleep in. It is made of canvass Nos. 3 or 5, sewed in the form of a " chest," about six feet long, one foot deep, and two or three feet wide, and is extended by a square wooden frame, with a canvass bottom, on which the bed or mattress is laid. It is reckoned much more convenient at sea than either hammocks or fixed cabins.

Courses.—The mainsail and foresail, main-staysail, fore-staysail, and mizen-staysail.

Cringles.—Small bows formed on the bolt-ropes, or through two holes made in the tabling of sails, by intertwisting the strand of a rope alternately round itself and through the hole, or through the strand of the bolt-rope, till it assume the shape of a ring, in which an iron thimble, having a groove formed in its outer circumference, is put. To the cringles the end of a rope is fastened, for different uses.

Cross-Gore.—The length measured from the nock, or height of gaff on the mast, to the place of the clue. (See Plate I.)

Down-Haul.—A rope passing up along a stay through the hanks of the stay-sails or jib, and made fast to the upper corner of the sail, to pull it down when shortening sail.

Drabbler.—An additional part of a sail, sometimes laced to the bottom of a bonnet on a square sail, in sloops and schooners.

Driver.—Another name for *Spanker,* which see.

Eating in Seaming.—The length of the gore which overshoots the creasing of the seam.

Earings.—The upper part of the leech-rope, worked into the shape of a cringle, and used to extend the upper corners of sails to their yards or gaffs, with small ropes also called earings.

Eyelet-Holes in sails, are round holes made of rope-yarns, worked in a sail, to admit a small rope through, chiefly the rope-yarns or lacing of the head of mizens, trysails, &c., and for seizings on sails that bend to hoops and hanks. Eyelet-Holes are likewise made across the sail in the reef-bands; at the clues, and in the leeches, for sticking cringles.

Fid.—A round, tapering piece of hard wood, to thrust between the strands of a rope, and make a hole to admit the strand of another rope, in splicing. *Driving-Fid* is much larger, being for rounding the cringles to admit thimbles which are fixed in the cringles of sails.

Fore.—The distinguishing character of all those sails of a ship which are attached to the foremast.

Fore-and-Aft.—Throughout the ship's whole length, or from end to end; it also implies in a line with the keel. *Fore-and-Aft Sail,* the sail in a line with the keel. *Fore-Bowline,* the bowline of the foresail. (See *Bowline.*)

Fore-Braces.—Are ropes applied to the fore-yard-arms, to change the position of the foresail occasionally.

Foot of a Sail.—The lower edge, or bottom. *Foot-rope,* the rope to which the lower edge of a sail is sewed or fixed.

Fixed or Fixing.—Another term for marling, which see.

Furling.—The operation of wrapping or rolling a sail close up to the yard, stay, or mast, to which it belongs, and winding a cord or gasket spirally about it, to fasten it thereto. *Furling in a body,* is a particular method of rolling up a topsail, only practised in harbour, and is performed by gathering all the loose part of the sail into the top, about the heel of the topmast, whereby the yard having as little rolled on it as possible, appears much thinner and lighter than when the sail is furled in the usual manner, which is sometimes termed, for distinction sake, furling in the bunt. *Furling line,* denotes a cord employed in this operation. *Furling lines* are generally flat, and are known by the name of gaskets.

Gaff.—A sort of boom, used to extend the upper edge of the mizen, and employed for the same purpose on those sails whose foremost leeches are joined to the masts by hoops or lacings, and which are usually extended by a boom below; such are the mainsails of sloops, brigs, schooners, &c.

Garnet.—A sort of tackle fixed to the clues of sails, and used to haul the clue up to the yard.

Gasket.—A sort of plaited cord fastened to the sail-yards of a ship, and used to furl or tie up the sail firmly to the yard by wrapping it round both, six or seven times, the turns being at a competent distance from each other.

Bunt Gasket.—Is that which supports or ties up the bunt of the sail, and should consequently be the strongest, as having the greatest weight to support; it is sometimes made in a peculiar manner.

Quarter Gasket.—Used only for large sails, and is fastened about half-way out upon the yard, which part is called the quarter.

The Yard-arm Gasket is made fast to the yard-arm, and serves to bind the sail as far as the quarter-gasket on large yards, but extends quite into the bunt of small sails.

Goose-Neck.—A sort of iron hook fitted on the inner end of a boom, and introduced into a clamp of iron or eye-bolt, which encircles the mast, or is fitted to some other place in the ship, so that it may be unhooked at pleasure.

Goose-wings of a Sail.—The clues or lower corners of a ship's mainsail or foresail, when the middle part is furled or tied up to the yard. The goose-wings are only used in a storm, to scud before the wind, when the sail, even diminished by a reef, would be too great a press on the ship in that situation. *Goose-wings* of a windsail, are two breadths of canvass, sewed to the opening at the top, which are braced to the wind so as to receive the full current of air, which fills the tube. (See page 70.)

Gores.—Angles cut slopewise at one or both ends of such cloths as widen or increase the depth of a sail.

Goring, or Goring Cloth.—That part of the skirts of a sail where it gradually widens from the upper part or head towards the bottom or foot. The goring-cloths are, therefore, those which are cut obliquely, and added to the breadth.

Grommet.—A sort of ring or small wreath formed of a strand of rope laid in three times round, used to fasten the upper edge of a sail to its stay, in different places, by means of which the sail is accordingly hoisted or lowered. Instead of grommets, hanks have been lately introduced. (See *Hanks.*)

Halyards.—The ropes or tackles usually employed to hoist or lower any sail upon its respective masts or stay, except the lower square sails.

Hanks.—A sort of wooden rings, fixed upon the stays to confine the stay-sails thereto at different distances: they are used in lieu of grommets, being much more convenient, and of a later invention. They are framed by the bending of a tough piece of wood into the form of a wreath, and fastening it at the two ends by means of notches, thereby retaining its circular figure and elasticity.

Head-Sail.—All the sails belonging to the foremast and bowsprit:—it also applies to all the square-sails.

Hoist.—The foremost leeches of stay sails, mast leech of boom sails, and drop of topsails to the lower yards, when their own yard is hoisted to the hounds.

Home.—To haul home the topsail sheets, is to extend the bottom of the topsail to the lower yard arms by means of the sheets.

Sheet-Home.—The top gallant sails, in order to extend the clues of those sails to the topsail yard arms.

Hounds.—The parts of a mast-head which gradually project on the right and left side beyond the cylindrical or conical surface. These hounds support the frame of the top, together with the topmast, and the rigging on the masts.

Hounded the Topsail Yard.—Signifies the length of the two yard arms deducted from the whole length.

House-Line.—Small lines of three strands, used to marl the clues and foot of the sail to the bolt rope, and to seize the corners of sails.

Housing.—The height from the step of the mast to the uppermost deck.

Jib.—The foremost sail of a ship, being a large staysail extended from the outer end of the bowsprit, prolonged by the jib-boom towards the fore-top-mast-head.   In cutters and sloops;the jib is on the bowsprit, and extends towards the lower mast head.

Jigger-Tackle.—A light small tackle consisting of a double and a single block, and used by seamen for hauling up the bunt of the topsail, &c.

Lacing.—The rope or line used to confine the heads of sails to their yards or gaffs.

Large.—A phrase applied to the wind when it crosses the line of the ship's course in a favourable direction, particularly on the beam or quarter ; for instance, if a ship is steering west, the wind in any point of the compass to the eastward of the south or north, may be called large, unless it is directly east, and then it is said to be right aft.

Sailing Large.—Is therefore the act of advancing with a large wind, so that the sheets are slackened and flowing, and the bowlines entirely disused.   This phrase is generally opposed to sailing close-hauled, or with a scant wind, in which situation the sheets and bowlines are extended as much as possible.

Latchings.—Loops formed on the line that is sewed to the head of a bonnet, to connect it with the foot of a sail.

Lateen-Sail.—A triangular sail, frequently used by xebecs, poleacres, settees, and other vessels navigated in the Mediterranean sea.

Leeches.—The borders or edges of a sail, which are either sloping or perpendicular ; those of the square sails, *i.e.* the sails whose tops and bottoms are parallel to the deck, or at right angles with the mast, are denominated from the ship's side, as the starboard leech of the mainsail, the lee-leech of the fore-topsail ; but the sails which are fixed obliquely on the masts have their leeches named from their situation with regard to the ship's length, as the fore leech of the mizen, the after leech of the jib, &c.

Leech Lines.—Ropes fastened to the middle of the leeches of the mainsail and foresail, and communicating with blocks under the opposite sides of the top, whence they pass downwards to the deck, serving to truss those sails up to the yard.   *Harbour Leech Lines*, ropes made fast at the middle of the topsail yards, then passing round the leeches of the topsails, and through blocks upon the top sail-tye, serving to truss the sails very close up to the yard, previous to there being furled in a bunt.

Leech Rope.—A name given to that part of the bolt-rope to which the border or edge of a sail is sewed.   In all sails whose opposite leeches are of the same length, it is terminated above by the earing, and below by the clue.

Linings.—The canvass sewed on the leeches and other parts of a sail to strengthen and preserve it.

Lugger.—A vessel carrying three masts, with a running bowsprit, upon which she sets lug-sails, and sometimes has topsails adapted to them.

Lug Sail.—A quadrilateral or four sided sail bent upon a yard which hangs obliquely to the mast at one-third of its length.   These are more particularly used in the barca-longas, navigated by the Spaniards in the Mediterranean.

Lug Sail Boat.—A boat carrying sails of the preceding description.

Marline Spike.—An iron tool, either with or without a short wooden handle, used to separate the strands of a rope in order to introduce those of another, when they are to be spliced or joined evenly without knotting.

Marling.—The act of winding any small line, as house-line, marline, twine, &c., about a rope, and through holes made in the canvass, so that every turn is secured by a kind of knot or hitch, and remains fixed in case the rest should be cut through by friction. It is commonly used to fix the foot of a sail to its bolt rope.

Mast Cloth.—The lining in the middle on the aft side of topsails and top-gallantsails, to prevent the sails being chafed by the mast.

Middle Band.—A lining of one-half to a whole breadth across the sail, at half-way between the lowest reef and foot of courses and topsails, to strengthen them.

Mizen.—The aftermost or hindermost of the fixed sails of a ship, extended by a gaff, and the foot by a boom.

Moment of the Sails.—(See Note, p. 115.)

Nock or Neck.—The upper and fore-corner, and the after and upper corner of the sail is called the peak, (which see).

Parcelling.— Long narrow slips of canvass, frequently bound about a foot rope in the manner of bandages, previous to its being served. They are laid in spiral twines, as smoothly upon the surface as possible, that the rope may not become uneven and full of ridges.

Peak.—A name given to the upper corner of those sails which are extended by a gaff, and the upper corners of the triangular sails.

Points.—Pieces of white cordage of 5 to 8 thread a hook, whose lengths are nearly double the circumference of the yard, and used to reef the courses and topsails of a square-rigged vessel. They are fixed to the sails by passing one through every eyelet-hole in the reef-bands, and securely sewed to it on the aft side of the sail, by opening the strands with a pricker.

Poleacre.—A ship with three masts, usually navigated in the Mediterranean: each of the masts are commonly formed of one piece, so that they have neither tops or cross-trees, neither have they any horses to their upper yards, because the men stand upon the topsail yards to loose or furl the top-gallantsails, and upon the lower yards to loose, reef, or furl the topsails, the yards being lowered sufficiently down for that purpose.

Rake of the Masts.—A term applied to the masts when they are out of a perpendicular situation, as "that ship's mainmast rakes aft."

Reef.—A certain portion of a sail comprehended between the top or bottom and a row of eyelet-holes generally parallel thereto. The intention of the reef is to reduce the surface of the sail in proportion to the increase of the wind, for which reason there are several reefs parallel to each other in the superior sails; thus the topsails of ships are generally furnished with three reefs, and large topsails with four, and there are always three or four reefs parallel to the foot or bottom of those mainsails and foresails which are extended upon booms.

Reef Bands.—The pieces of canvass sewed across the sail to strengthen it in the place where the eyelet-holes of the reefs are formed.

Reef Lines.—Small ropes, stretched across the reefs, and spliced into the cringles, for the men to catch hold off.

Reef Tackle.—A tackle upon deck, communicating with its pendant, which, passing through a block at the topmast-head, and through a hole in the topsail yard-arm, is attached to a cringle a little below the lowest reef, generally about 3 feet. Its use is to pull the skirts of the topsails close up to the extremities of the topsail-yards, in order to lighten the labour of reefing.

Close-Reefed, is when all the reefs of the topsails are taken in.

Roach-Leech.—A term signifying the curve on the mast, and after-leeches of mizens, and fore and aft mainsails.

Royals.—Sails spread immediately above the top-gallantsails, to whose yard-arms the lower corners of them are attached ; they are sometimes termed top-gallant-royals, and are never used but in fine weather.

Saic.—A sort of Grecian ketch, which has no top-gallantsail nor mizensail.

Sail.—An assemblage of several breadths of canvass, or other texture, sewed together, and extended on or between the masts, to receive the wind, and impel the vessel through the water. The edges of the cloths, or pieces, of which a sail is composed, are generally sewed together, with a double seam, and the whole is skirted round at the edges with a cord called the bolt-rope.

Seams.—The two edges of canvass where laid over each other and sewed down.

Seizing.—The operation of fastening any two ropes, or different parts of one rope, together, with several round and cross turns of small cord or spunyarn. *Seizing* implies also the cord which fastens them.

Selvage.—The edges of cloth as finished in weaving.

Serving.—The winding anything round a rope to prevent it from being rubbed: the materials used for this purpose, which are called service, are generally spunyarn and old canvass.

Settee.—A vessel of two masts, equipped with triangular sails, commonly called lateen sails. These vessels are peculiar to the Mediterranean sea, and are generally navigated by Italians, Greeks, or Mahometans.

Sheet.—A rope fastened to one or both the lower corners of a sail, to extend and retain it in a particular situation, and the after-clue of other sails, except studdingsails. The tacks draw the outer corner of the sail to the extremity of the boom, while the sheet is employed to extend the inner corner.

Shoulder-of-Mutton Sail.—Is triangular, similar to the lateen sail, but is attached to a mast instead of a yard.

Slab Lines.—Small ropes passing up behind a ship's mainsail or foresail, and reeved through blocks attached to the lower part of the yard, and thence transmitted each in two branches to the foot of the sail, where they are fastened. They are used to truss up the sail, but more particularly for the convenience of the steersman, that he may look forward beneath it.

Slack-Cloth.—A certain quantity of cloth gathered up in sewing on the bolt-rope to the sail, so that the cloth measures more than the length of bolt-rope, which, stretching in the wearing, might otherwise occasion the sail to split. *Slack-Seams* imply a certain quantity of canvass allowed for gathering in the seaming-up of the after-leech of fore and aft-mainsails, or puckering the seams in a gradual manner. The seams thus sewed, by the slack being allowed in the cutting out, forms the curve on the after-leech.

Slings of a Yard.—Iron chains fixed to a hoop in the middle of a yard, and serving to suspend it for the greater ease of working.

Sloop.—A small vessel furnished with one mast, the mainsail of which is attached to a gaff above, to the mast on its foremost edge, and to a boom below: it differs from a cutter by having a fixed steering bowsprit, and a jib-stay; the sails also are less in proportion to the size of the vessel.

Smack.—A small vessel commonly rigged as a cutter, and used in the coasting and fishing trade.

Smoke-Sail.—A small sail hoisted against the foremast when the ship rides head to wind, to give the smoke of the galley an opportunity of rising, and to prevent its being blown aft on to the quarter deck.

Snow.—A vessel equipped with two masts, resembling the main and foremasts of a ship, and a third small mast just abaft the mainmast, carrying a sail nearly similar to a ship's mizen. The foot of this mast is fixed in a block of wood, or kind of step, upon the deck, and the head is attached to the after-part of the main-top. The sail is called a trysail, and hence the mast is termed a trysail-mast.

Spanker.—A sail similar to a ship's driver; it differs in name from a mizen by having a short boom rigged outside of the taffrail.

Splice.—Two ends of a rope united, by interweaving the strands in a regular manner. There are several methods of splicing, according to the purposes for which they are intended, all of which are distinguished by particular epithets. The *short-splice* is used upon the foot of sails, under the service, or where the splice is not required to be made very long. The *long-splice* occupies a greater extent of rope, but by the three joinings being fixed at a distance from each other, the increase of the bulk is divided; hence it is much neater and smoother than the short-splice, and better adapted to ropes which are of the same size, for which it is generally used. The *eye-splice*, or *earing splice*, forms a sort of eye or circle at the end of a rope, and is used for splicing-in thimbles. The strands are, therefore, untwisted, and their extremities thrust through the three strands in that part of the rope whereon the splice is to be formed, and thence passing over the surface of the second strand, they are again thrust through the third, which completes the operation. There are other names for splices, such as the *left-handed splice, one-stranded splice, &c.*

Sprit.—A small boom, or pole, which crosses the sail of a boat diagonally from the mast to the upper aftmost corner, which it is used to extend and elevate; the lower end of the sprit rests in a sort of wreath called the snotter, which encircles the mast at that place. These kinds of sails are accordingly called spritsails.

Spunyarn.—Two, three, or more ropeyarns twisted together by a winch. Spunyarn is used for serving the foot of sails, seizing clues, and serving cringles.

Square.—A term peculiarly appropriated to the yards and their sails, either implying that they are at right-angles with the mast or keel, or that they are at greater extent than usual.

Square Cloths.—The cloths cut square to the depth, or cut by a thread of the weft of the canvass.

Square-rigged.—A vessel used in contradistinction to all vessels whose sails are extended by stays, lateen or lugsail-yards, or by gaffs and booms, the usual situation of which is nearly in a plane with the keel.

Square-Sail.—Any sail extended to a yard suspended by the middle, and hanging parallel to the horizon, as distinguished from other sails, which are extended obliquely. *Square-Sail,* is also the name of a sloop's or cutter's sail, which hauls out to the lower yard, called the square-sail-yard. This sail is only used in fair winds, or to scud in a tempest. In the former case it is furnished with a large additional part called the bonnet, which is then attached to its bottom, and removed when it is necessary to scud.

Standing.—As the standing-jib. (See jib).

Stay.—A large, strong rope, employed to sustain the mast on the fore part, by extending from its upper end towards the stem or bowsprit of the ship, and on which the upper edges of the several staysails are attached, and derive their names from them.

Staysail.—Any sail extended upon a stay.

Stay-holes.—Holes made at certain distances along the hoist, through which the seizings of the hanks on the stay are passed.

Steering.—The angle of elevation which a ship's bowsprit makes with the horizon.

Stiff.—The quality by which a ship is enabled to carry a sufficient quantity of sail without over-setting.

Strand.—One of the twists or divisions of which a rope is composed.

Studding Sails.—Certain sails extended in moderate and steady breezes beyond the skirts of the principal sails, where they appear as wings to the yard-arms.

Sweep of the Sail.—The circular edge on a sail.

Tabling.—A sort of broad hem, formed on the heads, skirts, and bottoms of the sails, to strengthen them in that part which is attached to the bolt-rope.

Tack.—A rope used to confine the foremost lower corners of the courses and staysails, in a fixed position, and also to confine the foremost lower corners of boomsails, and the outer lower corners of studdingsails.

Tack of a Sail is also applied, by analogy, to that part of any sail to which the tack is usually fastened.

Tarpauling.—A broad piece of canvass, well daubed with tar, and used to cover the hatchways of a ship at sea, to prevent the penetration of the rain or sea water, which may at times rush over the decks.

Taunt.—An epithet, at sea, signifying high or tall. It is particularly expressed of the masts, when they are of an extraordinary length, as square is applied to the yards on the same occasion.

Thimble.—An iron ring, whose outer surface is hollowed throughout its whole circumference, in order to contain in the channel or cavity a rope which is spliced about it, and by which it may be hung in any particular situation. Its use is to defend the eye of the rope which surrounds it from being injured by another rope which passes through it, or by the hook of a tackle or a chain which is hung upon it.

Throat.—A name given to that end of the gaff which is next the mast, and is opposed to peak, which implies the outer end: hence, *Throat Brails* are those which are attached to the gaff close to the mast. *Throat Halliards,* ropes or tackles applied to hoist the inner part of the gaff, and its appendant portion of the sail.

Top-Lining.—The lining sewed on the aft side of topsails and topgallantsails, to preserve the sail from chafing.

Trysail.—A sail used by cutters, luggers, sloops, &c., in lieu of their mainsail, during a storm. *Trysail* is also the name of a sail on board of a snow, (which see).

Twine.—Strong thread used in sailmaking, and is of two kinds: extra for sewing the seams, and ordinary for the bolt-ropes. These two sorts are generally called seaming and roping twine.

Vangs.—A sort of traces to steady the mizen peak, extending from the peak downwards to the aftermost part of the ship's quarters, where they are hooked and drawn tight, so as to be slackened when the wind is fair, and drawn in to windward when it becomes unfavourable to the ship's course.

Waist Cloths.—Coverings of canvass or tarpauling for the hammocks, which are stowed on the gangways, between the quarter deck and forecastle.

Weather Helm.—A ship is said to carry a weather helm when she is inclined to come too near the wind, and therefore requires the helm to be kept constantly a little to windward.

Weft or Woof.—The threads drawn across by means of the weaver's shuttle, and others extended in length, and called the warp.

Working to Windward.—The operation by which it is endeavoured to make a ship progress against the wind.

Xebec.—(See page 131).

OPINIONS OF THE PRESS.

THE ELEMENTS OF SAILMAKING.—An excellent little treatise, developing the whole art and mystery of Sailmaking as adopted in the Merchant Service, is here designed by the principal sailmaker of the port of Newcastle-upon-Tyne, and the first number of which is now before us. We can confidently recommend it to the attention of seamen, as giving the rules exemplified by cases for cutting out sails of all kinds on the best founded principles.— *Nautical Magazine, for June.*

THE ELEMENTS OF SAILMAKING.—This is a first part of a treatise which promises to be of great use to sailmakers, nothing of the kind having hitherto been published. The author has for several years been practically engaged in the pursuit on which he treats, and has now thrown together a variety of rules for the guidance of sailmakers—directing them how to cut out their work to the best possible advantage, and av..id the waste of canvas which but too frequently happens, through ignorance and the want of the necessary arithmetical processes. The object of the author is to give an exposition of everything connected with the art, with the view to the "thorough scientific construction, and ultimately permanent maintenance, strength, and stability of the sails." To accomplish this he has divided the work into sections, and the first part elucidates the measurement of masts and yards; rules for finding the numbers of cloths and determining the size and roaching of the sails, and the mensuration of the gores; the dimensions for cutting the sails, and copious tables showing the length of the gores corresponding to the depth of the selvage, and the eating in seaming. The value of a publication of this nature hardly needs to be pointed out by us, but we cannot refrain from calling the attention of those whom it concerns to it, accompanied with the strongest recommendations. The rules are full and complete, clearly expressed, and constructed to meet every emergency.— *Shipping Gazette.*

THE ELEMENTS OF SAILMAKING.—It is always interesting to hear a sensible person talk on matters which he understands well, and is at home in, however remote the subjects may be from those in which one has any immediate concern. So it is when a practical man, of competent ability, supplies a work relating to his own business: it gains attention, and is felt to be a real contribution to the stock of public information, differing as much as may be from the recastings of old ideas which too often characterise new books coming from hackneyed pens and authors by profession. We cannot be supposed to be judges of sailmaking; still we possess an instinct, in common with the generality of mankind, which tells us when an individual is discoursing intelligently, and on things coming within his own knowledge. There is about Mr. Kipping's treatise a stamp of authority, a sort of self-evident propriety and power, which entitle it to the special consideration of those for whom it is written; and we are much mistaken if these pages do not, by degrees, gain much more attention than the author anticipates. Such works are not calculated for the million; no stir is therefore made on their appearance; but they make their way gradually, and in the department to which they belong, they often accomplish great though not noisy revolutions. Mr. Kipping has made out, to our satisfaction, the following particulars, which attach no little importance to his book in relation to the maritime interests of this kingdom:—first, that the construction of new sails—their dimensions, form, and the mode of fixing them—has an essential bearing upon the safety and efficient navigation of a ship; secondly, that in point of economy to the owner, it is of much consequence for a vessel to have her sails rightly managed; and thirdly that there are certain principles which may be applied with mathematical certainty to sail-making, which have not as yet been sufficiently developed nor generally acted upon.— *Newcastle Courant.*

THE ELEMENTS OF SAILMAKING.—Mr. Robert Kipping, of the establishment of Messrs. T. & W. Smith, St. Peter's, Newcastle, has long been known as an eminent mathematician, and a proficient in the art of sailmaking; and certainly the work before us amply justifies the celebrity he has attained both in science and practice. By the trade it will doubtless be regarded as a boon of invaluable and lasting worth; especially when it is borne in mind, as the author correctly states in his preface, that "there was no existing work of this nature, applicable to the state of sailmaking; nor even any which contained the various calculations necessary for the scientific construction of sails." To supply this obvious and widely-acknowledged defect, the able author has happily combined his mathematical and geometrical knowledge with the results of his vast experience—"gained," as he observes, "in fitting with sails the largest Indiamen afloat." Hence, as a consequence, he has constructed rules and supplied draughts for cutting, at once so exact and ample, and (considering the difficulties of the science) so concise and easy, as to put his useful art within the comprehension and practice of any one who possesses even a moderate share of elementary mathematical knowledge, and will bend his attention to make himself fully master of his trade. Those who are the least acquainted with the art of sailmaking will not fail to perceive that this admirable work possesses several pre-eminent recommendations. One is, that the rules it supplies and the conclusions it works out may be relied upon with all the *certainty* of mathematical truth. Another is, that as the dimensions of sails of all sizes are distinctly laid down, masters of ships, in cases of emergency, though altogether unacquainted with the principles of the science, could cut out, by the exercise of a little attention, any sail that might be needed—supposing the old one might be blown away from the yards, or torn so as to leave no traces of its original construction to go by. Of course, in such circumstances, the value of those finished plans must be inconceivable. To young men learning the trade, the work will also be eminently beneficial—it not being a part of their master's duty (or, perhaps, we ought to say, practice) to teach them the art of cutting; and as such persons, after their apprenticeship is finished, generally go to sea in the capacity of sailmakers, Mr. Kipping's work will be of essential service, both in assisting them to fulfil the duties required, and also affording immense aid in obtaining the important knowledge of draughting.— *Gateshead Observer.*

PLATE. I

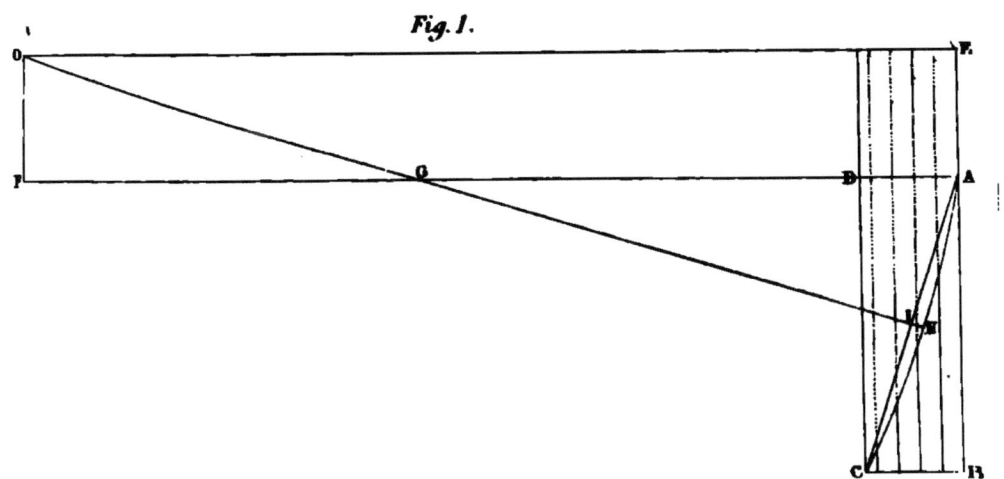

Fig. 1.

Fig. 2.

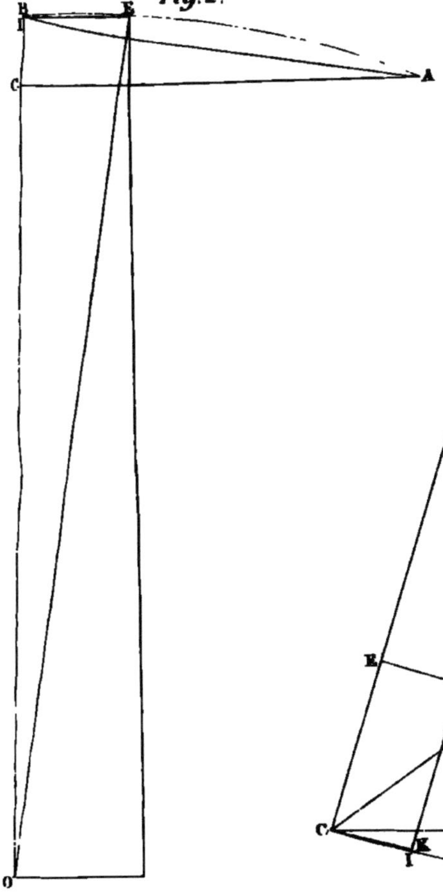

Fig. 3.

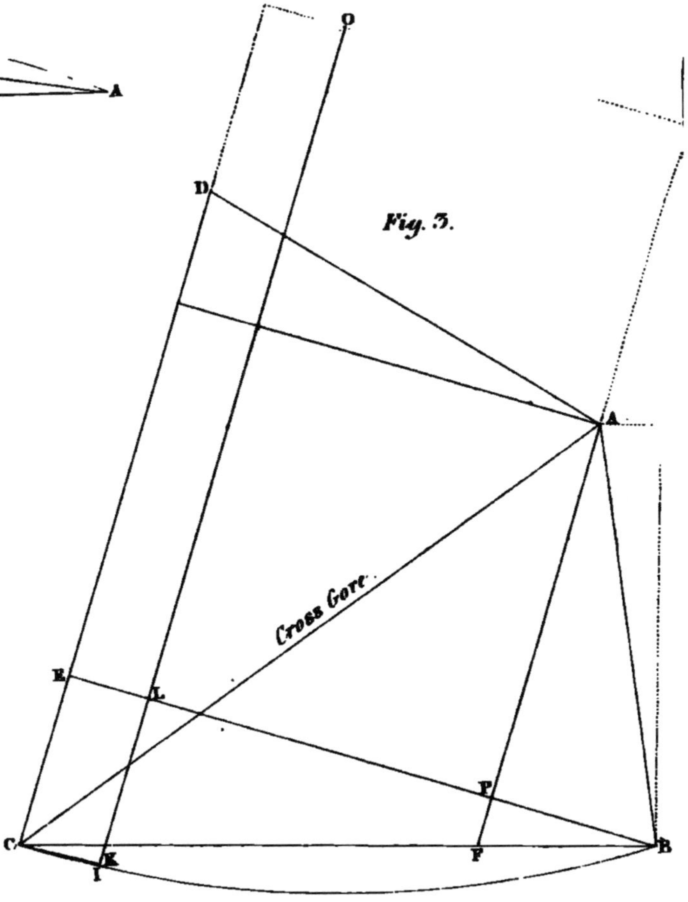

Cross Gore

SAILS ON MAIN MAST.

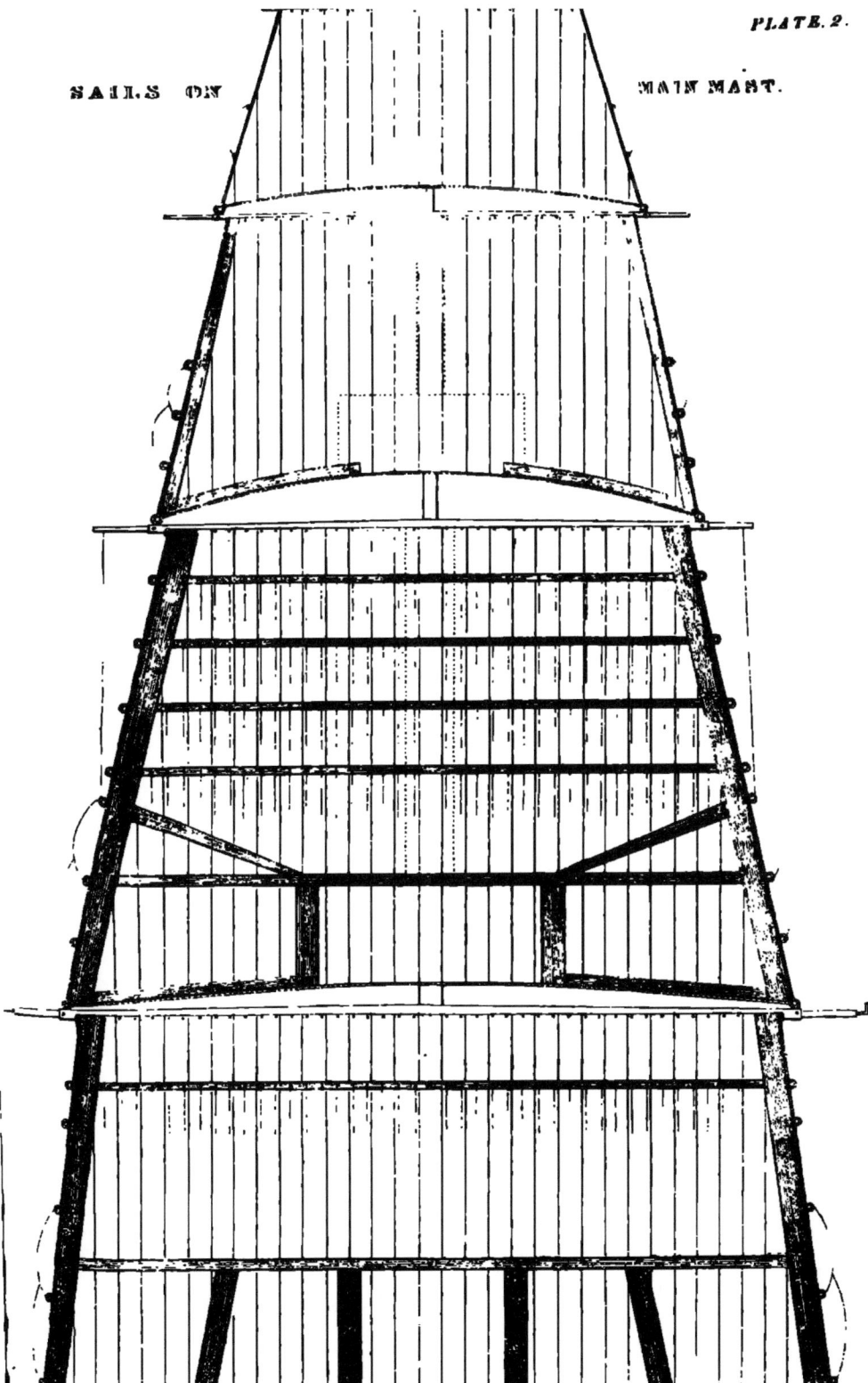

PLATE 3.

SAILS ON FOREMAST

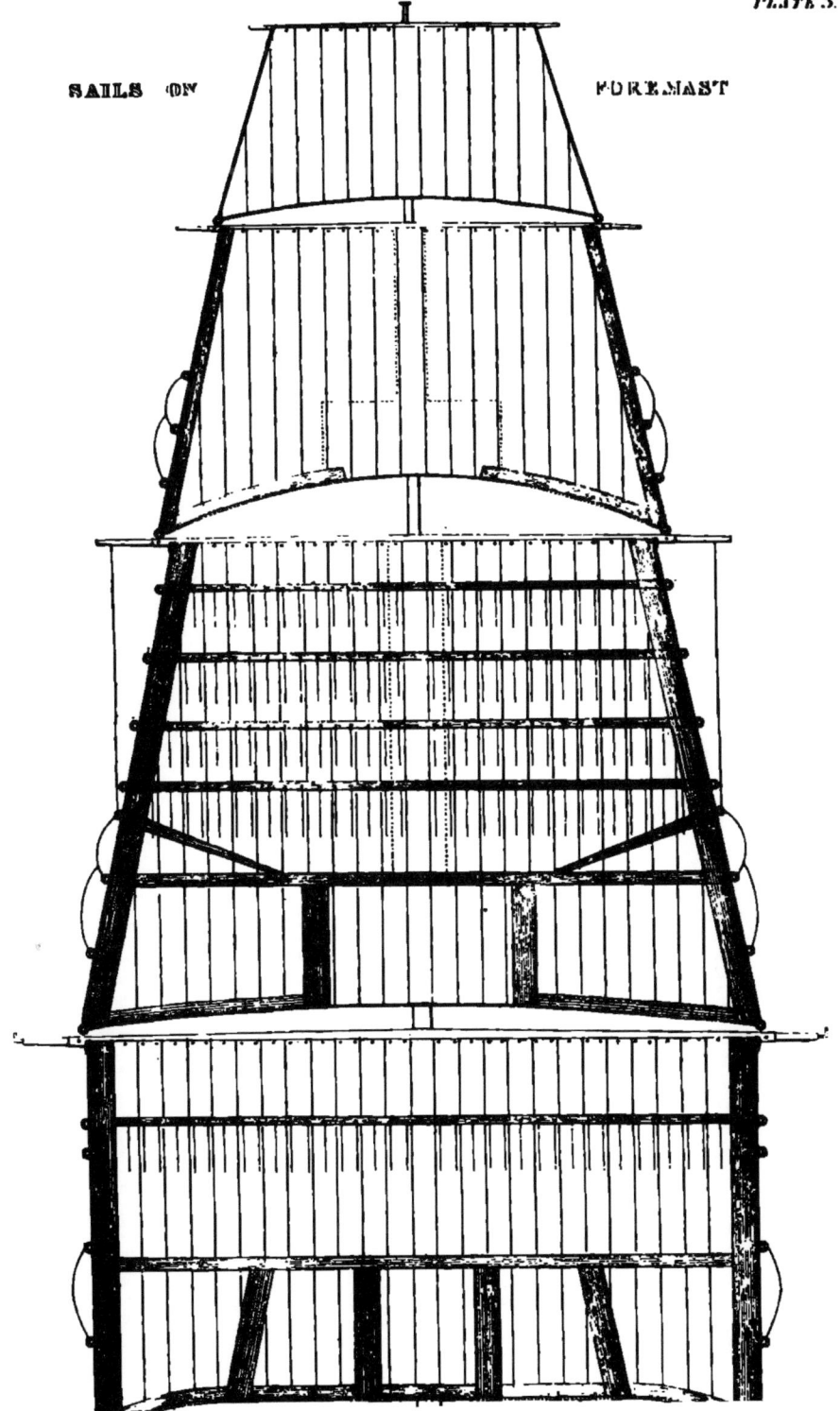

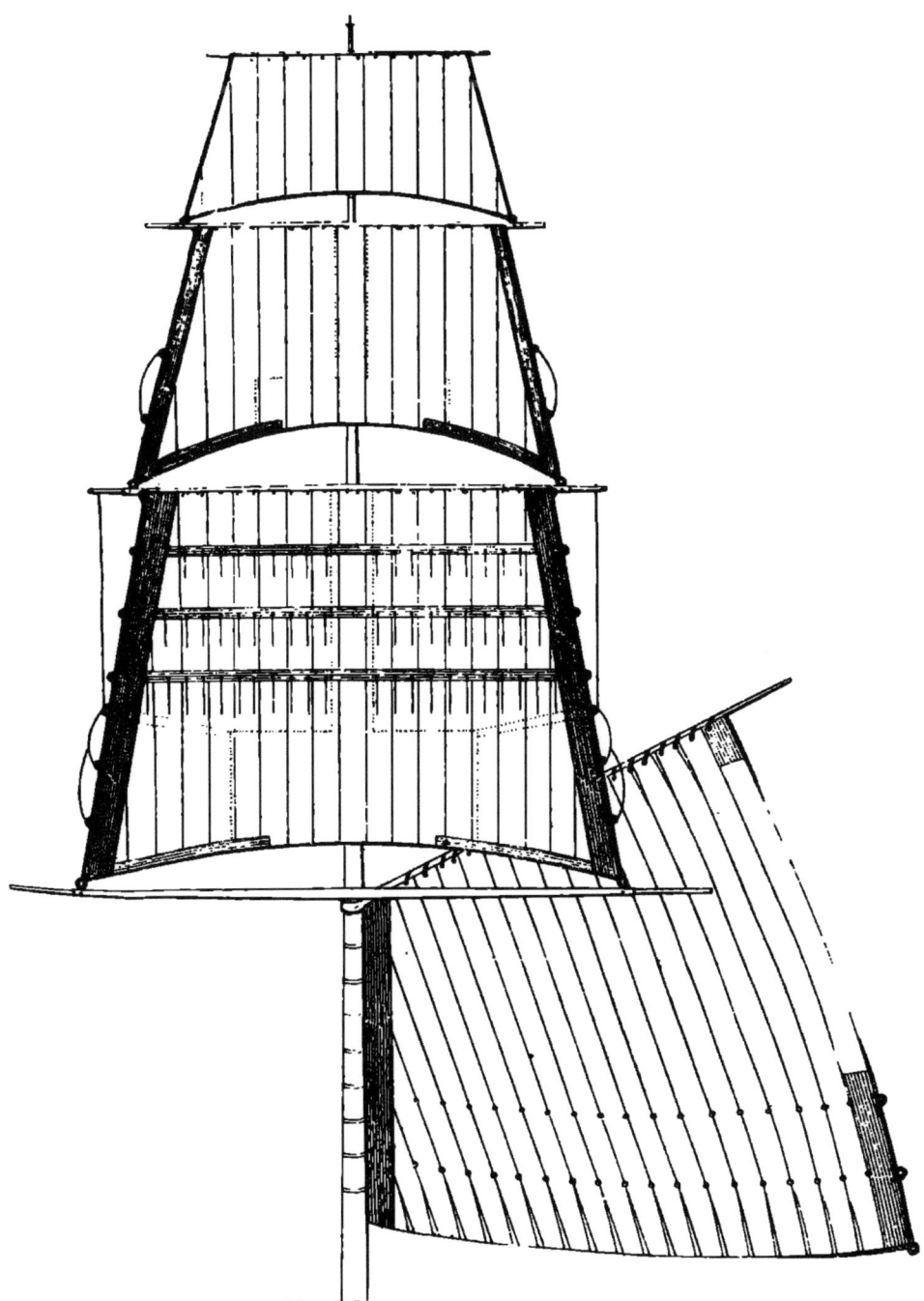

PLATE I.

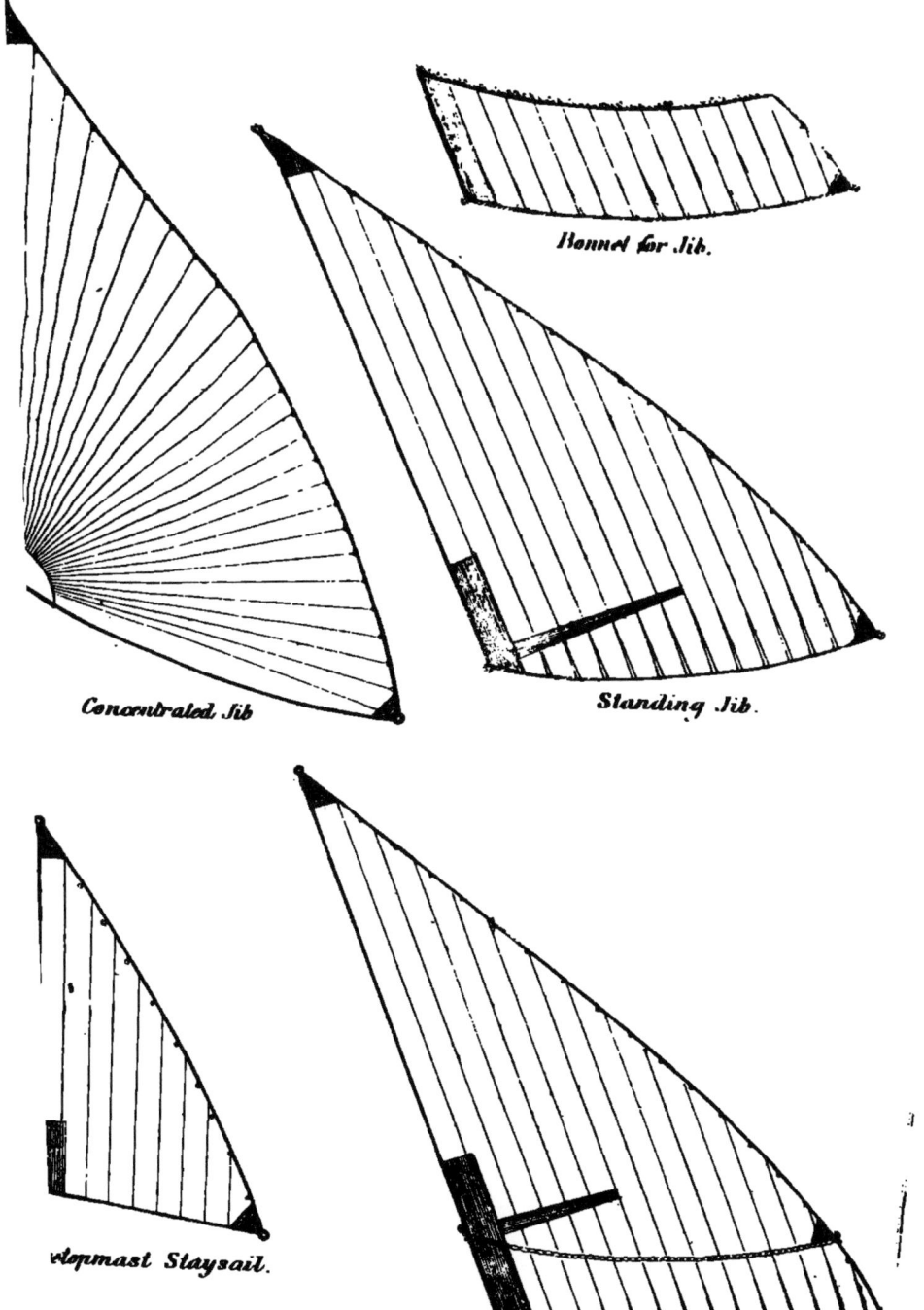

Concentrated Jib

Bonnet for Jib.

Standing Jib.

Topmast Staysail.

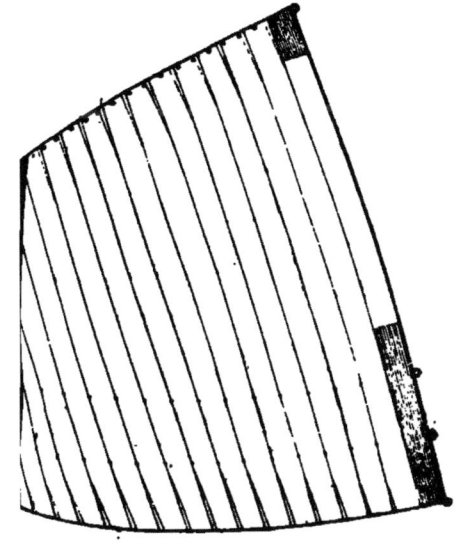

Barque's Mizen.

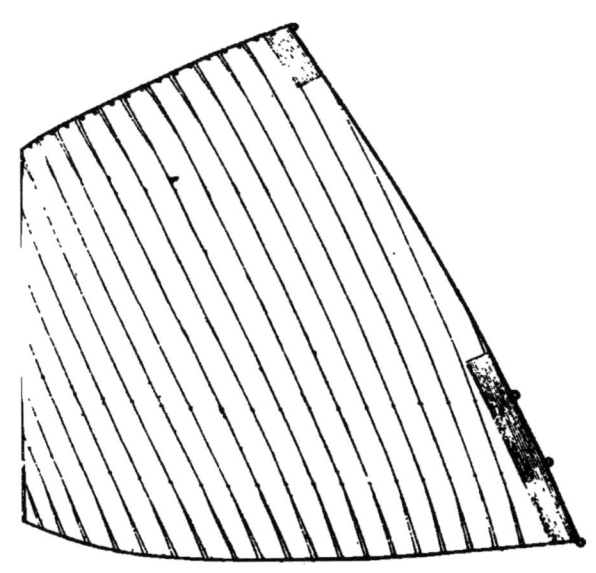

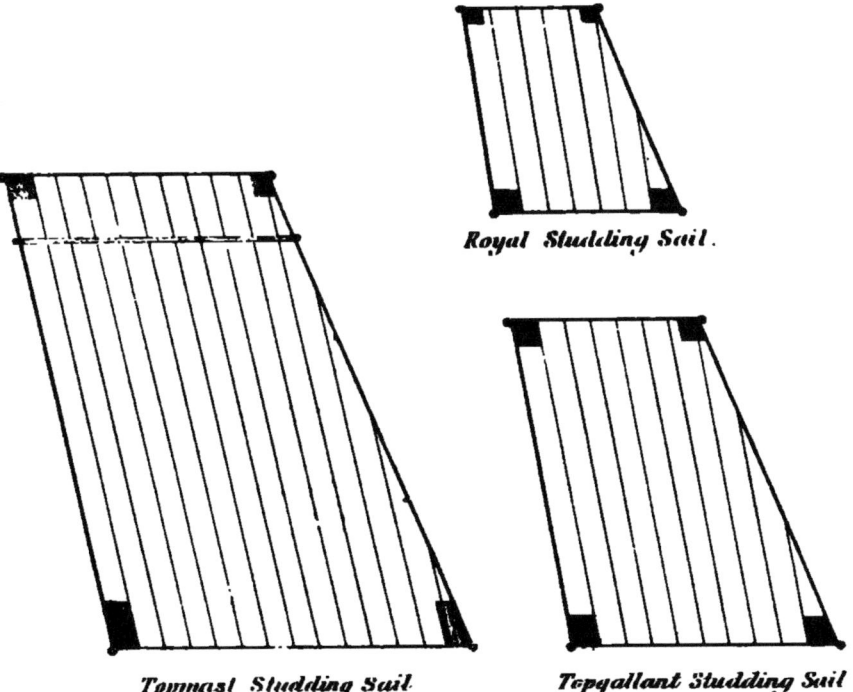

Royal Studding Sail.

Topmast Studding Sail

Topgallant Studding Sail

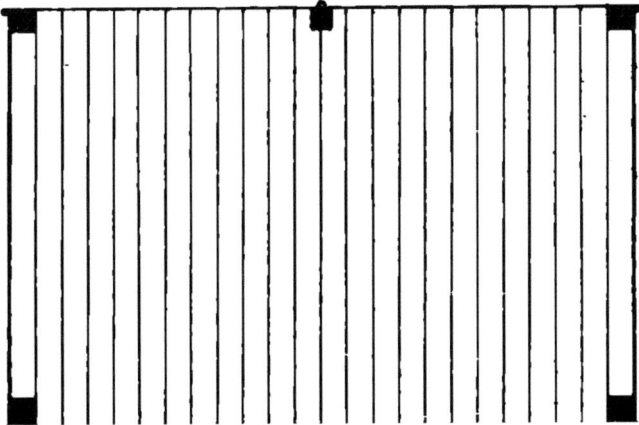

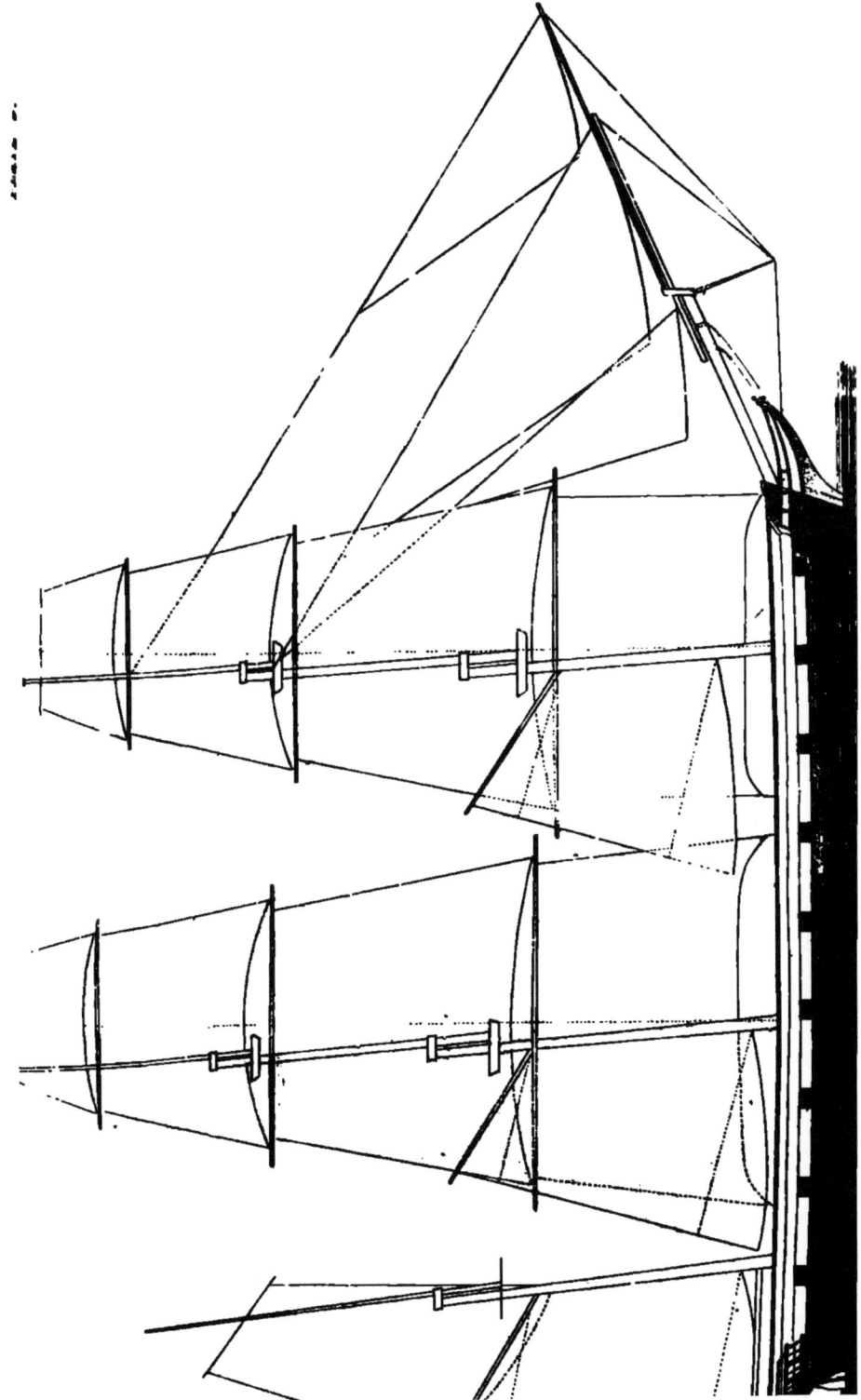

PLATE 10.

PLATE II.

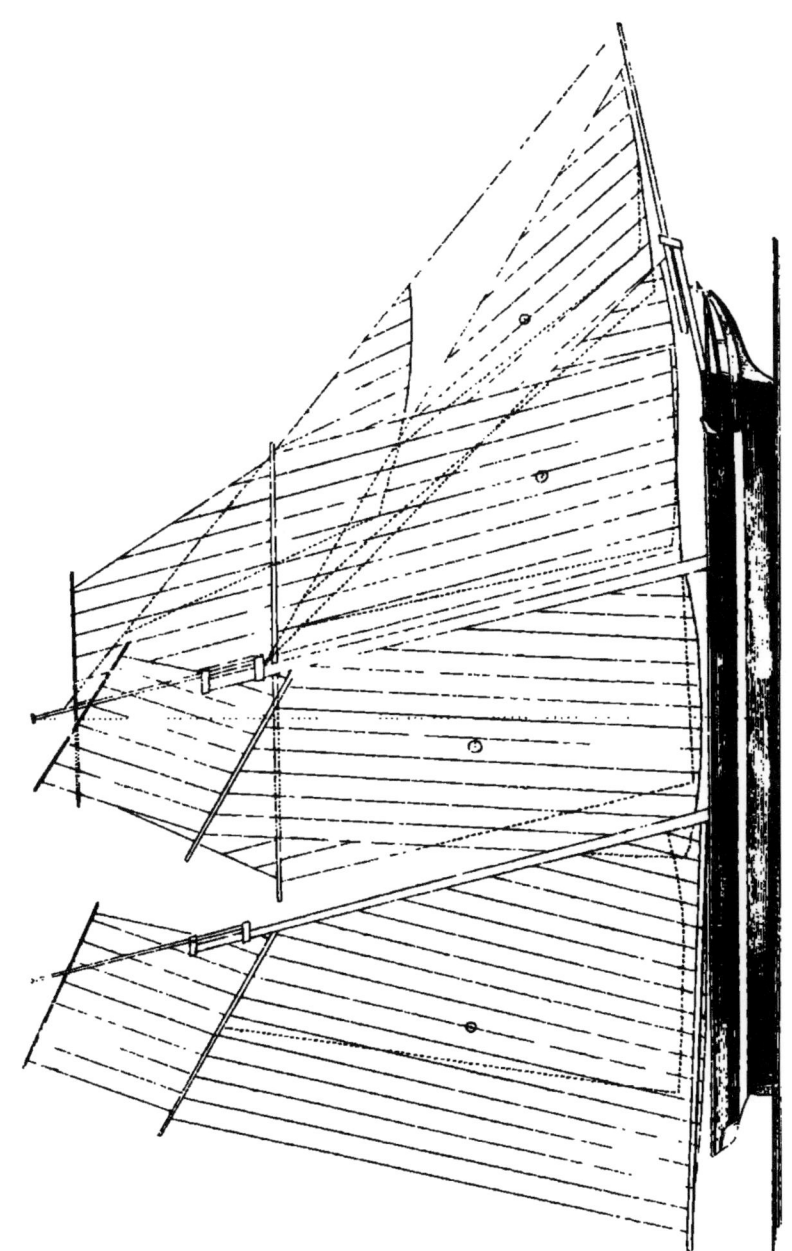

Three Lugsails square at the Heads.

Three Sprit-sails and a Jib.

PLATE 13.

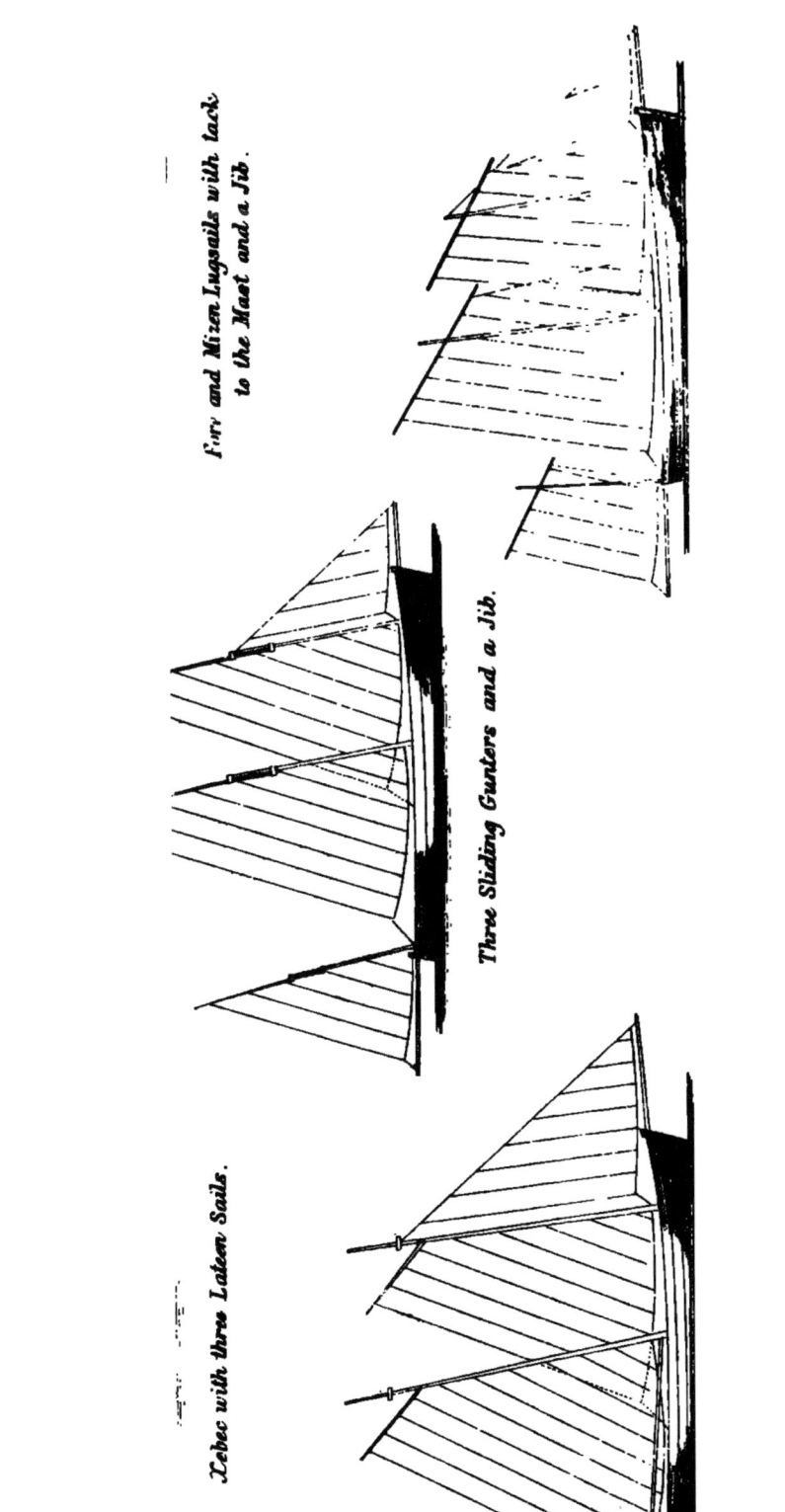

Xebec with three Lateen Sails.

Three Sliding Gunters and a Jib.

Fore and Mizen Lugsails with tack to the Mast and a Jib.

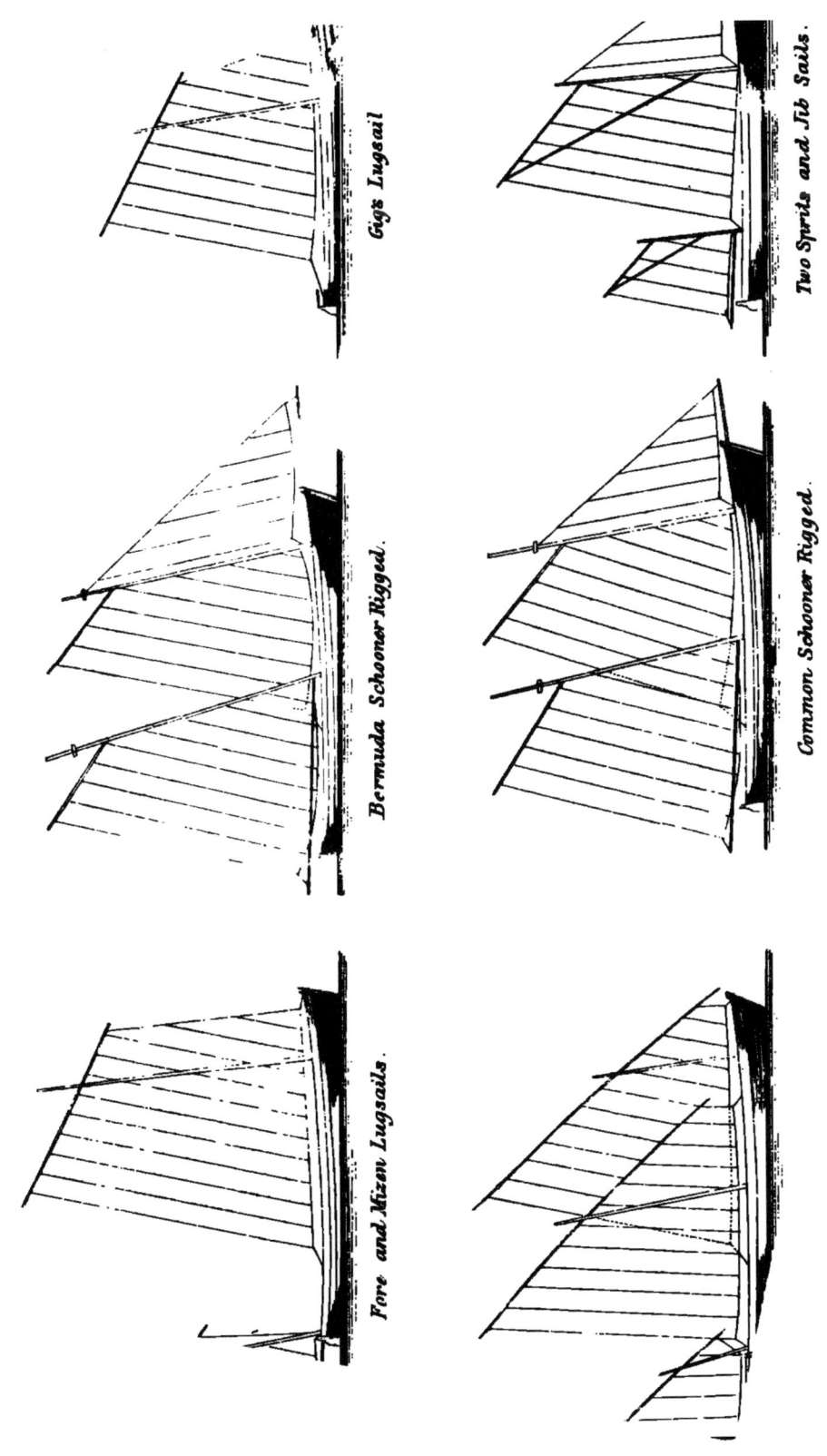

Gig's Lugsail.

Two Sprits and Jib Sails.

Bermuda Schooner Rigged.

Common Schooner Rigged.

Fore and Mizen Lugsails.

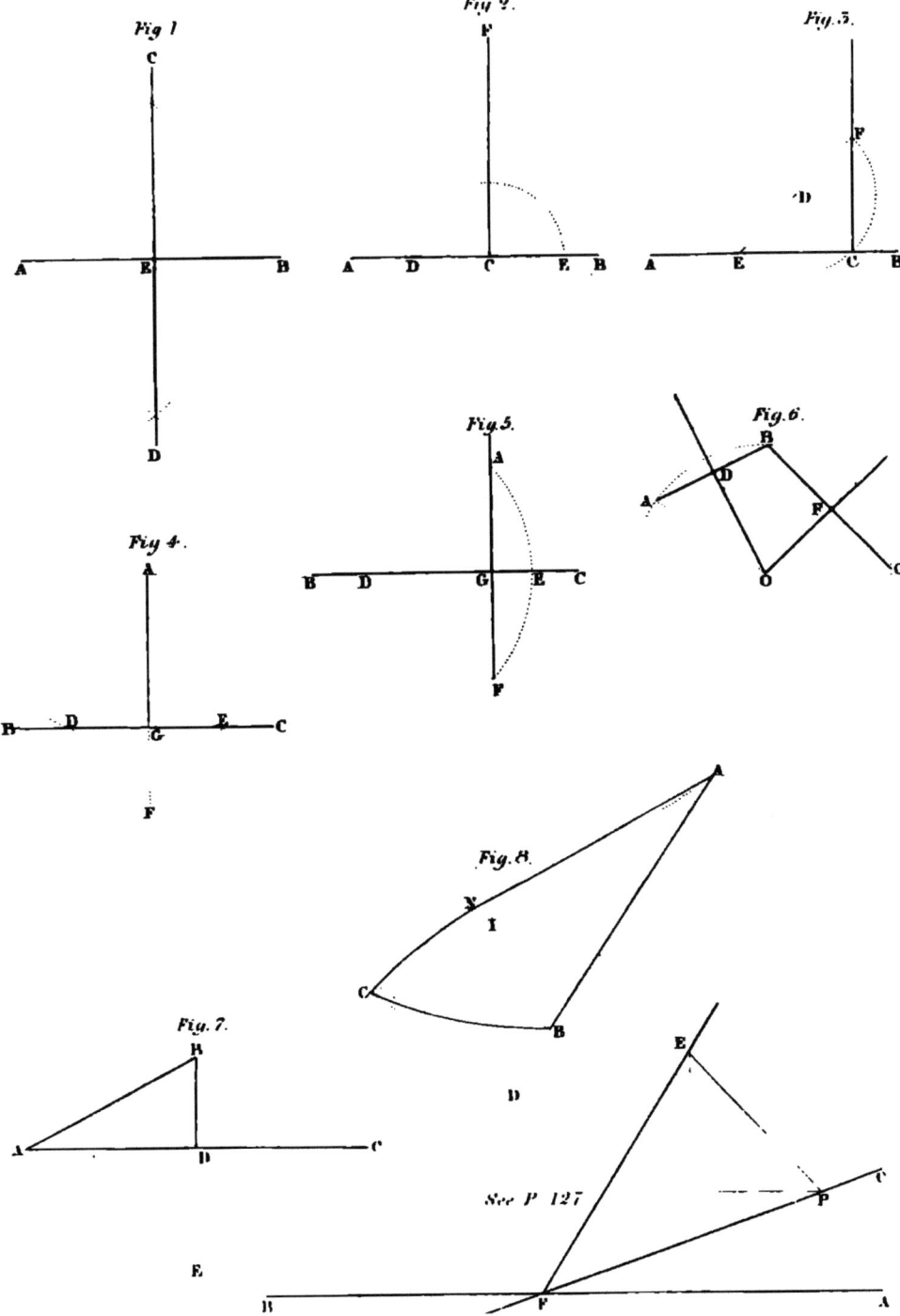

Fig 1.

Fig 2.

Fig 3.

Fig 4.

Fig 5.

Fig 6.

Fig 7.

Fig 8.

See P 127

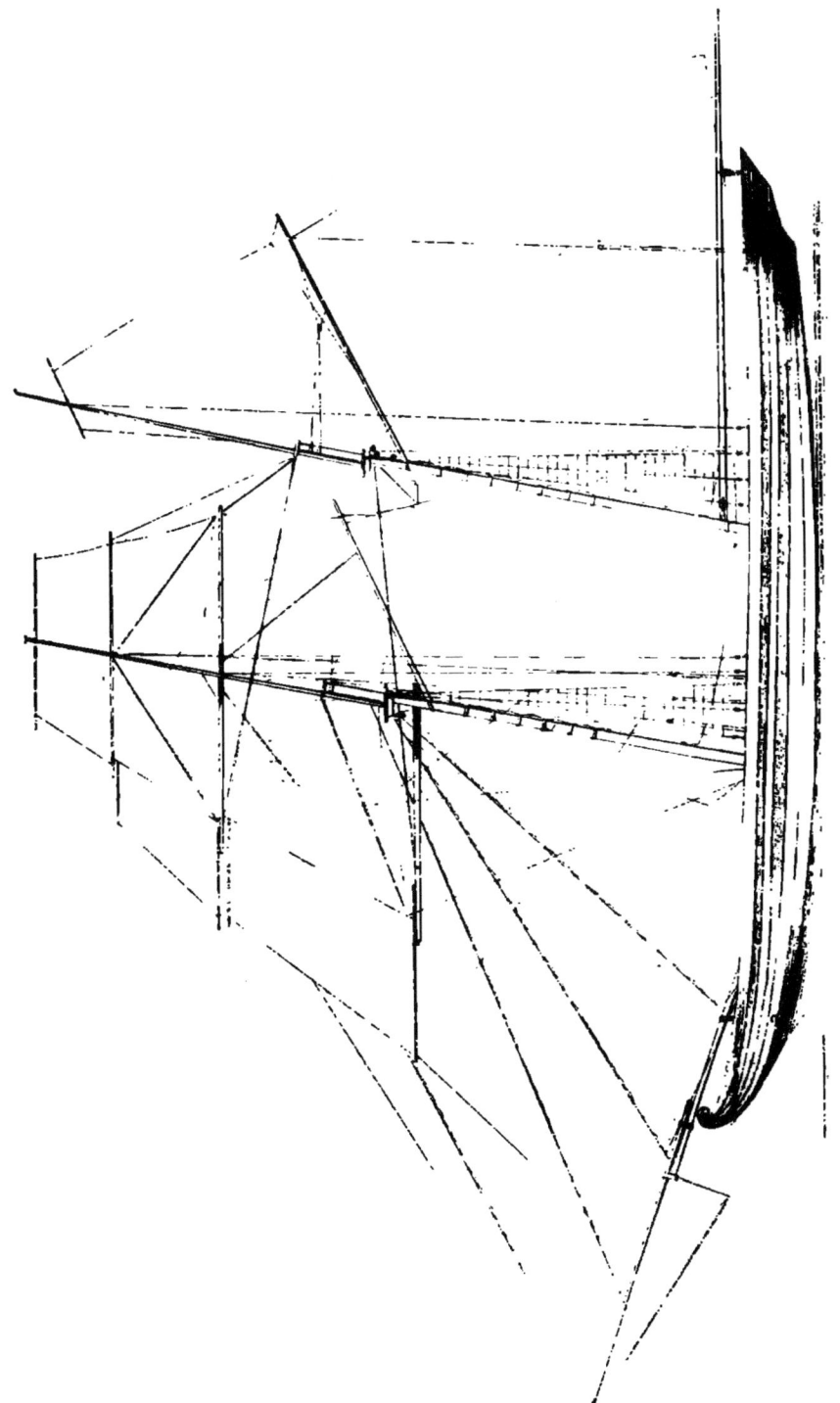

CLIPPER SCHOONER.